THRACIAN MAGIC
past & present

This book is dedicated to all,
who are worthy and proud to call themselves
'offspring of the Heavy Earth and the Starry Heaven'

Georgi Mishev

Published by Avalonia

BM Avalonia
London
WC1N 3XX
England, UK

www.avaloniabooks.co.uk

Thracian Magic

Copyright © 2012 Georgi Mishev

ISBN (10) 1-905297-48-3

ISBN (13) 978-1-905297-48-1

First Edition, September 2012

Design by Satori
Cover Art 'Mother of the Sun' by Georgi Mishev

About the Author

Georgi Mishev holds a bachelor's degree in German and Russian language, specialising in *"Applied Linguistics"*. He also studied *"Ancient magical formulae"* with Prof. Johann Tischler at the Dresden University of Technology in Germany, and holds a masters degree in *"Preservation of the cultural-historical heritage in the Republic of Bulgaria"* having presented his thesis on *"Thracian material and immaterial cultural-historical heritage in the region of Thracian cult centre Starosel"*.

Previous published work includes:

1. Mishev G., *Cultural memory in the region of Thracian cult centre Starosel* // The Bulletin of the National Museum of Bulgarian History, XXII, Veliko Tarnovo 2010

2. Mishev G., *Solar disk on peak Eldermen, region of Starosel*

online: http://godsun.thracica.com/library/publication/13

3. Mishev G., *The regulations of the Iobacchoi*

online: http://www.thracica.com/library/epublication/14

4. Mishev G., *Threskeia* // Hekate Her Sacred Fires, London 2010:67-71

Media consultation and participation:

1. *"She"* – a documentary dedicated to the cult of the Goddess, a production of Bulgarian national television – Plovdiv, 2011 (online: http://bntplovdiv.com/all-movies/movies-online/3641-tya.html).

2. *"Rhodope magic"* – documentary trilogy, co-production of Czech Republic Television and Golden Archer Productions, in collaboration with Bulgarian National Television, 2010.

If you wish to contact the author, please write to:

Georgi Mishev

c/o BM Avalonia

London

WC1N 3XX

United Kingdom

Alternatively you can contact him by e-mail, dadaleme@abv.bg

Georgi Mishev

THRACIAN MAGIC
past & present

Georgi Mishev
Foreword by Prof. Valeria Fol
Translated from Bulgarian by Ekaterina Ilieva

Published by Avalonia
www.avaloniabooks.co.uk

1 - Mountain Mother, by Georgi Mishev

Thracian Magic by Georgi Mishev

This book contains an overview of magical spells and rituals drawn from the ethnographical records and traditional folklore culture of the Balkan Peninsula, primarily from Bulgaria. It also contains practices drawn from other ancient sources including the *Greek Magical Papyri*.

DISCLAIMER

Although both Avalonia and the author of this book have taken great care to ensure the authenticity of the information and the techniques contained therein, we are not responsible, in whole or in part, for any injury which may occur to the reader or readers by reading and/or following the instructions in this book. It is understood that many of the techniques, rituals and meditations are only discussed for scholarly purposes, and that there exists a potential for injury when using the techniques or practices described in this publication, especially when the full text is not carefully studied.

It is essential that before following any of the activities, physical, meditative or otherwise, herein described, the reader or readers should first consult his or her physician for advice on whether practising or using the techniques, rituals or meditations described in this publication could cause injury, physical, mental or otherwise. Since the techniques and physical activities could be too demanding or sophisticated, it is essential that a physician be consulted. Also, local, state or federal laws may prohibit the practice of physical activities, rituals or exercises described in this publication. A thorough examination must be made of the federal, state or local laws before the reader or readers attempt to try or practice any of the exercises, techniques, rituals, meditations or any other activity described in this publication.

Neither Avalonia nor the author guarantees the legality or the appropriateness of the techniques, acts, rituals, exercises or meditations herein contained.

2 - Mistress of Fire by Georgi Mishev

ACKNOWLEDGMENTS

I have many people to thank for their help and support with the present book.

Firstly I give my gratitude and appreciation to all those carriers of the magical traditions, who throughout the years have shared and continue to share their experiences and knowledge with me.

Undoubtedly however, I owe my first steps and closeness to nature, as well as my great respect of folk wisdom to my grandmother Elena Misheva. I also express my honour and appreciation to my mother Sonya Misheva, who has shown me with her vocation as a physician that humaneness is to be experienced through acts and deeds.

I owe special recognition to Prof. Dr. Sc. Valeria Fol for her support, critiques, methodology help, advice and directions which I greatly value and am deeply grateful for. I cannot but express my huge respect and esteem for Prof. Alexander Fol and even though I have interacted with him only through his books, they are of great significance to the writing of the present volume.

I would like to express my gratitude to Ekaterina Ilieva, both for the opportunity to share a mutual spiritual path and quest and her exerted efforts in the English translation of this book. Thanks to her help and support, a small, but important part of Bulgarian folk belief and art became available to a wide range of readers around the world.

I thank all my colleagues and friends who have supported and keep supporting me: to Borislava Stambolieva for some of the lovely pictures, which are in my personal archive; to Iglika Mishkova from the *National Ethnography Museum* in Sofia, for help on searching a number of ethnographical records and as well for the jointly conducted terrain research; to Gena Gerovska for the opportunity to get closer to the beliefs and knowledge preserved in the area of the Thracian cult centre of Starosel; to Irina Sedakova of the *Russian Science Academy* for the granted materials.

Most certainly the above mentioned names do not exhaust the list of people to whom I owe acknowledgement, therefore may all the others with whom I have spent time, experiences and knowledge, know that I deeply value their presence in my life.

Last, but not least, I want to thank *Avalonia* and in particular Sorita d'Este, for their help in editing and publishing this book.

Georgi Mishev

TABLE OF CONTENTS

Georgi Mishev

FOREWORD

FROM THE OTHER SIDE OF THE MOON

By VALERIA FOL

I chose this title for the foreword to Georgi Mishev's work *Thracian magic: past and present*, because this book is unusual. One writes about magical practice most commonly either from the position of a scholar or from the position of a practitioner. The book, which G. Mishev offers us, leads the reader into the secrets of the magical with the dignity of a descendant and carrier of millennial traditions, preserved in the South-eastern European area, and with the passion of an explorer, rushing towards the light of knowledge. Figuratively, the book can also be defined as a valuable aspiration towards understanding the secrets of the hidden side of the moon, because all the original records of beliefs and magical ritual practices from the South-eastern European region presented in it reveal the living embers of the living traditions which have preserved the connection with antiquity over the millennia.

However, history of culture and political history have different rhythms, chronology and transformational regularity. Diachrony is particularly visible nowadays when the new information and communication technologies dynamise the intercultural dialogue and interactions and what used to take centuries in the past, now is literally happening in front of our eyes. It is seen only too vividly in the *'dialogue'* between oral and literary culture, in the process of folklorising scientific research and vice versa – literalisation of folk beliefs and practices.

Cultural collective and ancestral heritage preserve the knowledge of this harmony with the Great Goddess-Mother-Nature and her Son-Sun achieved in ancient times even when nations and religions changed. The faith that light and the cave's darkness, as well as love and the birth of the world, each year give power to those who have gained perfection and strength. This aids the community they belong to, bringing about transformation, adjusting to new religious systems, but never completely disappearing.

In today's Bulgarian lands magical operators have been called healers, witches, herbalists; and as G. Mishev shows with rich documentary material, they haven't been put under the so called *'condemnation of memory'* in spite of the efforts made by the monotheistic religions. Of all the reasons given by the author in the text the most important, according to me, is the incapability of the Church[1] to overcome the millennial faith and the necessity to express tolerance and get associated, throwing a Christian veil over ancient practices and beliefs. It doesn't mean that faith and ritual tradition don't go through transformations. On the contrary – they are visible and in many cases it has been clarified how the innovations have occurred.

From an ontological point of view, magic is a universal human phenomenon. Those who perform the rites possess the knowledge to subordinate the will of the deity to their own. During the period of kingship in the Mediterranean world, magic was part of religion and ritual tradition, as it is seen from Homer's epos, Hittite, Egyptian and other texts. In ancient Thrace the Mycenaean type of society headed by a king-priest continued to function until its conquest by the Romans. After the synoecism in Hellas the reality changed, but even in the classical age the polis' religion preserved bright elements of magic, especially in the rites for fertility, initiatory rites and the receiving of an oracle. In Thrace magical rites continued their life. In spite of the inevitable transformations during the Hellenistic period and Late Antiquity characterized with syncretism between cultures, cults, beliefs and ritual practices of Asia Minor and the Mediterranean, as well as profanation of aristocratic doctrinal rites, cultural memory puts the magical in the traditional culture of newly formed Danube Bulgaria. After Christianisation, Medieval Bulgaria found itself in the sphere of Byzantine culture. But it must be taken into account that in Byzantium and even in Constantinople the belief in the magical power of ancient statues, talismans, the conviction that ancient magical practices can help people, were inherent to the common folk, as well as to the aristocratic elite, and even to emperors and patriarchs. The historical discourse which Georgi Mishev offers to the reader is concise, but sufficiently comprehensive in order to outline the specifics of South-eastern European societies during different periods.

---

[1] I write Church with a capital "C" as an institution.

In my opinion the book's merit lies in the fact that the author doesn't slide on the modern terminology, where the beliefs and rites of community, when different from those approved by monotheistic religion, are defined as *'private sphere'* and *'religious initiative'*, ancestral folk healers are called *'religious actors'*, prophetic dreams – *'religious activism'* and so on. In G. Mishev's book people are alive, active, following the strong tradition of the lands they inhabit. In South-eastern Europe it can even be felt physically how priesthood has been transformed gradually in healing/herbalism through the centuries. The transformations are not always innovations, far more often they are an archaisation, a return to archetypes preserved in cultural memory. And this often happens during periods of deep social, political and moral crises of society. In the book charlatans are not discussed, nor those who claim to have received a vision in a dream or awake, but only people to whom magical practices are lineal and acquired knowledge; people, who are carriers of action-duty towards the society they belong to. More often unconsciously than consciously they believe that the individual and the community must always be in rhythm with the Nature-Great Goddess and in synchrony with the daily and annual cycle of the Sun-God.

G. Mishev's work is firmly based on written sources, analysis of depictive language and scientific literature. It may provoke anger, fear or joy that someone has dared to divert from the beaten paths we follow when talking and writing about magic, and to enter without fear and with love in the enchanting world of his ancestors. The book is read in one go. And please be careful! A wrongly performed rite may lead to the opposite effect!

Prof. Dr. Sc. Valeria Fol

valeriafol@gmail.com

Georgi Mishev

CHAPTER 1

INTRODUCTION

The present book aims to represent the Thracian traditions that have reached us today through Bulgarian folk and magical practices. Most of the rites, especially the collective ones, are the result of many years of syncretism and it can be difficult to determine particular features in them that have a direct connection with Thracian antiquity. Some of these rites are described in this book, because I feel certain elements in them contain clear references to the Paleo-Balkan and respectively Thracian culture. Other rites, like the magical, which are part of secret ritual practices, are strongly conservative and hardly yield to external influence, and as a result they retain a lot of archaic elements.

The interdisciplinary method was used during the research for this project. The materials introduced are primarily from the fields of ethnography, folklore, history and archaeology. Personal observations and conversations with magical practitioners in Bulgaria today have also been included. With time my own personal interest and knowledge of the subject grew and within the framework of my education – Russian and German philology, I had the opportunity to become familiar with the written magical rituals of a number of Slavic and Germanic peoples; and my subsequent study of them continued outside the walls of the university lecture halls. A tremendous contribution to my understanding of the ancient *Greek Magical Papyri* was the seminar *'Ancient magical formulae'* of Prof. Johann Tischler at the Dresden University of Technology, Germany in 2003/2004, and it was during the same period that my research into Hittite ritual practices also commenced.

Bulgarian scholars of Thracian history give special attention to the problem of relics from Thracian antiquity being present in Bulgarian traditional culture. Continuing research on the *nestinari* and masquerade rituals, as well as on the folk cults of saints, including St Marina, St Elijah, St Athanasius, St Constantine, Helen and others, shows that a lot of ancient characteristics which originated in Balkan antiquity are clearly present. When such discoveries are observed in common celebrations and mainstream ritual practices, it can be assumed with certainty that this hidden magical culture will also be a beneficial area when searching for Thracian remnants.

I am personally also an inheritor of this hidden ritual tradition, and this to some extent was the motivation for the personal challenge in researching the present book. In my maternal line, my great-grandmothers were famous healers in my hometown and the surrounding areas. The emergence of a similar interest in me when I was around the age of thirteen to fourteen years old showed me that the family tradition, in the field of the magical, is truly strong and manifests through the generations. Thus with time I was initiated by my relatives into the practices of healing rituals – including healing of the evil eye, of fear, dissolving spells and others. The old healers handed down their knowledge, because they saw a young person seeking who would become the subsequent carrier of the sacred knowledge. As time passed, my interest in the field grew and inspired me to meet with even more fascinating interlocutors and teachers. Each of those carriers of magical knowledge was a person with a fascinating destiny, carved from numerous vicissitudes, difficulties, visible and invisible forces. If I was to decide on something which all of them had in common it has to be their great fortitude. Their tough spirit is one of their main characteristic features, the irreconcilability against hardship made them search and use the knowledge of how to give rise to effects with their will and knowledge and to force the visible by means of the invisible. All of them felt the same admiration and reverence for nature and its beauty and power. For them the plants, the animals, the stones, the springs and even everyday life objects, were not only a part of the material world, but assistants, support and comfort in woe. Along with linear time, which they lived in, they aligned their lives with another type of time: cyclical. The celebrations which recur each year and the recurrent rites wove them in their infinity, and they felt themselves to be part of a ritual faith passed on for thousands of years, which changes its carriers, but continues to live.

Over the years I was impressed by the fact that a lot of the plants, to which magical powers are ascribed, had to be picked not only on particular days, but also at particular locations. Washing with specially prepared water, in which specified magical herbs have been infused, is done not at any time, but is bound with definite calendar days and holidays, which in spite of their Christian hues, carry another type of spirit – the spirit of a faith deeply connected with nature and its powers.

3 - Kalina Misheva – Healer, Great-Grandmother Of The Author
(Deceased during the early 1900's)
Personal Archive Of The Author.

In the region of my hometown there are several ancient Thracian sanctuaries. The coincidence of ritual requirements for the picking of plants on particular dates and at particular locations, which was sacred as far back as Thracian antiquity and which was consequently turned into a Christian or Muslim topoi of faith, led me even at that time to the conclusion that the succession of beliefs and rituals is a lot stronger than it is believed to be. Furthermore, that behind a number of Bulgarian magical practices there are hidden successors of the spiritual practices of our ancestors, the Thracians.

The present book aims to present some searches for Thracian elements in ritual practices with a magical nature. Perhaps some readers will evaluate my personal position in this case as a disadvantage. Conversely it is one of the big advantages of this book that the introduced subject is commented on from the position of both a carrier and practitioner of this knowledge, because the empirical side is also included, and not just the view of an outside observer.

The book primarily discusses the subject of the Thracian heritage of Bulgarian magical practices, but as a basis for comparison some practices of the neighbouring Balkan nations are also shown – Greek, Romanian, Serbian, i.e. the geographical region where the ancient Thracians used to live.[2] Unfortunately I lack enough information and knowledge regarding Turkish magic, to also include it in the analysis. For purpose of identification of possible Paleo-Balkan elements in the rites a comparison is made with similar rites among the other Slavic peoples, mostly Russians, Ukrainians, Polish, Czechs, as well as comparisons with those of the Germanic peoples, mostly on the basis of German magical practices. Moreover for this purpose some magical rites of other peoples have also been taken into consideration, for example those of the Chuvash pagan people. As a comparative example for ancient magic, the Hittite ritual texts, the *Greek Magical Papyri*, and curse tablets, as well as secondary sources on this subject (elaborations in the sphere of literature) are used.

For the majority of the published magical rituals in this book this is the first time they have been made available in an English translation. This makes the present book one of

---

[2] The ethnographic materials from FYROM (Former Yugoslav Republic of Macedonia) are discussed as an integral part of the Bulgarian traditional culture, because I consider their independent examination impossible in linguistic, as well as in historical perspective.

the few opportunities for the English speaking part of the world to acquaint itself with such ancient exemplars of Balkan folklore. Consequently, this makes it possible for researchers, as well as practitioners, to now include in their area of activity, these particular sparks of antiquity that have survived to the present day. The great variety of examples in the comparative analysis give an opportunity for rites and ritual elements, unique to Bulgarian traditional culture, as well as others which have their parallels among the other Balkan peoples, to be singled out. Finding a number of parallels and similar rites among Serbs, Greeks, Romanians and others, in which there can be supposed a Thracian basis, should not surprise the reader. Thracian culture is the unifying element for the countries from Southeastern Europe, because traces of it are found in a huge territory, which includes Bulgaria, Turkey, Greece, Romania, Moldova, Ukraine, Russia and FYROM.

But first of all, let me introduce the reader, in summary, to the history of South-eastern Europe, because the ritual practices and the beliefs are not abstractly acting systems, but are interconnected with social and community development and processes occurring within them.

Georgi Mishev

CHAPTER 2

BALKAN ANTIQUITY, THRACIANS & BULGARIA

South-eastern Europe and the Balkan Peninsula in particular, are not coincidentally regarded as the cradle of European civilization. The first Neolithic settlements on the Balkan Peninsula appeared in the seventh millennium BCE and were products of autochthonic inhabitants and settlers from Western Asia and Asia Minor. Archaeological finds show that in the period from the sixth-fourth millennium BCE, in the region of Varna, a prosperous society existed with its own hierarchical structure, attested by the rich burials. The researched necropolis, belonging to a big settlement which presently lies under the water of the Varna Lake, shows, besides the fairly poor graves of the masses comparable to other necropolises in South-eastern Europe, some exceptional burials in terms of richness. Inside them numerous objects made of gold, copper, bone and ceramics are found, including golden sceptres and diadems – presumably insignias. The rich burials presume the formation of a part of the society which centralised in its hands secular and religious authorities. The usage of gold as a symbol of spiritual power, rather than economical as many contemporaries think, attests to the honouring of the God-Sun, rationalised and believed even then.

The attested finds of a rich male burial with a sceptre as well as numerous golden adornments, could be interpreted as the first clear indications of the formation of an aristocratic circle of initiates who honour the Sun and identify themselves with its sacred cult symbols.

Even in this age, evidence for the sacral rationalisation of the home is found - in the foundations of the buildings, under the floor level, near the hearth or the oven, different cult objects are found. Many models of buildings, ovens, cult tables, idol sculptures have been discovered. Since they are found in the very buildings, this suggests the execution of regular rituals, performed in the family environment.[3]

---

[3] Fol V., *Cultural and historical heritage of ancient Thrace* // Protection of the cultural and historical heritage in Republic of Bulgaria, Sofia 2010, 164-165 (Фол В., *Културно-историческо наследство на Древна Тракия* //

4 - Rich Burial From Varna Necropolis, Fifth-Fourth Millennium BCE[4]

Защита на културно-историчекото наследство в Република България, София 2010, 164-165); *History of Bulgaria, v.1, Primitive communal and Slave system. Thracians*, Sofia 1979, 9-10 (*История на България, т.1, Първообщинен и робовладелски строй. Траки, София 1979, 9-10*); Fol Al., Fol V., *The Thracians*, Sofia 2005, 8-11 (*Фол Ал., Фол В., Траките, София 2005, 8-11*).
[4]http://upload.wikimedia.org/wikipedia/commons/9/9b/Or_de_Varna_-_N%C3%A9cropole.jpg <20.01.2012>

An interesting find is the cult scene from Ovcharovo village, dated in the later Chalcolithic. The scene represents an ensemble of twenty-six miniature objects, found on the floor level of a structure that belongs to IX building horizon (layer) of the Late Chalcolithic tell (settlement mound) Ovcharovo. Despite the interpretation of some scholars that the scene pictures officiators at the ritual meal, in my opinion it is more likely to be divinities that are depicted. The four cult figurines are depicted seated and three altars are placed in front of them. Especially common is the portrayal of the Great Goddess on a throne. The seated position in later periods is quite common for hypostases of the Great Goddess like Cybele, Demeter and others. I interpret the raised up arms not as a gesture of adoration, as some explain, but rather as stylised wing representation, which is symbolically bound with depictions of the Goddess.

5 - Cult Scene From Ovcharovo Village[6]

In the Early Bronze Age, belief in the Great Goddess and her Son – the Sun is attested to by the paintings in cave sanctuaries. The material evidence of this and the later ages, show that during this period, there was movement of tribal groups, mainly from the northern side of Danube in a southern direction. The finds from that time deflate the migration hypothesis of a population change. There are traces of meeting but not of clash and end:

---

[6]http://godsun.thracica.com/modules/gallery/items/2/img-kultova-stsena-s.-ovcharovo-nuid169-mid.gif <20.01.2012>

"The first participants in this (ethnic-consolidation) process are the local settled farmers. The other participant in the ethnic-genetic process and interaction is the population arriving from north, which has domesticated the horse and invented the wheeled wagon. The most eminent scene of meeting between the autochthonic population and the newly coming settlers is the necropolis at Varna (ancient Odessos).

The excavated graves of Varna Necropolis, along with the other finds from the Western Black Sea coast area, point to class stratification in a dynamic society headed by kings possessing religious power and by aristocracy. Near Varna and in other places at the Western Black Sea coast forms the first European civilization, i.e. the first spiritually rationalised organisation of the society. When settlements are planned and fortified, when sanctuaries are erected in order to attract and conserve the divine energy of the celestial objects, when pictograms begin to be written, then the awareness of community identification occurs."[7]

The ethnonym *'Thracians'* first appears in Homer's *Iliad* (Hom. II.2:844-850) in the description of king Rhesus' companions, who came to the aid of the Trojans. The ancient Greeks called the population of a rather vast area extending from the South Carpathian Mountain to the Aegean Sea and North-western Asia Minor, *'Thracians'*.[8] The core of this huge area is the territory of modern Bulgaria.

According to Arrian, the calling of the region *'Thrace'*, originates from the name of the nymph Thrake, who *"was clever in the epodai (chants) and herbs and on one hand could make the suffering go away with the help of herbs, and on another – could inflict it"* (Arrian. Bith. fr. 13).

According to some other evidence the older name of Thrace is Perke, which can be related to the Indo-European root *per-*, *pir-*, i.e. *'rock'*, which is the symbolic naming of the Great Goddess, called *'The Mountain Mother'*.[9]

---

[7] Fol V., *Cultural and historical heritage of ancient Thrace* // Protection of the cultural and historical heritage in Republic of Bulgaria, Sofia 2010, 166 (Фол В., *Културно-историческо наследство на Древна Тракия* // *Защита на културно-историчекото наследство в Република България, София 2010, 166*).

[8] The specification that the ancient Greeks use this name is in order to clarify that the Thracians have not identified themselves in this way, i.e. this is external naming and could not suggest a common ethnic self-awareness.

[9] About *per-*, *pir-* see Fol Al., Jordanov K., Porozhanov K., Fol V., *Ancient Thrace*, Sofia 2000, 76.

6 - The Thracian Tribes[10]

7 - Map Of Modern Bulgaria[11]

[10] http://wauchopes.com/Tribal_Areas_of_Thrace.jpg <20.01.2012>
[11] http://www.plovdivguide.com/images/maps/map.gif <20.01.2012>

Herodotus writes about the Thracians (Hdt. V. 3):

"The Thracians are the most numerous people in the world, except, of course, the Indians; and if they had one head, or were agreed among themselves, it is my belief that their match could not be found anywhere, and that they would very far surpass all other nations. But such union is impossible for them, and there are no means of ever bringing it about. Herein therefore consists their weakness. The Thracians bear many names in the different regions of their country, but all of them have like usages in every respect, excepting only the Getae, the Trausi, and those who dwell above the people of Creston."

This source text clearly reflects the complex political relations among the Thracians. In order not to encumber the readers with a detailed description of Thracian political history, which is part, but not the subject of the present book, let us look over the more important moments in a brief chronological review:

THRACE AND THE ANCIENT WORLD[12]

Synoptic table

BCE	THRACE	ANCIENT WORLD
Second half of 5th millennium	Chalcolithic necropolis in Varna – the first European civilization.	Pre-state period in Egypt. First settlements in Mesopotamia.
Second quarter of the 2nd millennium	Royal-priestly gold ritual set of Valchitran.	Culmination of the Minoan civilization in the island of Crete. Linear A.
Mid-2nd millennium.	Mycenaean Thrace	Mycenaean Greece. Linear B.
± 1275	Thracian king-priests in Homer's epic – Rhesus, Peiroos and Akamas.	Conquest of Priam's Troy by the Mycenaean Greeks (Homer's Achaeans) headed by Agamemnon.
11th – 10th century	Marine supremacy of the European and Asian Minor Thracians over the routes across the Dardanelles and the Bosporus.	Beginning of the transition to the cities-states in Greece.
8th – 7th century	The Thracians - Bythinoi moved from the Middle Strymon valley to Asia Minor and founded the Bithynian state in North-western Asia Minor.	First Olympic games. Founding of Rome. Start of the Greek settlement along the coasts of the Mediterranean Sea, the Aegean sea, the Sea of Marmara and the Black sea.
519/514/512(?)	The march of the Persian king Darius I against the Scythians across Thrace.	
Late 6th – early 5th century	Teres – the first known ruler of the Odrysian kingdom.	

---

[12] The present table is shortened form after the issue of Fol Al., Fol V., *The Thracians*, Sofia 2005, 192-202 (*Фол Ал., Фол В., Траките, София 2005, 192-202*)

BCE	THRACE	ANCIENT WORLD
431	The Odrysian king Sitalkes concluded an alliance with Athens.	Beginning of the Peloponnesian War between the First Athenian League and the Peloponnesian Alliance headed by Sparta.
424	Sitalkes died during or after a battle with the Thracian Triballoi. Seuthes I ascended the Odrysian Throne.	
407-406	The Odrysian kingdom was divided between king Medokos (Amatokos) and Seuthes II, who proclaimed himself as an independent dynasty.	On behalf of Athens, Alcibiades concluded a peace with the two Odrysian kings for military assistance against the Spartans.
383	King Kotys I ascended the Odrysian Throne. In an inscription he proclaimed himself to be Apollo's doctrinal son.	
359	Meeting between the Odrysian king Kotys I and the Macedonian king Philip II with the aim of establishing cooperation. Kotys I was killed by Athenian insurgents.	Philip II mounts the Macedonian throne after his brother Perdiccas died in a battle against the Illyrians.
357	Athens concluded treaties for alliances with the three Odrysian rulers, who divided the old Odrysian kingdom among themselves.	

BCE	THRACE	ANCIENT WORLD
356	The temple of Apollo in Delphi issues a decree in honour of the four sons of Kersebleptes – son of Kotys I.	Alexander, later known as Alexander the Great, was born. Philip II conquered the gold and silver mines in the Pangaion Mountain, which were exploited until then by the south-western Thracian kings.
341	Philip II invaded Odrysian Thrace and captured some Thracian cities, among which is Cabyle near modern Yambol.	
335	March of Alexander of Macedon, son of Philip II, against the Triballoi and the Getae.	Anti-Macedonian uprising in Thebes, the city was destroyed by Alexander of Macedon.
323	Alexander's strategist Lysimachus ruled Eastern Thrace, but did not penetrate into the kingdom of the Odrysian ruler Seuthes III.	Alexander of Macedon died in Babylon.
280-279	Celtic invasion of the Balkan Peninsula. The Celts established their kingdom in Thrace with its capital Tylis near Byzantion (modern Istanbul).	
214-213	The Thracians destroyed the Celtic kingdom.	
171	The Odrysian king Kotys offered help to Perseus, son of Philip V of Macedon, in his war against the Romans.	

BCE	THRACE	ANCIENT WORLD
88	Spartacus, the Future leader of the slave uprising in Italy, is captured.	
72-71		The slave army of Spartacus was defeated by Marcus Licinius Crassus in Southern Italy.
60-59	The governor of Macedonia Gaius Octavius, father of the future emperor Augustus, defeated the Bessi. He visited the biggest Thracian sanctuary of the god Dionysos and received a prophecy that his son Augustus would rule over the world.	
15-13	Revolt of the Bessi in Thrace against the Romans, headed by Vologases, priest of the Dionysian sanctuary in the Rhodope.	

CE	THRACE	ANCIENT WORLD
15	The Moesia province (present-day Northern Bulgaria, South-eastern Romania and Eastern Serbia) was established.	
44-45	Rome's vassal Thracian king Rhoemetalkes III was killed in a court coup. After his assassination, Emperor Claudius proclaimed Thrace as a Roman province.	
105-106	Second Dacian war. Defeat of the Dacians. Decebalus committed suicide. Dacia was proclaimed a Roman province.	
250	Gothic invasion in Moesia Inferior and Thrace	Constantine the Great was born.
11th of May 330	Byzantion, under the name of Constantinople, was proclaimed capital of the Roman Empire.	

The subsequent history of the Thracian lands is marked by dynamic events, movements of ethnic groups and heavy social turns. The times after Emperor Constantine are labelled by intensification of the religious shift, which occurred with the official position of Christianity. Some of the Thracians were baptised and the Bible was translated into the language of the Thracian tribe Bessi (known as *Biblia Bessica*), there is evidence that in some monasteries even the services were in Thracian. It is no coincidence the researchers of the time of Thracian Christianisation write:

"...The Thracian sanctuaries were left to desecration. They were turned into ruins. Their priests felt the horror of the no less violent death compared to the first martyrs of the Christian faith. But does that mean that their paganism was put to death; that it completely disappeared from the depths of the Thracian's consciousness and soul? No, it preserved itself by merging the pagan cults and rituals with the Christian ones, the worship of nature with the intrusive faith in the ethereal and consubstantial Christian God. The cross and the Christian temples, raised in Thracian land were only symbols to record the formal recognition of the religion, enforced on the majority of the population by the power of an imperial edict. On Thracian land Christianity set existence on pagan foundation, dressed in the attire of the peculiar syncretism which later transferred itself also to the new settlers in these lands..."[13]

This statement is also confirmed by the archaeological finds:

"The excavations show that over the ruins of the Thracian pagan sanctuaries in all the parts of the country, the early Christian ones have been built and therein the ritual continued to be respected in the spirit of paganism with all the characteristics of the local ethnos."[14]

From the sixth century CE a massive settling of Slavs in the Balkan Peninsula is described. Most scholars claim that the Slavic tribes found a sparse local population of heterogeneous origin. Whether this is completely true, we cannot be certain. Undoubtedly the population in the cities was of heterogeneous ethnic composition and has been such

---

[13] Gyuzelev V, *Knyaz Boris the First. Bulgaria during the second half of nineteenth century*, Sofia 1969, 94 (Гюзелев В., *Княз Борис Първи. България през втората половина на IX в., София 1969, 94*).

[14] *History of Bulgaria, v. 1. Primitive communal and Slave system. Thracians*, Sofia 1979, 429 (История на България, т. 1. Първообщинен и робовладелски строй. Траки., София 1979, 429).

from the Hellenistic age to the present day. But is this relevant to the villages and the mountain regions? I personally cannot agree with this assumption, particularly with the part concerning the ethnic composition. Thracian culture, with its millennial history, would be very hard to assimilate by the Slavic one which existed on a much lower level. In general, the finds from the Slavs are extremely few and in most cases uncertain. What I would presume to a greater extent is that the newly arrived groups, being pagan in their religious ideology, allowed a revival of the suppressed Thracian paganism and through this, it found a favourable ground to strike roots and survive into the future.

The Sixth century CE is also the century when the Thracians and Thracian language came off the historical scene,[15] although the use of the Thracian language in closed regions of the Rhodope Mountains can be presumed up to the Tenth-Eleventh century CE.[16] However in contemporary Bulgarian language there are a number of hydronyms and toponyms,[17] which have been preserved with their Thracian forms, which in turn speaks about interaction between Slavic ethnicity and the native Thracian population. According to some scholars, a possible relation between the Thracian dialect and the languages used by the Slavs cannot be excluded. Even if there isn't such a connection, the inheritance of names of places, rivers and others, suggests an active cultural interaction, which certainly didn't remain only at the level of language. The exchange of beliefs, rites and magical knowledge is an absolutely relevant part of the cohabitation of different ethnic groups. But when it comes to sacred places, springs or magical herbs for instance, the usual order is that the old inhabitants introduce the newcomers to their established places for ritual practice. The strong family tradition in the transmission of magical knowledge among the ancient people is well-known, which is another precondition to suppose that the native population transmitted their customs to the newcomers. The continuity in the sacred areas of sanctuaries, which were Thracian and after that Slavic and proto-Bulgarian, only reinforces this

---

[15] See Vlahov K., *Thraco-Slavic parallels*, Sofia 1969 (Влахов К., *Трако-славянски успоредици, София 1969*)
[16] Fol Al., *History of Bulgarian lands in Antiquity*, Sofia 2008, 250-251(Фол Ал., *История на българските земи в древността, София 2008, 250-251*).
[17] The most popular example is the name of Plovdiv, which derives its present name from the Thracian Pulpudeva in Slavicised form, but not from its Hellenic name – Philippopolis. See also Yanakieva S., *Thracian hydronymy*, Sofia 2009 (Янакиева С., *Тракийска хидронимия, София 2009*).

argument. Certainly, this process is bidirectional. The foundation of Slavic paganism is also based on the primary Indo-European layer. But no matter how bidirectional this process is, we can argue, with great certainty, for the superiority of the established traditional culture. Thracian religion has rationalised the local environment for millennia and it becomes a foundation for one of the new arrivals.

The situation is enriched even more with the proto-Bulgarians, who arrived last in the lands, to which they gave their name and we call Bulgarian. I would not contribute an opinion about the beliefs and religious views of the proto-Bulgarians, because the information about them is highly controversial and insufficient. Their nomadic way of life, the environment in which they had been forming their beliefs and their social structure itself, are very different. If we could presume that the Chuvash pagans have preserved these proto-Bulgarian beliefs in their most original form, then the proto-Bulgarians shared many common, religious views with the Thracians and Slavs they found, but also had many different views. This is valid to a greater extent for hidden ritual practices, which can be verified on the basis of comparative analysis and ethnographic records.[18]

The Bulgarian state emerged legally by treaty in 681 CE, being formed on the basis of three pagan ethnic groups, one of which autochthonic, i.e. indigenous, namely the Thracian. Therefore some scholars do not hesitate in stating:

"...Bulgaria, a country which has probably absorbed much of the ancient Thracian population."[19]

After the formation of the state known to this day as Bulgaria, it continued for almost two centuries to be a bearer of pagan culture, whilst at the same time having Christian neighbours. However, this is the reason for how the people's attitude towards Christianity formed. For the Thracians it was initially introduced by an act of a foreign emperor, and subsequently it turned into an instrument for political and spiritual influence from neighbouring Byzantium. This led to confrontation between the foreign Christian (mainly Byzantinian) and the local Bulgarian pagan culture which, among the common folk, is to a greater extent the one of the Slavicised Thracians and among the elite is more similar to

---

[18] Concerning the magical practices of the Chuvash pagans, of great importance is the work of the Hungarian ethnologist Meszaros D., *The monuments of ancient Chuvash religion*, Cheboksary 2000 *(Месарош Д., Памятники старой чувашской веры, Чебоксары 2000).*
[19] Farnell L., *Cults of the Greek States*, vol. V, Oxford 1909, 181.

the tradition of the proto-Bulgarians. Along the Slavs, the proto-Bulgarians do not remain away from the influence of the Thracian beliefs. It is no coincidence that one of the most eminent proto-Bulgarian sanctuaries in Madara has succeeded the Thracian sacred place where the goddess Bendis and the nymphs were venerated and after that there were consequently an early Christian building and a "kapishte" (proto-Bulgarian pagan shrine).[20] The Christianisation in such conditions is a process that certainly needed strong state support. Already in the first years of the appearance of Christianity in the lands of the ancient Thracians, it was strongly refracted through the view of the Thracian belief in the Son of the Great Goddess. In later stages it was adopted on a highly folkloric level and in heavy pagan attire and rationalisation.

In 1018 CE Bulgaria fell under a Byzantinian yoke. It continued during the eleventh and twelfth century CE and additionally contributed to the formation of a negative attitude among the people towards the strongly Christian neighbour country and towards Christian ideology itself. With this emerged the necessity of ethnic and cultural self-differentiation and self-preservation. On one hand this happened through the popularisation in the Bulgarian lands of different local and foreign Christian teachings, for instance Paulicianism, Bogomilism etc. On the other hand the alternative to these Christian teachings was the traditional folk culture, which remained pagan in its essence even after the official act of Christianisation of the Bulgarians in the ninth century CE. In 1187 CE came liberation from the Byzantinian yoke. The period from the Twelfth – Fourteenth century CE was marked by state support of the church, and to this period belong events such as the church council against the Bogomils in 1211 CE. The state support of the church did not last long enough for the church to succeed in its fight with its predecessor – the faith of the Thracians, Slavs and proto-Bulgarians.

With Bulgaria falling under the Ottoman yoke in the Fourteenth century CE, the Christian church once again lost state support and the people found a chance to protect their identity in the rituals and beliefs of their ancestors. In many regions and villages, there were no Christian priests and the religious power was in the hands of the local elders, who

---

[20] Ovcharov D., *For the essence of the pagan cult centre Madara* // *Madara. Excavations and researches*. Book 3, Shumen 1992, 99-108 (Овчаров Д., *За същността на езическия култов център Мадара.* // *Мадара. Разкопки и проучвания. Кн. 3, Шумен 1992, 99-108*).

followed the unwritten rules and beliefs of the old ages. Bulgarian culture encapsulated itself for the fairly long period of five centuries (Fourteenth-Nineteenth century CE) during the Ottoman yoke, and with its end a return to archaic models of organisation and religious behaviour is observed in the community.

All of the above has the purpose of indicating the difficulty when searching for a particular shade in some ritual act, with which to connect it genetically and cognately to a definitive type of culture. The typological resemblances are external signs, on the basis of which kinship is not to be claimed, but it is a different situation when the content, the spiritual message and ideas of the ritual act are part of the traditional memory and have a genealogy of their own.[21] An additional fact that complicates the search for connections with Thracian antiquity in magical beliefs even more is the relatively late recording of most of them (from the Eighteenth century CE until now). This temporal limit should not be considered as a reason for the dismissal of a Thracian basis in magical rites. It is expected that the hidden ritual tradition, which is far more archaic and conservative than the public one, has preserved an even greater number of cultural relics because the external influence on it is very restricted. Its transmission is made in a strictly ritual context, which makes its change difficult. On the other hand the necessity of accomplishing a result forces the perpetrator of the ritual to follow in detail the exact order of the magical actions. We can be certain of the great stability of magical rites when we compare the identity of the magical formulae and ritual acts which can be observed today with those recorded two hundred years ago. In this case an expected hypothesis is that if something has been preserved almost unchanged for two centuries, it is very possible that it had been preserved for more centuries, even reaching back to the times when the ancient Greeks called their northern neighbours Thracians.

Magic and faith in the Thracian notion remain one interweaved whole, as in both there is a basic presence of the concept of a Goddess, who is Everything, the Cosmos, the birth giver of the God, believed and perceived as earthly and celestial fire – the Sun in the sky and the fire at the altar and/or at the hearth. In archaic Bulgarian magical practices

---

[21] In this connection see Neykova R., *Shamans – Did They Exist in the Balkans?*, Sofia, 2006, 191 (Нейкова Р., *Имало ли е шамани на Балканите?*, София 2006, 191).

these divine concepts continue their presence and though they obtain new appellations they never change their identity to a great extent. The divine is honoured, called and sworn through the "*image, name, number, tone, matter, form, colour, movement and function.*"[22] The Goddess and the God in their different hypostases remain not only in the ancient invocations and hymns but also in the rituals that have survived to the present day. Even today under the veil of new images the ancient Goddess in her manifestations is called and propitiated as a Genetrix of everything. The God continues to be believed in and venerated as the giver of light – the Sun-God, from whom people seek comfort and help, and he is also the Horseman who hunts, the Great Hunter. The magical traditions keep the belief in the divine, and that is why the divine appearance still happens when it is believed - even in the present day.

---

[22] Fol Al., *Orphica magica*, Sofia 2004, 51 (Фол Ал., *Orphica magica*, София 2004, 51).

CHAPTER 3

MAGICAL FAITH & THE THRACIANS

Thrace has been related from antiquity until the current day with images of a number of authorities who were initiators into the secrets of the rites, and carriers of the magical faith. The names of Orpheus, Musaeus, Eumolpus, Zalmoxis, and Rhesus have all reached us. The eponym of the very land absorbed the image of a nymph skilled in herbs and spells called Thrake. Ancient authors mention the priestess who predicts the future at the famous Dionysian sanctuary of the Thracian Bessi tribe (Hdt. 7.111). All these images are known to a greater or lesser degree by those interested in antiquity, but without going into details it is still necessary to introduce what views and perceptions that ancient authors have left us regarding them. In that way we will be able, from our contemporary position, to go behind what connects them, what exactly is magical in them and why we mention them at all regarding the traditions and rituals which survived until today.

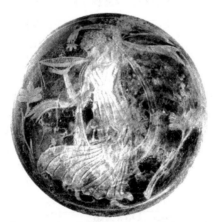

8 - Dancing Female Figure (Maenad)
With A Phiale (bowl) And Herbs In Her Hands, C3rd-4th CE, Augusta
Traiana[23]

---

[23]http://nauka.bg/forum/index.php?app=core&module=attach&section=att ach&attach_rel_module=post&attach_id=9944 <10.01.2012>.

9 - Orpheus Depicted On The Ceiling Of A Roman Catacomb In Domitilla, Around Him Biblical Scenes, C3rd BCE[24]

ORPHEUS THE BRILLIANTLY FAMOUS

First among the listed names is undoubtedly the most famous initiator in the mysteries and rites of the gods – Orpheus, called *"the brilliantly famous"* by Ibikos Rhegium as far back as the sixth century BCE. There have been many comments about him from antiquity to today and on the basis of most of the records an image has formed of a teacher who leads in initiation.[25] According to the ancient Greek authors he introduced amongst them the mysteries and sacraments of the gods, but he has also been described as an active magician. This is not accidental because according to some of the ancient legends Orpheus was trained by the Idaean Daktyls in charms, incantations,

---

[24] http://www.metahistory.org/images/OrpheusCeiling.jpg <10.01.2012>.
[25] I personally accept and share the opinion of a number of scholars that Orpheus is a composite image of the tutor. In this connection see the quoted literature and sources Fol V., *Orpheus the Thracian*, Sofia 2008 (Фол В., *Орфей тракиецът, София 2008*).

sacraments and mysteries.[26] This is exactly the depiction of Orpheus as a practitioner of magical rituals in his description in the *Orphic Argonautica* (Arg. Orph. 949), where he officiates together with Medea and only with her:

"Alone among the others, Medea followed me."

10 - Medea, Depicted On Her Dragon-Chariot, Late Antiqiuty[27]

In contrast to the widespread view of Orphic ritual practice as a male prerogative, we see here Orpheus officiating together with Medea. The implication of her attendance at the rite is that she was also initiated and in this case appeared as equal to Orpheus. The participation of women in mass mystery ritual practices was known with the maenads. However Medea differs typologically from them, she is a granddaughter of the sun Helios[28] and priestess of the great chthonic triple faced goddess Hekate,[29] so in this way she fits absolutely within the Orphic belief and ritual practices connected with the Great Goddess and her Son – Sun/Fire. The description of the sacred act (*Arg. Orph.* 951-971) also deserves attention:

---

[26] Fol Al., *The Thracian Dionysos. Book three: Naming and faith*, Sofia 2002, 128 (Фол Ал., *Тракийският Дионис. Книга трета: Назоваване и вяра, София 2002, 128*).

[27] http://www.theoi.com/image/M26.2Drakones.jpg <10.01.2012>.

[28] Apollonius Rhodius, *Argonautica* 4. 726.

[29] Apollonius Rhodius, *Argonautica* 3. 250.

"...I dug a three-leveled pit in some flat ground.
I broke some trunks from juniper bushes and dry cedar,
from prickly boxthorn and leaves from weeping black poplars,
and I quickly put them in the pit and made a pyre of them.
Skilled Medea brought to me many magical drugs,
taking them from the innermost part of her altar smelling of incense.
Soon under a woven veil kneaded dough from barley-meal
and I threw it over the pyre, and before the underworld gods,
I sacrificed three black puppies, with no signs.
I mixed with their blood copper sulphate, soapwort, a sprig of safflower,
and in addition odourless fleawort, red alkanet, and bronze-plant.
With all this, I filled the bellies of the puppies and placed them on the wood.
Then poured water and made a libation around the pit,
Dressed in a black (orphninos) mantle, I hit the ominous copper vessel
and started singing a magical song. To my call quickly answered
the three erinyes from the caverns of the gloomy abyss:
Tisiphone, together with Allecto, and divine Megaira,
waving torches that radiated ominous brilliance.
Suddenly the pit blazed up, and the deadly fire crackled,
the woods burned and the flame sent high its smoke."[34]

In the original:[35]

χώρῳ ἐνὶ πλακόεντι βόθρον τρίστοιχον ὄρυξα,
Φιτρούς τ' ἀρκεύθοιο καὶ ἀζαλέης ἀπὸ κέδρου,
ῥάμνου τ' ὀξυτέροιο, πολυκλαύτων τ' αἰγείρων
ὦκα Φέρων νήησα πυρὴν ἔμπροσθε βόθροιο.
Πολλὰ δέ μοι Φέρε πάμπαν ἐπισταμένη Μήδεια 955
Φωριαμοῦ ἀνελοῦσα θυώδεος ἐξ ἀδύτοιο.
Αὐτίκα δ' οὖλα πλάσμαθ' ὑπὸ πέπλους ἐπονεύμην,
ἂν. δὲ πυρὴν ἐπέβαλλον, ἰδ' ἔντομα θύματ' ἔρεζον,
σκύμνους παμμέλανας σκυλάκων τρισσοὺς ἱερεύσας·
αἵματι δ' αὖ χάλκανθον ἰδὲ στρούθειον ἔμιξα, 960
κνῆκόν τε σχιστὴν ἐπί τε ψύλλειον ἀηδὲς,
ἄγχουσαν τ' ἐρυθρὴν, ἰδὲ χάλκιμον· αὐτὰρ ἔπειτα
νηδύας ἐμπλήσας σκυλάκων, Φιτροῖσιν ἔθηκα·
ὕδατι δ' αὖ μίξας χολάδας χεόμην περὶ βόθρον,
ὀρφνινά θ' ἑσσάμενος Φάρη, καὶ ἀπεχθέα χαλκὸν 965
κρούων ἐλλισάμην· αἱ δ' ὀτραλέως ὑπάκουσαν,
ῥήξασαι κενεῶνας ἀμειδήτοιο βερέθρου,
Τισιφόνη τε καὶ Ἀληκτὼ καὶ δῖα Μέγαιρα,
πεύκαις ἀζαλέαις Φόνιον σέλας αἴσσουσαι.
Καίετο δ' αὐτίκα βόθρος, ἐπεσμαράγει δ' ὀλοὸν πῦρ, 970
Λιγνὺς δ' αἰθαλόεσσα χύθη περιμήκετα καπνῷ.

---

[35] Schneider J., *Orpheos Argonautika: Orphei quae vulgo dicuntur Argonautica*, Jena 1803, 38-39.

11 - The Ritual Platform At The Thracian Sanctuary Harman Kaya, Eastern Rhodope Mountains, On Which Can Be Seen Rock Cut Three-Leveled Pit (On The Right Of The Picture With 1m Scale In It). This Is One Of The Examples Of Archaeological Parallels In Thracian Cult Sites Of The Described Three-Leveled Pit In Argonautica. Picture – Personal Archive Of The Author, 2011

This Orpheus is far from the pure classical concept of the poet and the theologian. Here he is described in his guise of a theurgist, who compels the gods to fulfill his will. He calls them and communicates with them. In the quoted description we see a ritual act, whose parallels can be found starting from the Hittite ritual texts, where the dog is most often a purifying sacrifice. However, it is also offered as a sacrifice to the gods of the Heptad,[36] through until later periods, with evidence for dog sacrifices to the Great Goddess – Hekate Zerynthia at Samothrace, to Enodia in Kolophon, Genita Mana in Rome[37] and other deities throughout the archaic world. The act of digging a tree-leveled pit (which is an altar bothros (βόθρος)), the blood sacrifice of dogs into it, the use of different types of magical plants, walking around the sacred space, the colour code – the clothing in the colour orphninos, all depict this Orpheus as a practitioner of a particular magical belief and ritual tradition, being that of Thracian Orphism.

---

[36] Collins B., *The Puppy in Hittite Ritual* // Journal of Cuneiform Studies, Vol. 42, No. 2, 1990, 211-226, as well as Robertson N., *Hittite Ritual at Sardis* // Classical Antiquity, Vol. 1, No. 1, 1982, 122-140.
[37] Robertson N., *Hittite Ritual at Sardis* // Classical Antiquity, Vol. 1, No. 1, 1982, 124.

It is not accidental that we also learn in other literature fragments of the powerful spells of Orpheus. Euripides in his work *Cyclops* writes:

"Well, but I know a spell of Orpheus, a most excellent one, to make the brand enter his skull of its own accord, and set alight the one-eyed son of Earth."

This fragment emphasises the power of Orpheus' spells to compel the divine will; this is reliance through faith, which shapes the visible and invisible world. Orpheus knows the right way for calling the gods; this is the advantage of the magus-priest, who possesses the knowledge to unify his will with the divine and to guide it in one direction:

"But when Orpheus, as on the former occasion, offered up prayers to the deities of Samothrace, the winds ceased and there appeared near the ship Glaucus the Sea-god, as he is called." (Diod. Sic. IV, 48, 6)

The prayers in this case are spells, rather than pleading for the will of the initiate to be fulfilled. The corpus of ancient magical spells has preserved an example of a similar prayer:

Description of practice 1 PRAYER TO SILENCE THE SEA PGM XXIX 1-10

Translation:[38]

"I used to command the Rhodian' winds

And your regions of the sea

Whenever I'd want to set sail.

Whenever I'd want to stay there,

I'd say to the regions of the sea:

'Don't [smite] the seas with your blows;

Lay smooth the brine for seafarers.'

Then ev'ry fair wind is raised;

They shut out the blasts, and so, lord, grant:

The impassable to be passable."

---

[38] Betz H., *The Greek Magical Papyri in translation, including the Demotical spells*, Chicago/London 1986, 265-266.

Original text:[39]

'Ροθίοιc ἐκέλευον ἀνέμοιc |
καὶ μέρεcι coῖc πελαγίοιc, |
ὅτε πλέειν ἤθελον ἐγώ. |
ὅτε μένειν ἤθελον ἐκεῖ, |
ἔλεγον μέρεcιν πελαγίοιc· |
'μὴ τύπη⟨τε⟩ τὰ πελάγη, |
ἀλ' ὑποτάξατε ναυβάταιc.' |
ὅλοc ἄρ' ἄνεμοc ἐπείγεται· |
ἀπέκλειε⟨ν⟩ τὰ πνεύματα.
καὶ, 'ν[α]ξ, | δὸc τὰ [ἄβ]ατα εὔβατα.

The legend of Orpheus travelling to the underworld and his ability to persuade the underworld deities to bring his beloved Eurydice back to life with music is widely known. Certainly this is one of the most well known forms of katabasis, which has thrilled people from antiquity to today. This poeticised tale of initiation introduces us to one key moment, which we will see repeated also among the other famous Thracians mentioned above. Specifically this is the notion that the initiation occurs in the darkness of the womb and in the depths of the earth. It is not by chance that one of the experts in ancient magic, Fritz Graf, writes:

"A higher knowledge always results from the subterranean meeting with a superhuman being."[40]

MUSAEUS, SON OF THE MOON

Connected with the image of Orpheus and indicated as his disciple or even his son is Musaeus.[41] The collection of the preserved Orphic hymns begins with an address to him:[42]

"Attend Musaeus to the most sacred sacrificial hymns, and learn..."

---

[39] Preisendanz K., *Die griechschen Zauberpapyri, II*, Leipzig 1931, 155.
[40] Graf F., *Magic in the Ancient World*, Cambridge/Massachusetts/ London 1997, 91.
[41] Henrichs A., *Zur genealogie des Musaios* // Zeitschrift für Papyrologie und Epigraphik, Bd. 58, 1985, 1-8.
[42] Kern O., *Das Prooimion des Orphischen Hymnenbuches* // Hermes, 75 Bd., H. 1, 1940, 20-26.

The ancient authors connect Musaeus with the knowledge of techniques for obtaining a revelation from the gods and learning the future, as well as methods of healing:

"First, Orpheus taught you religious rites, and from bloody murder to stay your hands: Musaeus healing and oracle lore..."[43]

12 - Musaeus (On The Right) Taught By The Muse Terpsichore, Red-Figure Amphora 450-420 BCE[44]

Within the Orphic concept of Musaeus we find that the evidence supports the belief that he is a child of Selene – σεληνογενης,[45] who is also sometimes called Pandia, i.e. Goddess of everything.

"He [Musaeus] was theologian after Orpheus and the opinions around him are different: some consider him to be a son of Moon, and others – a son of Orpheus, whose disciple, as it is known he was: it is to him [Musaeus] that he [Orpheus] dedicated his first song from the poem, entitled «Crater»"[46]

---

[43]   Aristophanes,   *The*   *Frogs*,   online: http://www.gutenberg.org/cache/epub/7998/pg7998.html <10.01.2011>.
[44] http://www.theoi.com/image/K20.6BTerpsikhore.jpg <10.01.2012>.
[45] Luppe W., [σεληνογενης] // Zeitschrift für Papyrologie und Epigraphik, Bd. 55, 1984, 8.
[46] Servius, *Commentary on Aeneid*, VI, 667. The translation is from the Russian edition of Lebedev A., *Fragments of ancient Greek philosophers*, part I, Moscow 1989, 67 (*Лебедев А., Фрагменты ранних греческих философов,*

This wonderful naming defines the initiate as a child of the Goddess. He possesses the secret knowledge exactly for that reason, because he has obtained them from her. It is not by accident that in the magical papyri there is a preserved prayer, which in my opinion is wrongly attributed to Moses,[47] but actually it would be more correct to suppose that it is a spell of Musaeus to Selene. This would be absolutely appropriate bearing in mind his connection with the Goddess and the complete absence of a connection between Moses and Selene.

Description of practice 2 THE SECRET PRAYER OF MOSES (MUSAEUS – MY SUGGESTION) TO SELENE
PGM XIII 1059-1062

"OINEL of life, CHNOUB OUER AKROMBOUS OURAOI OYER AI HAPH HOR OKI. ANOCH BORINTH MAMIKOURPH AEI AEI E AEI EIE EIE TETH OUR OUR OUER ME CHROUR CHOU TAIS ECHREZE ECHRINX MAMIA OURPH,[48] goddess in woman's form, mistress Selene, do the NN thing."[49]

In original:[50]

15   Μοϋςέως ἀπόκρυφος Cεληνιακή· | 'Οινελ βιου Χνουβ ουηρ, ακρομβους ‖ ουραοι 1059

ουηρ αι 'Αφ 'Ωρ οκι ἀνοχ | βωρινθ μαμικουρφ αει αει η αει | ειε ειη, Τεθ ουρ ουρ ουηρ με χρου|ρ

20 χου ταις εχρηζη εχριτε μαμια | ουρφ, γυναικόμορφε θεά, δεσπότι Cελήνη, ‖ ποίηcον 1064

τὸ δεῖνα πρᾶγμα.'

часть I, Москва 1989, 67). For the original Latin text see the edition of Diels H., *Die Fragmente der Vorsokratiker*, Berlin 1903, 496.

[47] For the ambition of the Jews to represent Musaeus as Moses and in the same time Moses as a teacher of Orpheus relying on the idea that the older is also better and in this way to seek superiority on a spiritual level see Bloch R., *Orpheus als Lehrer des Musaios, Moses als Lehrer des Orpheus* // Antike Mysterien. Medien, Transformation und Kunst, Dill U., Walde Chr., Berlin/New York, 2009, 469-486.

[48] The beginning of the ritual formula starts with the so-called nomina barbara, barbarian names, which are untranslatable to date. I say to date, because a number of researches prove the meaning and origin of separate words from different ancient languages and their semantic as naming of separate divinities and divine forces. In this connection there are possible interpretations in Gager J., *Curse Tablets and Binding Spells from the Ancient World,* New York/ Oxford 1992, 256-269, as well as a development dedicated to the so called Ephesia grammata - Wessely K., *Ephesia Grammata* aus Papyrusrollen, Inschriften, Gemmen etc., Wien 1886, and McCown C., *The Ephesia Grammata in Popular Belief* // Transactions and Proceedings of the American Philological Association 54, 1923, 128-31.

[49] Betz H., *The Greek Magical Papyri in translation, including the Demotical spells*, Chicago/London 1986, 195.

[50] Preisendanz K., *Die griechschen Zauberpapyri*, II, Leipzig 1931, 131.

13 - Musaeus And Linos, The Two Thracian Characters Are Depicted With Tablets And Scrolls Of Sacred Writings In Their Hands, Red-Figure Vessel 440-435 BCE[51]

In addition to the fact that the Goddess of the moon is mentioned as Musaeus' mother, is that his teacher, according to the words of Euripides in *Rhesus* (945-947), is Apollo. This places Musaeus in the role of an initiate to the God-Sun and the Goddess-Moon, i.e. he unifies the light and the dark and in this way possesses knowledge of the future. Therefore a lot of collections containing oracle poems are accredited to him.[52]

---

[51]http://upload.wikimedia.org/wikipedia/commons/thumb/b/bd/Palaistra _scene_Louvre_G457.jpg/602px-Palaistra_scene_Louvre_G457.jpg <10.01.2012> .
[52] Oliver J., *On the Exegetes and the Mantic or Manic Chresmologians* // The American Journal of Philology, Vol. 73, No. 4, 1952, 406-413.

EUMOLPUS, THE HIEROPHANT OF THE EARTH MOTHER

Following this line of great initiates in antiquity we reach the image of Eumolpus, who is considered the progenitor of the high priests in the Eleusinian Mysteries.[53]

"From the time when Eumolpus, the son of Musaeus, initiate of Orpheus, founded the mysteries in Eleusis and the father Musaeus gave to the people the poetry, 1100 years passed; in this time at Athens the king was Erechtheus, son of Pandion. [1373 BCE]"[54]

The pre-Hellenic antiquity of these mysteries has been commented in the scientific basis of archaeological research and findings[55] and what is important for this study is the mention of the Thracian origin of Eumolpus. The leading role in the line of the Eumolpidae in the mysteries of the two Goddesses is of great importance, because it reflects a historical tradition in the notion of the ancient Greeks ascending to a pre-Hellenic age. This belief supposes transmission of the secret knowledge of the Goddess to her officiate, in whose family the leading role in the mystery rites is preserved. In this sense the priest is recognised as an offspring of the Goddess.

---

[53] For the priest communities in Eleusis see Clinton K., *The Sacred Officials of the Eleusinian Mysteries* // Transactions of the American Philosophical Society, Vol. 64, 1974, 1-143, also for an interesting article regarding the possibility that on the famous relief from Eleusis is depicted Eumolpus, but not Triptolemus see Harrison E., *Eumolpos arrives in Eleusis* // Hesperia: The Journal of the American School of Classical Studies at Athens, Vol. 69, No. 3, 2000, 267-291.

[54] Parian Chronicle, FGrHist 239 A15, the translation is from the Russian edition of Lebedev A., *Fragments of ancient Greek philosophers*, part I, Moscow 1989, 67 (Лебедев А., *Фрагменты ранних греческих философов, часть I, Москва 1989, 67*). For the original ancient Greek text see the edition of Diels H., *Die Fragmente der Vorsokratiker*, Berlin 1903, 496.

[55] For the dating of the findings in the region of the telesterion in Eleusis in the pre-Mycenaean and Mycenaean age see Persson A., *Der Ursprung der eleusinischen Mysterien* // Archiv für Religionswissenschaft Bd. 21, Leipzig/Berlin 1922, 292, както и Fol V., *The Rock Antiquity of Eleusis* // von Domica bis Drama. Gedenkschrift für Jan Lichardus, Sofia 2004, 171-180, as well as Fol V., *Rock topoi of faith in Southeastern Europe and Asia Minor during Antiquity*. Studia Thracica 10, Sofia 2007, 43-51, 53-61, 229-230, 242 (Фол В., *Скални топоси на вяра в Югоизточна Европа и Мала Азия през древността, Studia Thracica 10, София 2007, 43-51, 53-61, 229-230, 242*).

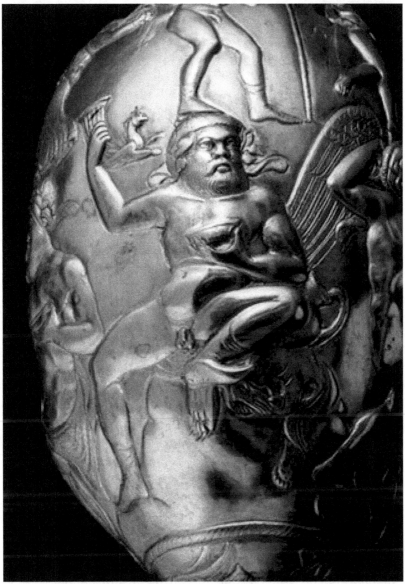

14 - Rhyton Jug From The Borovo Findings With A Depiction Interpreted By Some Scholars As Zalmoxis, Sitting On A Bear Hide[56]

---

[56] For this interpretation of the depiction see Venedikov Iv. *The copper threshing-floor*, Stara Zagora 1995, 210-215 (*Венедиков Ив., Медното гумно на прабългарите, Стара Загора 1995, 210-215*).
Image: http://www.runitravel.com/wp-content/gallery/borovo/borovo_035.jpg <10.01.2012>.

ZALMOXIS, THE GIVER OF IMMORTALITY

Zalmoxis lines up in the same row of initiates and initiators. According to some authors he is related mostly to the North Thracians – the Getae, but some data shows that his image is known in a vast area of the Thracian region. The first ancient author that mentions him is Herodotus (Hdt. IV, 94-96) and he tells the following story:

"IV, 94 Their belief in their immortality is as follows: they believe that they do not die, but that one who perishes goes to the deity Salmoxis, or Gebeleizis, as some of them call him. Once every five years they choose one of their people by lot and send him as a messenger to Salmoxis, with instructions to report their needs; and this is how they send him: three lances are held by designated men; others seize the messenger to Salmoxis by his hands and feet, and swing and toss him up on to the spear-points. If he is killed by the toss, they believe that the god regards them with favour; but if he is not killed, they blame the messenger himself, considering him a bad man, and send another messenger in place of him. It is while the man still lives that they give him the message. Furthermore, when there is thunder and lightning these same Thracians shoot arrows skyward as a threat to the god, believing in no other god but their own.

IV, 95 I understand from the Greeks who live beside the Hellespont and Pontus, that this Salmoxis was a man who was once a slave in Samos, his master being Pythagoras son of Mnesarchus; then, after being freed and gaining great wealth, he returned to his own country. Now the Thracians were a poor and backward people, but this Salmoxis knew Ionian ways and a more advanced way of life than the Thracian; for he had consorted with Greeks, and moreover with one of the greatest Greek teachers, Pythagoras; therefore he made a hall, where he entertained and fed the leaders among his countrymen, and taught them that neither he nor his guests nor any of their descendants would ever die, but that they would go to a place where they would live forever and have all good things. While he was doing as I have said and teaching this doctrine, he was meanwhile making an underground chamber. When this was finished, he vanished from the sight of the Thracians, and went down into the underground chamber, where he lived for three years, while the Thracians wished him back and mourned him for dead; then in the fourth year he appeared to the Thracians, and thus they came to believe what Salmoxis had told them. Such is the Greek story about him.

IV, 96 Now I neither disbelieve nor entirely believe the tale about Salmoxis and his underground chamber; but I think that he lived many years before Pythagoras; and as to whether there was a man called Salmoxis or this is some deity native to the Getae, let the question be dismissed."[57]

I quoted the full story by Herodotus, because there are numerous commentaries and scholastic research works on this topic, but let us see what becomes clear from the words of the ancient author. First of all he tells that trust in the teachings of Zalmoxis makes the Getae believe in immortality. They don't believe that they die, but that they are making a transition and go, pass Beyond, to where their God awaits them. After that, in the text of Herodotus it becomes clear that this belief is also practiced, i.e. ritually expressed as we see from the described rite. The Getae, as they are described in that passage, are not afraid of the natural elements, but they threaten them with the power of their divinity, to whom they are devoted, i.e. they threaten the elements, because they believe in their own power to control them. Additionally the ancient author shares the

---

[57] The Ancient Greek original as follows:

94 Ἀθανατίζουσι δὲ τόνδε τὸν τρόπον· οὔτε ἀποθνήσκειν ἑωυτοὺς νομίζουσι ἰέναι τε τὸν ἀπολλύμενον παρὰ Σάλμοξιν δαίμονα· οἱ δὲ αὐτῶν τὸν αὐτὸν τοῦτον ὀνομά ζουσι Γεβελέϊζιν. Διὰ πεντετηρίδος δὲ τὸν πάλῳ λαχόντα αἰεὶ σφέων αὐτῶν ἀποπέμπουσι ἄγγελον παρὰ τὸν Σάλμο ξιν, ἐντελλόμενοι τῶν ἂν ἑκάστοτε δέωνται. Πέμπουσι δὲ ὧδε· οἱ μὲν αὐτῶν ταχθέντες ἀκόντια τρία ἔχουσι, ἄλλοι δὲ διαλαβόντες τοῦ ἀποπεμπομένου παρὰ τὸν Σάλμοξιν τὰς χεῖρας καὶ τοὺς πόδας, ἀνακινήσαντες αὐτὸν μετέωρον ῥιπτέουσι ἐς τὰς λόγχας. Ἢν μὲν δὴ ἀποθάνῃ ἀναπαρείς, τοῖσι δὲ ἵλεος ὁ θεὸς δοκέει εἶναι· ἢν δὲ μὴ ἀποθάνῃ, αἰτιῶνται αὐτὸν τὸν ἄγγελον, φάμενοί μιν ἄνδρα κακὸν εἶναι, αἰτησάμενοι δὲ τοῦτον ἄλλον ἀποπέμπουσι. Ἐντέλ λονται δὲ ἔτι ζώοντι. Οὗτοι οἱ αὐτοὶ Θρήικες καὶ πρὸς βροντήν τε καὶ ἀστραπὴν τοξεύοντες ἄνω πρὸς τὸν οὐρανὸν ἀπειλέουσι τῷ θεῷ, οὐδένα ἄλλον θεὸν νομίζοντες εἶναι εἰ μὴ τὸν σφέτερον.
95 Ὡς δὲ ἐγὼ πυνθάνομαι τῶν τὸν Ἑλλήσποντον καὶ Πόντον οἰκεόντων Ἑλλήνων, τὸν Σάλμοξιν τοῦτον ἐόντα ἄνθρωπον δουλεῦσαι ἐν Σάμῳ, δουλεῦσαι δὲ Πυθαγόρῃ τῷ Μνησάρχου· ἐνθεῦτεν δὲ αὐτὸν γενόμενον ἐλεύθερον χρήματα κτήσασθαι συχνά, κτησάμενον δὲ ἀπελθεῖν ἐς τὴν ἑωυτοῦ. Ἅτε δὲ κακοβίων τε ἐόντων τῶν Θρηίκων καὶ ὑπαφρονεστέρων, τὸν Σάλμοξιν τοῦτον ἐπιστάμενον δίαιτάν τε Ἰάδα καὶ ἤθεα βαθύτερα ἢ κατὰ Θρήικας, οἷα Ἕλλησί τε ὁμιλήσαντα καὶ Ἑλλήνων οὐ τῷ ἀσθενεστάτῳ σοφιστῇ Πυθαγόρῃ, κατασκευάσασθαι ἀνδρεῶνα, ἐς τὸν πανδοκεύοντα τῶν ἀστῶν τοὺς πρώτους καὶ εὐωχέοντα ἀναδιδάσκειν ὡς οὔτε αὐτὸς οὔτε οἱ συμπόται αὐτοῦ οὔτε οἱ ἐκ τούτων αἰεὶ γινόμενοι ἀποθανέονται, ἀλλ᾽ ἥξουσι ἐς χῶρον τοῦτον ἵνα αἰεὶ περιεόντες ἕξουσι τὰ πάντα ἀγαθά. Ἐν ᾧ δὲ ἐποίεε τὰ καταλεχθέντα καὶ ἔλεγε ταῦτα, ἐν τούτῳ κατάγαιον οἴκημα ἐποιέετο. Ὡς δέ οἱ παντελέως εἶχε τὸ οἴκημα, ἐκ μὲν τῶν Θρηίκων ἠφανίσθη, καταβὰς δὲ κάτω ἐς τὸ κατάγαιον οἴκημα διαιτᾶτο ἐπ᾽ ἔτεα τρία. Οἱ δέ μιν ἐπόθεόν τε καὶ ἐπένθεον ὡς τεθνεῶτα. Τετάρτῳ δὲ ἔτεϊ ἐφάνη τοῖσι Θρήιξι, καὶ οὕτω πιθανά σφι ἐγένετο τὰ ἔλεγε ὁ Σάλμοξις.
96 Ταῦτά φασί μιν ποιῆσαι. Ἐγὼ δὲ περὶ μὲν [τούτου καὶ] τοῦ καταγαίου οἰκήματος οὔτε ἀπιστέω οὔτε ὦν πιστεύω τι λίην, δοκέω δὲ πολλοῖσι ἔτεσι πρότερον τὸν Σάλμοξιν τοῦτον γενέσθαι Πυθαγόρεω. Εἴτε δὲ ἐγένετό τις Σάλμοξις ἄνθρωπος, εἴτ᾽ ἐστὶ δαίμων τις Γέτῃσι οὗτος ἐπιχώριος, χαιρέτω.

opinion of the Ancient Greeks for the Thracian God, as he says himself that he doesn't believe that all they say is truth. The detail of the alien culture and the seeking of a way to discredit it is obvious, and in this case Herodotus very objectively disregards that. But it is unquestionable that in this story there are elements, which have a real basis and this is most probably the practice of initiating in underground premises or caves, which are their prototype. Even here Zalmoxis is associated with Pythagoras, as Herodotus says that *"he lived many years before Pythagoras."*

The motif of katabasis appears again. The seeker goes down in the depths of the chthonos (the earth), there he receives his initiation, i.e. he changes his status, after that he performs anabasis (he goes up again) and goes back to the upper world. After his return he is recognised as a deity, i.e. he has achieved immortality. This immortality is not of the body, but it is the immortality that is shared by anyone who recognizes the divine essence inside themselves and finds union with it. This initiate is a newborn, but this birth is done in the womb of the Mistress of the underworld, as the Goddess is called in the Orphic tablets and she immortalises him.

15 - Artistic Vision Of The Rite Performed By The Getae – Sending A Messanger To Zalmoxis[58]

---

[58] http://i242.photobucket.com/albums/ff223/fredyloy/sacrificiulsupremgeto -dac.jpg <10.01.2012>.

One story derives the name of Zalmoxis from the Thracian word zalmos – 'hide', because according to legend he was placed on a bear hide at his birth. The bear hide is interesting in this case, because the bear is a strong symbolic animal on a mythological level and in the Thracian area is connected with the Goddess (for instance Artemis Brauronia), as even until today in Balkan culture it is perceived as a female character – Baba Metsa (grandmother Bear). The bear hide and placing the child over it is possibly a symbolic recognition of the child from the Goddess and its acceptance as her offspring.

A variation of the story by Herodotus is given also by Strabo (Strab. 7.3.5), who tells that Zamolxis, as he calls him, came back to the Getae, after he was a slave of Pythagoras and became an adviser of the king, and at the same time a priest. Later he proclaimed himself a God and lived alone in a cave, and the only ones who went to see him were the king and his close associates. In this connection the cave and the mountain were worshipped as sacred. It is not by chance that a similar story is known about Pythagoras himself, who went down in an underground dwelling, where he lived receiving from the mother writings[59] regarding what was happening on the surface and after some time he came back to the upper world thin as a skeleton, claiming that he came back from Hades. A number of scholars see in the image of the mother[60] and her messages the chthonic mother, i.e. the Goddess, but not the real mother of Pythagoras. This is completely expected in the spirit of the ancient belief that the Goddess is the one who initiates in the mysteries and through her the uninitiated is born again as an initiate and knows the divine.

The image of Zalmoxis is particularly important for Thracian ritual practices in the light of Plato's story in his dialogue *Charmides* (Plat. Charm. 156d-157c):

"Most assuredly, he said. Then I, on hearing his approval, regained my courage; and little by little I began to muster up my confidence again, and my spirit began to rekindle. So I said, — Such, then, Charmides, is the nature of this charm. I learnt it on campaign over there, from one of the Thracian physicians of Zalmoxis, who are said even to make one

---

[59] These writings are called μητρος παραγγελματα, i.e. *"given messages from the mother"* see Burkert W., *Weisheit und Wissenschaft: Studien zu Pythagoras, Philolaos und Platon*, Nürnberg 1962, 159.
[60] See Graf F., *Magic in the Ancient World*, Cambridge/Massachusetts/London 1997, 9 and Jacoby F., *Die Fragmente der griechischen Historiker 4*, Leiden/Boston/Köln 1999, 267-276.

immortal. This Thracian said that the Greeks were right in advising as I told you just now: "but Zalmoxis," he said, "our king, who is a god, says that as you ought not to attempt to cure eyes without head, or head without body, so you should not treat body without soul"; and this was the reason why most maladies evaded the physicians of Greece—that they neglected the whole, on which they ought to spend their pains, for if this were out of order it was impossible for the part to be in order. For all that was good and evil, he said, in the body and in man altogether was sprung from the soul, and flowed along from thence as it did afrom the head into the eyes. Wherefore that part was to be treated first and foremost, if all was to be well with the head and the rest of the body. And the treatment of the soul, so he said, my wonderful friend, is by means of certain charms, and these charms are words of the right sort: by the use of such words is temperance engendered in our souls, and as soon as it is engendered and present we may easily secure health to the head and to the rest of the body also. Now in teaching me the remedy and the charms he remarked, — "Let nobody persuade you to treat his head with this remedy, unless he has first submitted his soul for you to treat with the charm. For at present," he said, "the cure of mankind is beset with the error of certain doctors who attempt to practise the one method without the other." And he most particularly enjoined on me not to let anyone, however wealthy or noble or handsome, conduce me to disobey him. So I, since I have given him my oath, and must obey him, will do as he bids; and if you agree to submit your soul first to the effect of the Thracian charms, according to the stranger's injunctions, I will apply the remedy to your head: otherwise we shall be at a loss what to do with you, my dear Charmides."

Here the ancient philosopher describes the concept held by the Thracian physicians of Zalmoxis that the body and the soul should be healed in unity and in the same unity the herb and the incantation should be used. In this sense the healing power and knowledge of the initiates in the cult of Zalmoxis strongly stands out, who as the ancients say could *"immortalise"*.[61]

---

[61] In this connection see Ustinova Y., *Greek knowledge of the Thracian and Scythian healing practices and ideas of afterlife and immortality* // Ephemeris Napocensis, XIV-XV, Bucarest 2004-2005, 41-52.

16 - The Dead Rhesus, Red-Figure Krater 340 BCE[62]

RHESUS THE ANTHROPODAEMON

The story about the cave in which Zalmoxis dwelled[63] reminds one a lot of the passage of Euripides in *Rhesus* (Eur. Rhes. 962-973), where the mother of Rhesus – the muse, says that after his death he will live again, when he recedes in a cave and he will be a god-man – anthropodaemon. Philostratus mentions a sanctuary of Rhesus in the Rhodope Mountains (*Heroic.* 149). There the animals were coming by themselves to be sacrificed[64] and he is also described as a healer, who drove back the plague from the mountain, where he lived. The belief about the deer that comes by itself to be

---

[62]
http://www.mediterranees.net/mythes/ulysse/guerre_troie/incursions.htm l <10.01.2012>.

[63] See also Ustinova Y., *"Either a Daimon, or a hero, or Perhaps a God:" Mythical Residents of Subterranean Chambers*, Kernos 15, 2002, 267-288; Ustinova Y., *Truth lies at the bottom of a cave: Apollo Pholeuterios, the Pholarchs of the Eleats, and Subterranean Oracles* // La Parola del Passato 59, Naples 2004, 25-44 as well as in the works of the same author Ustinova Y., *Caves and the Ancient Greek Mind*, Oxford/New York 2009, as well as in Fol V., *Rock topoi of faith in Southeastern Europe and Asia Minor during Antiquity.* Studia Thracica 10, Sofia 2007, 87-96 (Фол В., *Скални топоси на вяра в Югоизточна Европа и Мала Азия през древността, София 2007, 87-96*).

[64] The idea of the self-sacrifice of the deer is mentioned in a work for blood sacrifice among the Balkan peoples Kurban in the Balkans, Belgrade 2007 and respectively the following articles in the collection - Sobolev A., *On Balkan names for the sacrificial animal on the St George´s day* // Kurban in the Balkans, Belgrade 2007, 19; Dalipaj G. *Kurban and its celebration in the Shapti region* // Kurban in the Balkans, Belgrade 2007, 186; Popov R., *Kurban sacrificial offerings on the feastdays of the summertime saints in the calendar tradition of the Bulgarians* // Kurban in the Balkans, Belgrade 2007, 259-260; Bocev Vl., *Kurban among the Macedonians* // Kurban in the Balkans, Belgrade 2007, 271.

sacrificed is preserved even today among the Balkan peoples. This is not by chance as prof. Al. Fol writes:

"...the ancient Greek verbal naming of the Thracian Orphic ritual tradition is inherited in the Bulgarian folklore language environment because of the cultural-historical continuum of the ethnosness faith, which is not ethnic and in which the languages are not ethnic determinants."[65]

THE THRACIAN PROPHETESS OF DIONYSOS

Along with the images of initiated men and priests, we have evidence for the role of women in the cult practices of the Thracians. Herodotus (Hdt. 7.111) describes the sanctuary of Dionysos in Thrace and says that a priestess makes the divinations in it, just like in Delphi.

"7.111. The Satrae, as far as we know, have never yet been subject to any man; they alone of the Thracians have continued living in freedom to this day; they dwell on high mountains covered with forests of all kinds and snow, and they are excellent warriors. 7.111.2 It is they who possess the place of divination sacred to Dionysos. This place is in their highest mountains; the Bessi, a clan of the Satrae, are the prophets of the shrine; there is a priestess who utters the oracle, as at Delphi; it is no more complicated here than there."[66]

Why and in what manner Herodotus equates the Thracian priestess with the Pythia is questionable, because from latter information we understand that the rite consisted of pouring wine on the altar. But whether Herodotus has this rite in mind or another we cannot know. What matters is the role of the woman, called πρόμαντις, i.e. prophetess, by Herodotus. Because she is equated to the Pythia at Delphi we could suppose that she also made her prophecies inspired by the divine. This divinely inspired woman received and expressed the will of the gods.

---

[65] Fol Al., *The Thracian Dionysos. Book three: Naming and faith*, Sofia 2002, 126 (Фол Ал., *Тракийският Дионис. Книга трета: Назоваване и вяра, София 2002, 126*).

[66] The original in ancient Greek as follows:
"7.111. Σάτραι δὲ οὐδενός κω ἀνθρώπων ὑπήκοοι ἐγένοντο, ὅσον ἡμεῖς ἴδμεν, ἀλλὰ διατελεῦσι τὸ μέχρι ἐμεῦ αἰεὶ ἐόντες ἐλεύθεροι μοῦνοι Θρηίκων· οἰκέουσί τε γὰρ ὄρεα ὑψηλά, ἴδῃσί τε παντοίῃσι καὶ χιόνι συνηρεφέα, καὶ εἰσὶ τὰ πολέμια ἄκροι. Οὗτοι οἱ Διονύσου τὸ μαντήιον εἰσὶ ἐκτημένοι· τὸ δὲ μαντήιον τοῦτο ἔστι μὲν ἐπὶ τῶν ὀρέων τῶν ὑψηλοτάτων, Βησσοὶ δὲ τῶν Σατρέων εἰσὶ οἱ προφητεύοντες τοῦ ἱροῦ, πρόμαντις δὲ ἡ χρέωσα κατά περ ἐν Δελφοῖσι, καὶ οὐδὲν ποικιλώτερον."

THRAKE – THE NYMPH THAT CAUSES HEALTH AND ILLNESS

17 - As An Example Of Magical Objects I Give The Findings From The Burial Of The Thracian Priestess Leseskepra, Burgas[67]

Arrian writes about the nymph Thrake, who *"was clever in the epodai (chants) and herbs and on one hand could make the suffering go away with the help of herbs, and on another – could inflict it"* (Arrian. Bith. fr. 13). With this information the author shows the double possibilities when using magical and secret knowledge – for chasing away the pain, but also for causing it.

Archaeological findings also prove that some Thracian women performed magical activities and subsequently were buried with their ritual inventory. Clay figurines with magical signs that are categorically considered by archaeologists to be used for cult purposes[68] have been found in a number of burials. Some of those clay vessels and figurines have parallels in contemporary healing ritual practices. The ritual inventory is usually transmitted by inheritance and there are cases when the healer is the last in

---

[67]http://www.eidola.eu/data/5c77726358c5daf98ad9cdccd0882bca0f718b88/d94da96a6ab92f8e3ed64c24416d6ec7b0428678_full.jpg <18.02.2012> .
[68] Konova L., *Magic and the funeral rites. Clay cult objects from the necropolis of Apollonia Pontica* // Heros Hephaistos. Studia in Honorem Liubae Ognenova-Marinova, Veliko Turnovo 2005, 148-164 (Конова Л., *Магия и погребален обред. Глинени култови фигурки от некропола на Аполония Понтика* // Heros Hephaistos. Studia in Honorem Liubae Ognenova-Marinova, Велико Търново 2005, 148-164).

line and there is no successor, that this same inventory was placed with her body at her burial. Some of these findings are determined also as Orphic cult objects, the so-called toys of the god Zagreus, which is also a possible interpretation according to the context of the findings.

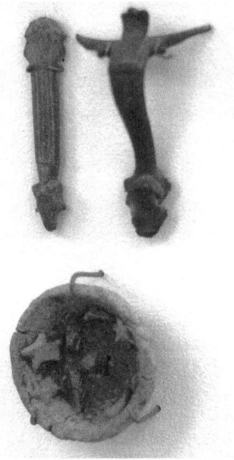

18 - Cult Objects From The Burial Of
The Thracian Priestess Leseskepra, Burgas[69]

[69]http://www.eidola.eu/data/5c77726358c5daf98ad9cdccd0882bca0f718b88/f5441108f0a86129f33998e518a6d8c4cde253c5_full.jpg <18.02.2012>.

CHAPTER 4

MYSTERIES AND MAGIC

As we have seen from the information about ancient initiates, most of them are connected with mysteries and with magical ritual practices. This approximation of mysteries and ritual practices, defined as magical, was made in ancient times and subsequently this notion was preserved also among the Christians. The fact that Christianity itself borrows elements of the mystery cults of antiquity and also from this same magical ritual practices, is interesting. We also understand the connection of the mysteries with magical ritual practices and the concept of the magical in them from Christian texts. In the confession of St Cyprian it is said that he was initiated into most of the mystery cults and there he was taught numerous magical practices.[70] But what is the connection between the ritual practices of the mysteries and magic, and also with those identified as magicians? On the one hand in antiquity there is a clear differentiation of the types of magical rites, i.e. the so called low and high magic, but also in more ancient times this artificial differentiation dissolves and we learn, for instance that the Idaean Dactyls were defined as γοητες, i.e. not magi in the late meaning of the word that attaches to it eminence, but exactly as magicians. These same Dactyls are also pointed out as teachers of Orpheus, as was previously stated.[71] In turn they are companions of the Goddess (Rhea, Cybele) and have received the secret knowledge from her.[72] It is not until the Hellenistic age that goeteia (γοητεία) acquires such a negative connotation and that is why people begin to use the term mageia (μαγεία) and magi aiming to show the different, the sublime orientation of the magical actions, but this also supposes a division of the knowledge. The mysteries of antiquity were also focused on the improvement of the whole human state in this life, as well as in the other and

---

[70] See Nilson M., *Greek Mysteries in the Confession of St. Cyprian* // The Harvard Theological Review, Vol. 40, No 3, 1947, 167-176.

[71] See Fol Al., *The Thracian Dionysos. Book three: Naming and faith*, Sofia 2002, 128 (Фол Ал., *Тракийският Дионис. Книга трета: Назоваване и вяра, София 2002, 128*).

[72] One of the legends for their birth described in *Argonautica* 1122 is very interesting: *"...the Idaean Dactyls of Crete, whom once the nymph Anchiale, as she grasped with both hands the land of Oaxus, bare in the Dictaean cave."*

therefore they are related to magical ritual practice, which has a similar purpose.[73] The ancient initiates like Orpheus, Musaeus, Eumolpus and others, established festivals and celebrations of the divinities, but at the same time introduced mortals to the knowledge and techniques for self-perfection with the goal of achieving even the ability to 'immortalise', as we learn for the initiates of Zalmoxis. In the magical papyri from the Graeco-Egyptian period, which carry preserved archaic notions, we see that the magician is recognised as an adept and initiate of a certain cult. It is not accidental that in the prayer to the Goddess in PGM LXX the one who pronounces the magical formula says:

"I have been initiated, and I went down into the (underworld) chamber of the Dactyls, and I saw the things down below, the Virgin, the Bitch and all the rest..."[74]

In original:[75]

τετέ[λ]εσμαι

καὶ εἰς μέγαρον κατέ[βη]ν Δακτύλων
καὶ [τ]ὰ ἄλλα εἶδον κάτω, παρθένος, κύων,
καὶ τὰ λοιπὰ πάντα.

In a similar way this notion is depicted in another magical papyrus PGM IV.2251-2255:

"You will, willy-nilly, do the NN task because I know your lights in full detail, and I am your priest of good offices, your minister and fellow witness, Maid."[76]

In original:[77]

τὸ δεῖνα ποιήσεις, | κᾶν θέλῃς κᾶν μὴ θέλῃς, ὅτι οἶδά cου τὰ | φῶτα πρὸ⟨c⟩ cτιγμῆc μέτρον καὶ τῶν καʹλῶν cου μυcταγωγὸc πραγμάτων ὑπο υρ⟨τόc⟩ εἰμι καὶ cυνίcτωρ, παρθένε.

From this statement we understand that the swearer must be a carrier of the mystery knowledge, he must be an initiate in order to have the cognition and be capable, not simply know the technique of the rite. Only then could he swear by the gods and accomplish the action vertically (i.e. through the three worlds of earth, heaven and underworld),

---

[73] See Graf F., *Magic in the Ancient World*, Cambridge/Massachusetts/London 1997, 101.
[74] Betz H., *Fragments from a Catabasis Ritual in a Greek Magical Papyrus* // History of Religions, Vol. 19, No. 4, Chicago 1980, 287-295.
[75] Preisendanz K., *Die griechschen Zauberpapyri*, I, Leipzig 1928
[76] Betz H., *The Greek Magical Papyri in translation, including the Demotical spells*, Chicago/London 1986, 78.
[77] Preisendanz K., *Die griechschen Zauberpapyri*, I, Leipzig 1928, 142-143.

but not only on the basis of the horizontal sympathy (to the cardinal directions of east, south, west and north). This is the difference between the so called τεχνη μαγικη – *'magical technique'* and μαγικη εμπειρια – *'magical knowledge'*, that leads to γνωσις - *'gnosis'*.[78] In this sense the contents of the magical act are called mystery, i.e. something secret; the magical practice is telete (τελετή – meaning *'rite'*), a word also used for the mystery sacraments. The perpetrator is called mystes, i.e. initiate in a mystery; the teacher, who passes the knowledge is mystagogue, i.e. the one who initiates in the mystery; the others involved in the ritual act are synmystai (συνμύσται), i.e. co-initiates.[79] The ancient magical tradition left writings, such as the magical papyri. However the Thracians didn't leave such texts. Nevertheless a part of the Orphic magical belief and ritual practice is reflected in the written tradition. In a number of magical texts the name of Orpheus is mentioned as an authority on magical practices. In the ritual formulae there are a number of divine namings, which lead to the Orphic ones. From the region where most of the magical papyri are found also comes the papyrus of Gurôb, Egypt.[80] It contains ritual instructions for performing an Orphic type of worship of the Gods. All this confirms the developments of scholars that the late magical papyri are recordings of earlier oral belief, which has been written in its syncretised version. Examining the papyri this syncretism is not random and is made on the principle of the heard, but misunderstood. It would be unreasonable to underestimate the ancient priest-magi so much, who have left us these ritual texts, and to attribute such ignorance to them. The absence of similar texts in the Thracian environment is based on the fact that the Thracian ritual tradition is an act of expression of belief practiced in a non-narrative society.

---

[78] Hopfner Th., *Griechisch-Ägyptischer Offenbarungszauber*, Bd. II, Amsterdam 1983, 2-3.

[79] For the usage of this terminology see Abt A., *Die Apologie des Apuleius von Madaura und die antike Zauberei*, Gießen 1908, 106 -111; Graf F., *Magic in the Ancient World*, Cambridge/Massachusetts/London 1997, 97.

[80] The papyrus of Gurôb is dated 3rd-4th century BCE and is a record of Orphic ritual practice, see the quoted literature Hordern J., *Notes on the Orphic Papyrus from Gurôb* (P. Gurôb 1; Pack² 2464) // Zeitschrift für Papyrologie und Epigraphik, Bd. 129, 2000, 131-140; Jauregui M., *Orphism and Christianity in Late Antiquity*, Berlin/New York 2007, 54-57, 147; Schütz O., Zwei orphische Liturgien // Rheinisches Museum für Philologie 87, *Frankfurt* am Main 1938, 241-267, as well as Fol A., *Thracian Dionysos. Book one: Zagreus*, Sofia 1991, 131-134 (*Фол Ал., Тракийският Дионис. Книга първа. Загрей, София 1991, 131-134*). Interesting in this case is the fact that the so-called toys or cult objects, quoted in it, are quoted in a later time by Christian authors such as Clement of Alexandria, i.e. there is a preservation of the ritual practices from fourth century BCE to fourth century CE, which is a long period.

The carriers of this ritual tradition don't create ritual literature, because they don't need it. Through the oral initiatory tradition and the position of teacher–disciple the sacred knowledge preserves the line of succession and accessibility to a circle of initiates.

"Oral tradition preserves the intimate holiness of the hope as a pure energy of the melodeclamation, music, dance, mime and gesture, which spiritualises the sacred objects and the sacred texts."[81]

The belief in the power of the pronounced words is typical for Thracian ritual practice, as is the saying of the magical formula, *"swearing the named, so it could happen".*[82] It is not accidental that Herodotus (Hdt. V. 7) in his famous commentary about Thracian beliefs writes:

"They worship only these gods: Ares, Dionysos, and Artemis, while their kings, unlike the rest of the citizens, worship Hermes most of all, they swear to him and claim to be descended from Hermes."[83]

The kings, i.e. the initiated ones, swear, i.e. conjure Hermes so he could *"make the creation of the energies".*[84] The voice of the one pronouncing the ritual words is also the instrument which unifies the human and the divine in the ritual; while at the same time pushing them to act together, which is directed to the fulfillment of the operator's will.[85] Some of the ancient authors who belong to the circle of the carriers of literary Orphism have left us an explanation of the power of the speech and the words. Thereby the pupil of Empedocles,[86] Gorgias writes:

"...speech is a mighty ruler, who even with the smallest and invisible body could achieve the most divine deeds. Because it can put an end to fear, to chase away sorrow, to inspire joy, and to increase kindness... the power of the spells

---

[81] Fol V., *Megalithic and Rock-cut Monuments in Ancient Thrace*, Sofia 2000, 138 (Фол В., *Мегалитни и скално-изсечени паметници в Древна Тракия, София 2000, 138*).

[82] Fol A., *Orphica magica*, Sofia 2004, 21 (Фол А., *Orphica magica*, София 2004, 21).

[83] The ancient Greek original states:
θεοὺς δὲ σέβονται μούνους τούσδε, Ἄρεα καὶ Διόνυσον καὶ Ἄρτεμιν. οἱ δὲ βασιλέες αὐτῶν, πάρεξ τῶν ἄλλων πολιητέων, σέβονται Ἑρμέην μάλιστα θεῶν, καὶ ὀμνύουσι μοῦνον τοῦτον, καὶ λέγουσι γεγονέναι ἀπὸ Ἑρμέω ἑωυτούς.

[84] Fol A., *Orphica magica*, Sofia 2004, 20 (Фол А., *Orphica magica*, София 2004, 20).

[85] Fol A., *Orphica magica*, Sofia 2004, 45 (Фол А., *Orphica magica*, София 2004, 45).

[86] For the Orphic element in the views of Empedocles see Trepanier S., *Empedocles: An Interpretation*, New York 2004, 116; Toohey P., *Epic lessons: an introduction to ancient didactic poetry*, London/New York 1996, 41.

and incantations reversing the perception of the soul, convince and change it through the ways of magic... the power of speech has the same relation to the order of the soul as the order of healing means have to the nature of the body. Because some of those means chase away certain moods of the body, others put an end to a disease, and others to life, and thereby some words provoke sorrow, others joy, some fear, others make those that hear them brave, while some enchant and bewitch the soul...[87]

From these words we understand that for the ancients the power of speech was of great importance and this is valid on an even greater scale for non-narrative cultures, such as the Thracians. Among most of the Indo-European peoples this rule is also valid. The Germanic people also don't write their sacred knowledge and use signs, but not for expressing the whole belief system, rather because they realise the inability of the record to hold this content. Late records of ritual traditions play a double role – on one hand they leave us written data, but on the other they have led to the profanation of what is in them. It is not by chance that in the Orphic papyrus from Derveni is written:

"XX. For [those] of the people that have performed and saw the rites in the cities I am not at all surprised that they have no knowledge: it is impossible to hear the ritual words and in the same time to understand them. But those who have (received) the rituals from an expert in them; they deserve the surprise and the pity. Surprise, because before they have been initiated they have supposed that they are going to obtain knowledge, but have passed through the initiation before they have acquired that knowledge and didn't ask, as if they already knew what they see or hear or learn. Pity, because not only that they have to pay their tax before that, but also they have walked away without finding knowledge.

Before they perform the rites, they were hoping that they find knowledge, and after the performance, one way or another, they remain devoid even of their hope."[88]

---

[87] McPherran M., *Socrates and Zalmoxis on Drugs, Charms, and Purification* // Apeiron: A Journal for Ancient Philosophy and Science, Vol. 37, 1, 2004, 17.

[88] For this version the Bulgarian translation is used offered by Yordanova-Aleksieva M., *Hellenic Orphic evidences*, Sofia 2004, 186 (Йорданова-Алексиева М., *Елински орфически свидетелства*, София 2004, 186), but because of inaccuracies and differences are also used the English translations of Betegh G., *The Derveni papyrus: cosmology, theology, and interpretation*, New York 2004, 43 и Graf F., *Derveni and Ritual* // Proceedings of the Derveni papyrus conference 2008.

The author tells quite clearly that for understanding the ritual words additional explanation is needed, which has to come from the one who performs the rite. When the ritual act is done together with the pronouncing of ritual words, they are not always understandable for the people participating in the ritual. Often additional training is needed, as well as explanation of certain ritual meanings. The explanation is done by the initiator, as it is emphasised in this case namely in the meaning of the initiatory rite – it is a moment of passage with which the door opens and after that comes the time for transformation of the newly initiated. The ones seeking transformation in the rite itself, but not in the knowledge, which derives from knowing its whole meaning, leave *"...devoid even of their hope"*.

I gave this quote of part of the Orphic papyrus from Derveni with the goal of highlighting again the role of magical knowledge, but not knowing the magical technique. In this sense there is always a necessity for a mystagogue, i.e. someone experienced in the rite, who can initiate the new one and give him the directions for obtaining the knowledge.

The sacredness of the oral tradition and the stability of the belief that in the secret knowledge there is a need of succession is a phenomenon, which in passing out of the utilitarian society of the mystery initiates has transferred into the folklore environment and been preserved in the ritual tradition of the Balkan peoples and in particular among the Bulgarians. Of course a number of the characteristics of Thracian belief and ritual practice disappear. The cultural succession is selective – some rites, notions and beliefs are transferred from age to age, and others remain in the past. The ethno-cultural and political changes also have influence, but only to a certain degree. Most often they affect this part of the culture, which is directly connected with them. The other part, which is connected with essential human desires such as health, luck, prosperity, love and so on, is sustainably preserved.

The ancient Greek original is following Rusten J., *Unlocking the Orphic Doors: Interpretation of Poetry in the Derveni Papyrus between Pre-Socratics and Alexandrians* // Proceedings of the Derveni papyrus conference:

ὅσοι μὲν οὖν] ἀνθρώπω[ν ἐμ] πόλεσιν ἐπιτελέσαντες [τὰ ἱε]ρὰ εἶδον, ἔλασσον σφᾶς θαυμάζω μὴ γ[ι]νώσκειν (οὐ γὰρ οἷόν τε ἀκοῦσαι ὁμοῦ καὶ μαθεῖν τὰ λεγόμενα), ὅσοι δὲ παρὰ τοῦ τέχνην ποιουμένου τὰ ἱερά (sc. εἶδον), οὗτοι ἄξιοι θαυμάζεσθαι καὶ οἰκτε[ί]ρεσθαι, θαυμάζεσθαι μὲν ὅτι δοκοῦντες πρότερον ἢ ἐπιτελέσαι εἰδήσειν ἀπέρχονται ἐπιτελέσαντες πρὶν εἰδέναι οὐδ' ἐπανερόμενοι ὥσπερ ὡς εἰδότες τ[ι] ὧν εἶδον ἢ ἤκουσαν ἢ ἔμαθον·[οἰ]κτε<ί>ρεσθαι δὲ ὅτι οὐκ ἀρκε[ῖ] σφιν τὴν δαπάνην προανηλῶσθαι ἀλλὰ καὶ τῆς γνώμης στερόμενοι προσαπέρχονται πρὶμ μὲν τὰ [ἱε]ρὰ ἐπιτελέσαι ἐλπίζον[τε]ς εἰδήσειν ἐπ[ιτελέσα]αν[τες] δὲ στερηθέντες κα[ὶ] τῆ]ς ἐλπί[δος] ἀπέρχονται.

The belief in immortality, which was typical for the ancient Thracians, can be found even today, but in a more unrealised version, followed through folklore reality and ritual practice. The ancient mystery cults officially disappeared, but before that happened they left the sanctuaries and were professed in the ordinary environment.[89] This connection is expressed in the opinion of prof. Al. Fol:

"Lowing (profanation) of one teaching-faith, actually ensures its continuity..."[90]

In this regard the secret knowledge is passed among the families of the former officiators and only a part of it continues to exist. Losing its relevance with time from the mystery ritual traditions there remains only one part – mainly this one, which is connected with ordinary existence. The complicated system of cosmological knowledge and ritual practices deliquesces with time in its span and loses a part of its intimate sanctity. Additional elements are the external influences, which even in a family environment can't be avoided completely. The strictly conservative nature of the hidden ritual tradition, as well as the inner conviction of its carriers becomes the main possibility for it to survive.

THE PRESERVED SECRET KNOWLEDGE

Priest-magicians are a notion also known to the autochthonous population of the Balkans. Ancient authors have left us assorted evidence for this, and this was discussed in the beginning of this chapter. Ethnographers leave us records of the perception of healers and magicians as a different part of society:

"All these individuals, who deal with magical herbs, with spells, with magic and with the other means from the field of the folk medicine, once have formed and even today still form one class separated from the other people. Everyone looks

---

[89] The late Neoplatonist Proclus writes in great details for the experiences during the Eleusinian Mysteries, although that the mysteries were closed before his time, and the very temple at Eleusis was destroyed 15 years before Proclus was born. An explanation for this could be the fact that Proclus knew Asclepigenia, grand-daughter of the last hierophant in the Eleusinian Mysteries Nestorius. The biographer of Proclus says that she was initiated in the mysteries, see Marinus of Samaria, *The Life of Proclus or Concerning Happiness*, 28, online: http://www.tertullian.org/fathers/marinus_01_life_of_proclus.htm <10.02.2012>.
[90] Fol Al., *History of the Bulgarian lands in antiquity*, Sofia 2008, 343 (Фол Ал., *История на българските земи в древността, София 2008, 343*).

upon such people with some veneration, religious respect and even awe. Everyone admits that with their knowledge and skills these people stand higher than them, higher than everyone. This veneration and respect results from the fact that not every man, not every woman possesses these skills, this proficiency; and the awe and the religious nature, with which this veneration is veiled, result from this that such men and women don't come from every community, from every house."[91]

The cultural memory preserves and additionally enriches these images. Healers and magicians in Bulgarian folk notion are carriers of the magical and similar in its character knowledge, connected with the imposition of personal will and turning the forces of Nature in accordance with it, but perceived as different images.

THE HEALER IN BULGARIAN TRADITIONAL CULTURE

Usually healers, called most often *"baiachki"* or *"baiachi"* (from the verb *"baya"*[92] i.e. *bhā-jō *'talk'*[93]) are known to everyone in the community and they don't hide that they possess knowledge, that can be defined as *'magical'*. They keep the knowledge itself a secret (the words, the meaning of the ritual objects and so on), but not the fact that they possess it. The performing of healing rituals, cleansing bad influences, as well as divination is not kept as a secret from the community in most cases. Frequently healers are believers, but they keep a distance from the Christian canon and religiousness. This position is due more to the attitude of the Christian church and its representatives towards the healers than to the attitude of the healers towards the church. The personal ritual tradition, to which the magical ritual practices belong, in most cases is stigmatised and censured by the church, claiming it continues pre-Christian worship, which is actually true. The attitude of the community towards the healers is most often positive, unlike the attitude towards the magicians, which is negative.

---

[91] Marinov D., *Religious folk customs – selected works in 5 volumes*, vol. I, part 1, Sofia 2003, 348 (Маринов Д., *Религиозни народни обичаи – избрани произведения в 5 тома, том I, част 1, София 2003, 348*).

[92] *Bulgarian etymological dictionary*, Sofia 1971, 38 (*Български етимологичен речник, София 1971, 38*).

[93] From the Sanskrit *"bha"* – to talk, Greek "φα", compare with "φάναι", Latin – "fama" – Krauss F., *Südslawische Hexensagen* // Mitteilingen der antropologischen Gesellschaft in Wien, Band XIV, 15.

Admiration is found in the reports of explorers of Bulgarian traditional culture for the great respect which people have for the healers:

"Healers and seers among the simple people are so respected, as no priest or teacher is."[94]

19 - Wall-Painting From The Rila Monastery, Called "Going To The Healer", Which Depicts The Idea Of The Church That Healers Are In Contact With Unclean Forces. Personal Archive Of The Author[95]

This is due to many reasons, primarily that communities have never followed written canons, norms and rules, but have built their relationships on the basis of what each person has done for that same community. Healers were often the closest medical aid and were also familiar with many key rituals – such as those for weddings, births etc. Most often the baiachki and baiachi are also carriers of other elements of traditional folklore, and additionally many of them are famous folk singers; familiar with other parts of oral folklore[96] – songs, tales, fables. This places them within a very dynamic social context, they are rarely isolated people, and to the contrary they often enjoy the respect and encouraging attitude of their fellow villagers.

---

[94] Lyubenov P., *Baba Ega: Compendium of different beliefs, folk healings, spells, incantations and customs from the region of Kyustendil*, Tarnovo 1887, 56 (Любенов П., *Баба Ега. Сборник от различни вярвания, народни лекувания, магии, баяния и обичаи от Кюстендилско, Търново 1887, 56*).
[95] It is interesting that in the time of the Bulgarian National Revival the folklore motifs also appear on the wall-paintings not only of rural churches, but also of large monasteries such as the Rila monastery. This turning to folklore reality is observed in Bulgaria, as well as in Western Europe.
[96] See also Halpern B., Foley J., *The Power of the Word: healing charms as an Oral Genre* // The Journal of American Folklore, Vol. 91, No 362, 903-924, as well as Foley F., *Word – Power, Performance and Tradition* // The Journal of American Folklore, Vol. 105, No 417, 275-301.

Georgi Mishev

With the passing of time and with the fading of the folklore preserved in song, only the knowledge of magical healing rituals has been preserved in many families. The healers were consulted not only for problems of a physiological nature, but also about psychological problems. The role of the healer, as a helper for personal and health problems, gives them a place in society, where they are not only mediators between the visible and invisible, but also between people in the community. Thus we see a continuation of the ancient officiator, who performs cleansing rituals, gives directions for the correct performance of the personal rites, as well as support with advice in particular life situations.

According to folk belief the healers are most often women, and particularly elderly women, who have their own sacred status in the community. A woman who has not yet had her first menstrual period or has already passed through menopause is considered to possess ritual purity and also closeness to the divine. This sacredness is determined by the proximity of these two age periods to the two life thresholds – birth and death. Connected with them, women of these ages are capable of performing the transition between the worlds and accomplishing the unification of the human with the divine. The woman-mother on the other hand is perceived as an earthly face of the Great Goddess and she bears other functions, and also has other responsibilities. Of course along with that there are exceptions, because most of those women initiated in the healing rituals way back in their childhood practice them during their whole life, but their active occupation with this activity begins only when they reach the old age.

Along with the women, known as healers and *baiachki*, there are also a lot of cases of men healers, respectively *baiachi*. For the men the ritual requirements and characteristics are similar. Usually the man healer is an old man and his tuition begins before his first sexual contact with a woman. The difference in this case in the ritual restrictions may be due to the folk belief of the self-conceiving woman, i.e. the presence of the menstrual cycle makes her capable of being a mother, even without the presence of a man. For the man the situation is different, because only their contact with a woman gives them the opportunity to become fathers. There is also one other difference for the men, and it is that most often they do a particular circle of healing rituals – picking the sickness, as well as that they possess knowledge for the properties of the herbs, etc. Another difference in the rituals made by men is the evolved ritual side, i.e. there is a priority of the action over the pronouncing of sacred text.

Following the ancient tradition, in Bulgarian traditional culture there is also the necessity of initiation, so that the new healer can perform the magical actions. The magical knowledge is handed down orally,[97] i.e. the oral initiatory tradition carries on. Oral transmission is not necessarily a result of the illiteracy of its carriers,[98] but it exist namely because of the belief that pronouncing the ritual formula is a process of announcing of and bringing the cosmic forces into manifestation. During terrain surveys ethnologists often have difficulties with the announcing of the magical text. Healers refuse to pronounce the ritual words, but see no obstacle in writing them, because in that way, according to their beliefs, the power of the words won't be lost.[99] Additionally there is a known practice, during the transmission of the magic text, in which the transmitter (teacher) spits three times in the mouth or on the forehead of the trainee (newly initiated), which symbolises the saliva as a carrier of the words because of its contact with the tongue. Even if the words are pronounced and said to an extraneous person, for most of the magical formulae this is not a precondition for the one who knows the words to be able to perform the ritual, because the words aren't transmitted to him in a ritual context, i.e. no initiation is made and the new carrier of this knowledge is not accepted as part of the ritual lineage.

Apart from knowing the words and the technique of the ritual, in order for one to become a healer or a magician the folk tradition also requires a bloodline relationship, as well as the completion of a special rite for passing of the power. According to folk beliefs magical knowledge was the privilege of particular families and is inherited in them. The requirement for familial relationship and succession is dictated by the belief that particular blood lines are predisposed to communication with the divine forces. This

---

[97] The oral form of preserving sacred knowledge is widespread among many peoples. Among some of the rest of the European peoples the so-called book magic appears, i.e. collections with magical instructions, but in the Balkans the ancient practice of such sacred knowledge being passed in a closed circle is preserved, most often in the family and especially in oral form. An exception is the apocryphal literature, which takes from the folklore but is not a part from the traditional folk culture.

[98] Even if we suppose illiteracy of the population in the past, nowadays in spite of the literacy of the carriers of this knowledge it is again passed in an oral form.

[99] Kazasova R., *Secret incantations and divinations*, Gabrovo 2003, 23 (*Казасова Р., Тайни баилки и гадания, Габрово 2003, 23*).

requirement is valid in its greatest form for the healers and seers. In their case the inheritance as a requirement is based on the belief that knowledge alone is not enough, but also abilities, passed through the blood line, are necessary. Information on such beliefs is known even from antiquity. Separate priestly families served a certain cult, sanctuary or mysteries. For the ancients this was also determined by the divine choice of a specific family. An example of this is the role of the Eumolpidae in the Eleusinian Mysteries, who were the descendants of Eumolpus, first hierophant in the mysteries.[100] These priestly families were responsible for the correct performance of the rites and for the maintenance of the sacred areas. A similar belief is preserved among the Bulgarian people[101] until today as it is connected not only with the esoteric, but also with the public (exoteric) ritual practices – specific families maintain the chapels of given saints, they organize the 'kurban' (sacrifices) and the celebrations.[102] In most of the cases those were, and to the present moment are, elderly people of good repute in their community. Their role in traditional Bulgarian culture is commented in the ethnographic records:

"From my personal observations and from the gathered personal information everywhere I came across the same elders, which we called above seers. These seers once used to make the animal sacrifice (the kurban), lead the festival, fumigate the meal and consecrate the sacrifice (kurban, breads, kolivo, wine and other things given). Where there were no such seers, other elders were chosen for such priests."[103]

It is not uncommon to see the opinion that in antiquity, and even until the present day, Balkan traditional cultures are patriarchal and this limits the role of women in many ways. This is probably a possible concept regarding social relations, but in ritual practices we can't speak of such an advantage to a particular gender. Just like in antiquity, today among the Balkan people the concept is known that there are ritual practices, which are performed by the man

---

[100] For the Thracian origin of Eumolpus, as well as for the Thracian etymology of the name of his son Himmarados, see Kerenyi K., *Eleusis. Archetypal Image of Mother and Daughter*, Princeton 1991, 22.

[101] As well as among other Balkan people, but of course with local differences and peculiarities.

[102] Fol V., *The Forgotten Saint*, Sofia 1996, 15 (Фол В., *Забравената светица*, София 1996, 15).

[103] Marinov D., *Religious folk customs – selected works in 5 volumes*, vol. I, part 1, Sofia 2003, 354 (Маринов Д., *Религиозни народни обичаи – избрани произведения в 5 тома, том I, част 1, София 2003, 354*).

and the woman, i.e. they officiate together, or are completely under the domination of women or men.

"I have mentioned above that there are rites in which a man cannot fumigate the meal or consecrate the sacrifice, but this is a right given only to a woman...

For these celebrations and rites the priest who makes the sacrifice (hen or rooster) and who fumigates the meal is an old woman. This old woman is none other than the soothsayer or seer. If by chance there is no such woman in a village, they choose another old woman, who in this case must have all those qualities, which we mentioned above for the old man, i.e. to have a good reputation, to be the grandmother in a numerous society or family; her sons, daughters-in-law, daughters and grandchildren to have a good name and behaviour. The folk belief in this case is not interested in whether the old woman has a husband or her husband has died."[104]

Some ethnologists define this society of elderly people, who watch over and lead the rites, as 'priesthood'. This definition is not accidental, because the real function and leading role in the community is what even today defines them and brings them closer to the image of the ancient pagan officiators. Of course they identify themselves as Christians, but this is done for other reasons, rather than on the basis of knowing the Christian canons and rules. We should bear in mind that the majority of the so-called elders were not familiar with the liturgical books and the church rules, but acted according to the will and the law of the tradition. Just like the requirements in antiquity, concerning the priesthood, in the present day we require the officiator to have a good reputation. The good name in a small and closed community is most often based on one hand on the apparent expressions of favour from the invisible forces for that person – good social status, pure living and healthy posterity, fertility in their home and lands, but also value for the group. From the quoted ethnographic record it becomes clear that most often these folk priests and priestesses .are also healers, i.e. they possess the sacred knowledge and skills to chase away evil forces, to purify and bring health to the person as well as to the community.

Let us consider in detail the ways for initiation in healing that are known from ethnographic research. Of course, we

---

[104] Marinov D., *Religious folk customs – selected works in 5 volumes*, vol. I, part 1, Sofia 2003, 355 (*Маринов Д., Религиозни народни обичаи – избрани произведения в 5 тома, том I, част 1, София 2003, 355*).

can't speak of one general rite, but there are common elements, which are known in the whole Bulgarian ethnic territory. As was mentioned above in earlier times the repertoire of a healer was much vaster than it is today. This also applies to the completeness of the practices, which were known to the healers. Today, for various reasons, simplification of the ritual techniques and relinquishing of some of them can be observed.

20 - Maria Kabadzhova, Born 1940 In The Village Of Starosel, Bulgaria. Healer On The Maternal Lineage. Heals Fear, Evil Eye And Eye Illnesses. Picture – Personal Archive Of The Author 2010

21 - Mara Georgieva Kostova, Born 1938 In The Village Of Stoilovo, Bulgaria. She Was Taught From Her Fellow Woman Villager, When She Became A Widow. Heals Fear, Evil Eye, Samodivi Illnesses, Eye Illnesses, Erysipelas. Picture – Personal Archive of the Author 2010.

22 - Radka Kakanasheva, Born 1934 In The Village Of Starosel, Bulgaria. Healer On The Maternal Lineage, Heals Fear And Evil Eye. Picture – Personal Archive Of The Author 2010

Description of practice 3 INITIATION IN A SUPERNATURAL WAY

(transferred, dream or from divine entities (saints, samodivi))

The rarest type of reception of healing skills is through a state close to death or through a revelation in a dream. Folk call the people who were close to death and even those declared as dead and who came back to life – transferred (in Bulgarian *preneseni - пренесени*).[105] This contemporary form of katabasis, i.e. going down in the underworld, is explained by people as a supernatural choice. Such healers and seers are still remembered. I say healers and seers, because most often those who were close to death consequently also have the tendency to anticipate the future, together with their ability to heal. In this case they perform healing either with words or with actions, which they say were showed to them during their stay Beyond, or through the suggestion of supreme forces, which they call saints, angels, *samodivi* or other. It is not uncommon for healers to say that they just know what to do, without describing the source of that knowledge. This state recalls to a great degree the initiations of antiquity, which were connected with katabasis. Back then this was part of an organised ritual tradition, but in later times and today these cases are incidental and are not performed in an organised manner under the guidance of anybody. It is not uncommon that in these states the one who receives the ability to heal *'meets'* supernatural entities – the Mother of God, Jesus, saints, *samodivi*, *zmey* and others. They give him instruction on what to do and subsequently he applies it. The role of the local healers, who were transferred according to the people, was of great significance to the community. Often they had huge social influence with which even the Christian clergy complied. This fact is interesting because it differs with what was happening in Western Europe. The local community, appreciating the importance of the healer, and especially when he was marked by a supernatural choice, listened to his words. This in turn was due to the actions of the very healers. There are records of a number of cases of building a

---

[105]In this connection see also Goev A., *Ritual healing through incantation in the Bulgarian folk medicine* // Ethnographic problems of the folk culture, vol. 1, Sofia 1989, 130 (*Гоев А., Обредното лечение чрез баене в българската народна медицина // Етнографски проблеми на народната култура, т. 1, София 1989, 130*), as well as Todorova-Pirgova Iv., *Traditional healing rituals and magical practices*, Sofia 2003, 56-57 (*Тодорова-Пиргова Ив., Баяния и магии, София 2003, 56-57*).

chapel, cleansing of old consecrated grounds, reviving of celebrations, refunding of *kurban* and others, under the influence of such healers. The position of the church towards them was and even now is twofold, because on the one hand it has seen support from them for the restoration of Christian temples, but on the other it is absolutely aware of the pre-Christian nature of the activity of those people. Building chapels following a dream, honouring sacred springs and making kurbani are not part of the official Christian canon, but were tolerated in the past by the Christian clergy. Direct contact with supernatural entities has always aroused the awe of society for the person who experienced it. Along with that, the appearance in dreams of saints (or at least they were called that by the ones who see them), as well as of *samodivi, zmeyove* and others, places them in the liminal space between this and the other world.

Description of practice 4 TRANSMITTING THE HEALING ABILITY IN THE FAMILY

(or to a person chosen by the healer)

The most common case of transmitting healing ability is in the family circle.[106] Usually hereditary healers have the richest repertoire of ritual practices and activities, as well as the most extensive range of knowledge. Many of the healers use a combination of herbs and ritual formulae, just like the Thracian physicians of Zalmoxis. Learning the healing plants, the methods of their preparation and usage together with the ritual practices, used to begin in childhood. The optimal practice for transmitting healing abilities is in a straight line over a generation from a clean woman (after the menopause) to a girl before her first menstrual period.[107] The transmission over a generation is based on the belief in some regions that the former healer must stop practicing after he or she has passed on their knowledge, but this is not always

---

[106] For the transmission of magical knowledge in the context of the traditional culture see Koiva M., *The transmission of knowledge among Estonian witch Doctors* // Folklore: Electronic Journal of Folklore, No 2 /1996, 41-72; Smalwood T., *The Transmission of Charms in English, Medieval and Modern* // Charms and Charming in Europe, New York 2004, 11-31; Poper J., *Towards a Poetics, Rhetorics and Proxemis of verbal charms* // Folklore: Electronic Journal of Folklore, No 24 2003, 18-19; Petreska V., *The Secret Knowledge of Folk Healers in Macedonian Traditional culture* // Folklorica. Journal of the Slavic and East European Folklore Association, Vol. XIII 2008, 25-50.

[107] Goev A., *Ritual healing through incantation in the Bulgarian folk medicine* // Ethnographic problems of the folk culture, vol. 1, Sofia 1989, 130 (Гоев А., *Обредното лечение чрез баене в българската народна медицина* // Етнографски проблеми на народната култура, т. 1, София 1989, 130).

obligatory. Usually if the healer is a woman the transmitting is done also to a girl, and if the healer is a man to a boy.[108] The requirement that the girl is ritually clean, i.e. not to have her menstrual period yet, is strictly observed, and if it is a boy – the transmitting to be before his first sexual contact. But there are also rites and incantations, which are considered the prerogative of only one gender and it is not allowed for them to be passed from man to woman or from woman to man. In other cases an exception is made and a boy is taught instead of a girl and vice versa, when there are no inheritors of the healing tradition from the gender of the healer in the family. It is considered a bad omen if the family of a healer contains no child with a tendency to this secret art:

"...this is bad, because it shows that these children are stolen, brought from somebody else's blood, it is not from this straight blood."[109]

In separate regions it is considered that it should be passed on to the firstborn child, and in others the requirement is for the last child in the family. The rite for transmitting the incantation formulae and rites has its local variations.

Description of practice 5 TRANSMITTING OF INCANTATION BY A RIVER[110]

In some regions the transmission is done in the following way – after sunset the old healer and the apprentice go to a willow by a river. Two of the branches of the willow must touch each other and must creak when there is wind. The apprentice gets up on the creaking branches and says the ritual text three times, and after that repeats the text again three times on another branch and in the end again three times on a third branch – altogether the text is repeated nine times. During the rite there must be no outsiders present.

The river as a limit appears as a place of initiation, which is present also in the initiatory rites of antiquity.[111] Because

---

[108] For instance it is different in Greece where the transmission is considered as most successful when it is to a person from the opposite gender, see Passalis H., *Secrecy and Ritual restrictions on Verbal Charms Transmission in Greek Traditional Culture* // Incantatio, Tartu 2011, 7-24.

[109] Marinov D., *Religious folk customs – selected works in 5 volumes*, v. I, part 1, Sofia 2003, 349 (Маринов Д., *Религиозни народни обичаи – избрани произведения в 5 тома, том I, част 1, София 2003, 349*).

[110] Goev A., *Ritual healing through incantation in the Bulgarian folk medicine* // Ethnographic problems of the folk culture, vol. 1, Sofia 1989, 131 (Гоев А., *Обредното лечение чрез баене в българската народна медицина* // *Етнографски проблеми на народната култура, т. 1, София 1989, 131*).

it is connected with the possibility of transmission, together with the night time when the rite is done, it emphasises the idea of one's fake death. The apprentice climbs up the tree and is placed in an even more liminal place, because he is neither in the sky, nor on the earth or in the water, but at the same time unifies them as elements. In this belonging to nobody and at the same time common space, he pronounces the ritual formula, which echoes in the three worlds. This trinity is achieved with the triple change of place when pronouncing the ritual words. They are repeated three times, which is expected for a magical formula, aiming to strengthen and echo the will of the one pronouncing it. The willow is connected with water, the feminine principle and new birth. It is also related to the idea of easily taking roots – when it is planted near water - and on the principle of similarity – in this way the work should also take roots, i.e. the spells of the apprentice.

Unlike the rite quoted above the ethnographic records have preserved one much more distributed variation of transmitting the healing abilities and because such full record is rare I will present it here in its entirety.

Description of practice 6 TRANSMITTING OF INCANTATION BY A HEARTH[112]

"The elderly woman lived in an old house, in which she had a room with a hearth. While we were talking about something else, she kneaded a small 'new' round bread and baked it in the ash of the hearth. She brought all the iron objects, which she uses to poke the fire and she arranged them on both sides of the hearth. She brought three dry ears of wheat, red wool thread, water from the well, a bunch of basil and wild geranium.

She made me kneel on the broom facing the fire and on my right side she put a wicker basket, in which she kept all of her ritual objects, necessary for the incantations which she practiced. She took three grains from the first wheat ear and put them on my right knee, then another three from the second to put them on my left knee, and another three from the third to throw them in the fire. After that she stood behind my back and began to pronounce clearly and slowly

---

[111] The river is present also in the magical papyri because it is a liminal place and a possibility for realizing a transmission between the worlds, see PGM IV 26-51, Preisendanz K., *Die griechschen Zauberpapyri*, I, Leipzig 1928, 68-69.

[112] Pirgova Iv., *Traditional healing rituals and magical practices*, Sofia 2003, 13-14 (Пиргова Ив., *Баяния и магии*, София 2003, 13-14).

the verbal text of the first incantation. I had to repeat every line of it like an echo.

After we repeated it in that way three times, she passed me the object which is used for this type of incantation. She told me to make the cross sign three times and to touch the object once to my forehead, once to my heart and once to my knees. After that I had to make the cross sign again and to leave the object on my left side. She verbally explained and showed me what I have to do with the objects, while I am doing the incantation, but I didn't have to repeat that as an action, but only to observe and to remember. In this way she taught me to all of the incantations, which she knew from her grandmother. Finally she took the basil and the bowl with water, she started to stir the water in a circle with the basil and she began to pronounce the following blessing:

"May God give that all becomes a cure,

to go from me into you,

to go from you into the person;

to go from mine into your hands,

to go from mine into your mouth,

to go from mine into your heart,

now and ever to become a cure!

When you lift up your hand, cure to become;

what you say, cure to become;

when you touch a stone, cure to become;

when you touch a fire, cure to become;

when you touch a water, cure to become;

whatever you do, to bring life and health,

to bring welfare and good to the man!

May God and saint Mother of God help you

whatever you do, cure to become!

To go from me into you,

to go from you into the person;

to go from mine into your hands,

to go from mine into your mouth,

to go from mine into your heart,

now and ever to become a cure!

When you lift up your hand, cure to become;

whatever you do, to bring life and health!"[113]

After that she sprinkled me using the bunch and gave me water to drink from three places in the bowl.

After that she broke off three bits from the round bread – one she ate, one gave to me, and the third she fixed high in the chimney. She gave me the rest of the round bread so I could use it as a remedy in one of the incantations. She gave me some of the *'zmey plants'* and objects, for which she supposed that there was no place I can find them. The rest I have to search for by myself as I was following the requirements in the ritual of each of them.

She tied on my right hand the red thread and she pinned the wild geranium on my clothing – to wear it until *"it gets lost somewhere"*.

The recorded rite shows us one initiation reduced to a folklore level, i.e. in its everyday life aspect. The carrier of the rite probably doesn't rationalise the practice in its whole, but following the will of the tradition preserves the separate ritual elements in their very archaic form. If we analyse the ritual act we will see the following elements:

- personages – the experienced healer and the apprentice;
- hearth;
- iron objects connected with fire;
- new round bread baked in the ash of the hearth;

---

[113] Text of the incantation in Bulgarian:
„Да даде Господ све на лек да иде,
от мене в тебе да иде,
от тебе в човеко да иде;
от мойте ръце в твойте да иде,
от мойта уста в твойта да иде,
от моито срце в твойто да иде,
съга и свекога на лек да иде!
Ръка да дигнеш, лек да стане;
све, що речеш, на лек да е;
камик да допреш, на лек да е;
огин да допреш, на лек да е;
вода да допреш, на лек да е;
све що магериш, на живот и здраве,
за благо и добро на човеко да е!
Да ти помага Бог и света Богородица
све на лек да ти става!
От мене в тебе да иде,
от тебе в човеко да иде;
от мойте ръце в твойте да иде,
от мойта уста в твойта да иде,
от моито срце в твойто да иде,
съга и свекога на лек да иде!
Ръка да дигнеш, лек да стане,
све, що магериш, на живот и здраве да е!"

- broom, on which the apprentice kneels facing the fire;
- wicker basket with ritual objects;
- three ears of wheat – from which three grains she places on the left knee, three grains on the right knee and three in the fire;
- red thread – tied after the ritual on the hand of the new initiate;
- water – the new initiate is sprinkled with it;
- a bunch of wild geranium – it is given to the new healer to wear it;
- the oppositions of stone-fire, fire-water, which through the rite are connected with the idea of giving a wholeness;

If we set aside the atmosphere in the rural home and we examine the described practice in its ritual and magical plan, we will get a record of ritual practice, which was done for thousands of years – of course in another context, but with a similar rationalisation. The experienced healer in this case appears as the mystagogue, who initiates the candidate neophyte. The temple and more specifically the altar is the home hearth, which possessed this sacred function in ancient times. Purifying the sacred area is done by placing iron objects around it, used to poke the fire, because in ritual tradition they possess strong purifying properties and can chase away evil and impurity. This is determined by the unity of iron and fire, power and burning all that is unclean. The wicker basket with the ritual objects used in the ritual is placed in the purified sacred area. Often these include metal or clay items, which are handed down by inheritance from the old healer to the new. The wicker basket reminds us of those baskets in the ancient mysteries, in which the sacred ritual objects were kept, the so-called *cista mystica*. Because in the folk notion there is supposed to be a transferring of the power for healing from one carrier to another, it is necessary to have a mediator in order to accomplish this transfer. This mediator in the rites for transferring the healing abilities is usually new round bread, baked in ash.[114] This archaic preparation of the ritual bread additionally emphasises the archaic nature of the whole practice. The ears of wheat are an expected element for those who are familiar with ancient sacrificial ritual practice, because they

---

[114] For the role of bread in cult ritual practice see Benko St., *The Virgin Goddess: Studies in the pagan and Christian roots of Mariology.* Leiden 1993, 174-191.

are used to sprinkle and consecrate the sacrificial animal and at the same time are an offering to the deities. Placing the wheat grains on the person, the candidate-neophyte, aims to purify and represent him or her as a vessel for the divine power.[115] Sacrificing the wheat continues with throwing three grains of it in the fire. The Great Goddess is present in the rite through the wheat ears, the hearth and the bread. The neophyte is kneeling on a broom, because from antiquity it has been a symbol of purification. The broom sweeps everything unclean from the house and in that way, on the principle of sympathy everything unclean must go away from the one who is in contact with it. Facing the altar, i.e. the hearth, the neophyte repeats the ritual words after the experienced healer. After that the neophyte takes the ritual object used in the practice from the wicker basket, touches it to their forehead, their hearth and their knees and in this way is in full contact with it. This succession is evidenced also for the circle of the Eleusinian Mysteries:[116]

- legomena – what is said;

- deiknumena – what is shown;

- dromena – what is done;

But is the order of the actions in this rite coincidental with the one described for the ancient mysteries:

- pronouncing the ritual text (legomena);

- showing the ritual object (deiknumena);

- explaining what is done with it (dromena);

Of course this is possible, but it is more likely that the skeptics will say that this is based on a similar model in mythological thinking, which would be a wonderful explanation if it was not concerning the same ethno-cultural area and if we didn't have in mind the cultural continuity and stability of the hidden magical ritual tradition. Per se

---

[115] This symbolism, which from the sprinkling of the sacrificial animal and the altar, transfers in the rites, where the initiated sprinkle themselves is preserved also in the *Homeric Hymn to Hermes* (551), where the diviners from Parnassus are besprinkled with barley meal and in this way they are presented as priestesses: *"their heads are besprinkled with white meal, and they dwell under a ridge of Parnassus"*, translation by H.G. Evelyn-White. For the same interpretation see also Eitrem S., *Opferritus und Voropfer der Griechen und Römer*, Kristiania 1915, 269, as well as the complete examination of the wheat ear and grain as part of the sacrificial rite ibid. 276 and 269-272.

[116] See Popov D., Zalmoxis. *Religion and society of the Thracians*, Sofia 1989, 125 (Попов Д., Залмоксис. *Религия и общество на траките, София 1989, 125*).

this record of the rite is an exception and rarity, because such a detailed description of transferring the magical knowledge is almost unknown in ethnographic literature. A similar rite, bearing in mind that the transferring is usually done from an elderly woman healer at the end of her life time to a girl before her first menstrual period, happens one or two times, and even if it is three times, in a century, i.e. for a period of thousands of years it can be supposed that on average it is done twenty-thirty times. The conservative nature of the practice doesn't allow significant changes, but only shallow modifications and such of linguistic character.

Like the ancient mystagogue the healer gives additional explanations to the new initiate.[117] And finally the moment comes when the old healer blesses the young one and with this blessing makes her part of her power. It is not by chance that in the words is said: *"to go from me into you"*. The healer perceives herself as a vessel, in which the divine has put power, which heals and brings life. Now she transmits this power to another carrier. The ritual formula calls the elements, which are metaphorically named as speech (air), stone (earth), fire and water. After that she calls the deities, which even in a seemingly Christian form – God and the Mother of God, completely correspond to the ancient divine couple – the God and the Great Goddess. The blessing and the advice are sent in three directions – the mouth, the hands and the heart. With this the new initiate is given guidance to speak the things which bring health and life, to do also these things and to feel them and experience them with her heart. She sprinkles her with the water, which has to bring the divine power into her, just like the ancient priestesses used to sprinkle themselves with the water from sacred springs. After that the initiator ties on the hand of the new initiate a red thread – an action symbolically identical with the handing of the purple cloth to the new initiate in the mysteries of Samothrace. The red thread placed on the right hand of the new healer must protect her in the same way, in which the purple cloth protected the ancient neophytes who were wreathed with it.[118] Finally the ritual bread is shared between them and also part of it is placed as a sacrifice in

---

[117] This moment reminds of the warning of the teacher in the *Derveni Papyrus*, that while the words are said during the rite, they cannot be understood and additional explanations and specifications are needed (see above in this chapter). Although in this case the experienced healer herself has lost the knowledge of some of the ritual elements, she again gives guidance and leads the newly initiated in their use.

[118] See Dimitrova N., *Theoroi and Initiates in Samothrace: the epigraphical evidence*, Princeton 2008, 142.

the chimney. With this last act they share their power. Probably because of this there is an opinion that the new healer can practice fully only after their teacher dies.

The healers usually don't require payment for doing healing rituals, but a common practice and unwritten rule is to leave something, so the rite 'catches'. Generally regardless of the sum (or the thing, because the payment could also be an object – fruits, clothes and others), which is left it is claimed that is good to give a coin, on which the healer steps and blesses: *"So much from me, from God health!"*[119] When some years ago I asked healers why this is done and why the payment must be left on the ground, one of the elderly women said that this is so because all the herbs and remedies come from the ground. There are known cases, when the ill person is really poor and has nothing to pay with, that they pick a thread from their clothing and the healer steps on it instead of on the usual coin. Not requiring payment is even one of the main differences between the respected healers of good name and the negatively perceived magicians, who demand wages for making a particular spell. In the folk notion a basic and very important consideration is the motive for performing a certain action – the healer acts led by their own spiritual development and position to be a mediator of the life-giving forces, and the magician takes part in an action which is led by selfish incentives, which aim to benefit the one who orders it and the one who performs it. Unfortunately today a profanity in this field can be seen. Often the traditional sacred knowledge becomes a part of the repertoire of the contemporary so-called psychics and alternative healers, who use them as their profession and way of earning a livelihood. This fact is perceived negatively by the hereditary carriers of the healing rites, who always make a comparison with times in the past, when people's lives were far from being easier than they are today, but the cases of such exploitation of the sacred knowledge were much rarer. In this sense the process of desacralisation affects the magical ritual tradition and it becomes a source for enrichment – a fate similar to the one of festive ritual practice, which in turn transforms and demeans to an ordinary tourist attraction. Of great importance in this connection is the rationalisation of the inheritors of the former respected healers and their role for the preserving not only of the form and contents of the ritual practices; but in

---

[119] This formula varies in the different regions of the country and among the different healers, but its contents are similar.

continuing their morally-ethical function as part of the means for mutual aid without venal goals. The ancient healer is a respected part of a fraternity not only because of their knowledge, which is inaccessible to others, but also for their spiritual development, which in traditional society is recognised in their deeds and in their willingness to act for the good of the community.

Passing through the rite of initiation is only the beginning for the new healer. After that she must establish herself in the community as such and prove her abilities.

Along with performing healing rites the folk healers, especially some of them, are also sought by people for making diagnoses. The healer's task is to determine the impact of what relevant issue has occurred – whether it is a health issue or another. In a number of cases the same person makes the diagnosis and the healing. There are different techniques for making a diagnosis, but some of the most widespread are those with extinguishing coals, an example of which is seen in the following rite:

Description of practice 7 EXTINGUISHING CHARCOALS FOR DIAGNOSING THE CAUSE OF THE DISEASE[120]

The sick person brings a sign with him, which is the so-called *materia magica*, and is most often a thread from his clothes. The sign is dropped in a bowl of water, but before that a movement with the hand in the shape of a cross is made over the bowl.[121] After that *'alive embers'* (i.e. still burning) from the hearth or the stove are dropped in the water in succession, and for each the same hand movements for making a cross over the bowl of water are made. For each of them is said:

"Is it for healing eyes?" (is it necessary to heal evil eye)

"Is it for measuring" (is it necessary to perform a healing ritual for fear, measuring the height of the ill person with a thread, which according to the healer's repertory could be replaced with naming another healing ritual)

---

[120] Markov Gr., *Folk spells from Godech region as a means for psychotherapy* // Bulgarian ethnology 56, Sofia 1992, 102 (Марков Гр., *Народни баяния от Годечко като средство за психотерапия* // *Българска етнология 56, София 1992, 102*).

[121] This cross reflects the four directions and the harmonization of the Cosmos.

"*Is it for preklapane?*"[122] (whether it is necessary to perform a healing rite for separating a *ednomesets*[123] or unlocking the luck, it could be replaced with another question for other reasons)

"*Is it for church?*" (should the sick person seek help in a Christian or other temple, i.e. it is not for help from the healer)

"*Is it for a doctor?*" (if this is the case medical help should be sought, because the cause is absolutely and only physiological)

The charcoal which the sign '*catches*', decides the healing method which should be applied. After the cause of the illness is determined, the healer gives the ill person a drink from the water in which the charcoals were extinguished, and the sign (the thread from the clothes) is put in the hem of some other clothing of the ill person, so it won't be noticed.

The healing ritual could consist of speaking a ritual text, doing ritual acts or a combination of both, which is the most common case. The ritual texts are pronounced an exact number of times, according to the nature of the rite. During the conducting of the ritual act a number of ritual instruments are used, which every healer has and uses in their activities. Most often those are objects rich with specific symbolic meaning and mythological identification. Examples include:

- clay bowl with green hues – used for pouring water in, over which certain incantations are made. It is used most often in healing of the evil eye and fear. The green colour is associated with reviving life and its validation;

- broom made from white chicken feathers, which have to be found, but not plucked, rye spike and a basil sprig, tied up with red thread, but with no knots – used for healing evil eye, fear and other. The symbolism is that just like the feather has detached, so the illnesses should detach from the healed person; as the feather is light, so he feels light too. The rye spike has purifying symbolism, most often it

---

[122] *Preklapane* is a ritual in which the suffering person is tied up with a hearth chain and a ritual untying is performed.

[123] *Ednomesets* is a person who is born in the same month as another person. According to the folk belief, when these people are relatives by blood and one of them dies, a special rite for their separation should be done in order to prevent the living one from having bad luck.

is associated with shaking off and lightness in ritual formulae. The red thread and its symbolism to protect were discussed supra in this chapter.

- knife with black handle – used for healing fear and evil eye. The symbolism is the cutting, which must be made on a ritual level, to cut the illness and its connection with the ill person.

- mandible or bone from the front right foot of a lamb, sacrificed on *Gergiovden* (Day of St George) – used for healing body swellings, for wart removing and other. As part of the sacrificial animal, these bones are considered to carry a purifying power, which can repulse the illnesses.

- skull from a dog (firstborn) – used for healing rashes caused by stepping in a dangerous (from a ritual point of view) place. The dog is connected with purification rites from antiquity and through to today it has been used in magical ritual practice in exactly such a way.

- horse or ox shoe – used for healing evil eye, *samodivski* illnesses and others. In the samodivi rites it replaces the horseshoe of the horses of the samodivi themselves.

- *sablekalo* (moulted snakeskin) – for healing fainting and other. The symbolism of the snake is complicated, but in Balkan ritual tradition it is related to the idea of rebirth and in this connection the sablekalo is a sign for liberation from the old essence. Using it for healing fainting is caused by the severity of the disease. The person must be born again, change their skin and then they will find healing.

- hearth chain – for healing fear, unlocking luck, separating of *ednomesetsi*[124] and other. The hearth as a cult place in the home is connected with many magical rites. It is the ancient altar, which stays intact through external social changes. In this regard all the attributes connected with it are considered as highly sacred.

- hair-comb – for healing body rashes. The use of the comb is based on the principle of similarity and horizontal sympathy.

---

[124] See previous note.

- Oakum – hemp fibre used to create a circle around the patient which is subsequently set on fire to invoke the symbol of the Sun on earth, during purification and healing.

The ritual practice connected with the making of a healer is close to the mystery rites, because it introduces the uninitiated into the secret knowledge and makes him an initiate. After the initiation the new healer becomes a part of a ritual lineage that ascends from antiquity. He begins to perform ritual practices, which are different from normal social activity, and becomes a carrier of thinking different from the usual. Folk belief lends to healers the ability to chase away illnesses, personified as unclean spirits, with their power. The healer has one basic ability and responsibility and it is to purify and awaken the beginning of life. As it was said previously in the incantation of the old healer - *"...what you say, cure to become; when you touch a stone, cure to become; when you touch a fire, cure to become; when you touch a water, cure to become; whatever you do, to bring life and health."*

Knowing the ritual techniques, ritual words and the properties of the herbs and other natural elements is only a part of the preconditions for acquiring the skills of the healer. An important element in the creation of the healer is the authority of the initiated teacher, who must open the gate and initiate the new carrier in the old magical faith. The carrier of this faith is appealed to by his or her teacher to experience it daily with word, deed and heart.

THE MAGICIAN IN TRADITIONAL BULGARIAN CULTURE

The figure of the magician is perceived in a different way. The community doesn't accept his activity, because in most cases that activity is directed against it and aims only for personal benefit – someone's death, sickness, separating a married couple, stealing fertility and others. The fear of these people, who gained the appellation of magicians, was great.[125] There are rare cases of isolation and rejection by the

---

[125] See also Mihaylov N., *The witch as an archetypical character* // Balkan readings 2, Symposium on the structure of the text, Moscow 1992, 50-52 (*Михайлов Н., Ведьма как архетипический персонаж // Балканские чтения 2. Симпозиум по структуре текста, Москва 1992, 50-52*), as well as Kasabova-Dincheva A., *Magic – social necessity* // Ethnographic problems of the folk culture 5, Sofia 1998 (*Касабова-Динчева А., Магията –*

community of a person believed to be a magician, but in cases where he is seen doing his evil acts it leads to undertaking penalties – denigration and physical punishments.[126] Usually magicians don't share their knowledge with other people, but unlike the incantations the reason is not because of eventual loss of the effectiveness of the practice with its dissemination and knowing by the uninitiated. Handing down the techniques for doing magic is done either to a relative (the most common case, because that guarantees keeping the up-to-date deeds of the magician in secret) or, in some cases, to a suitable person chosen by the magician, who differs with particular qualities.[127]

Although according to folk beliefs magicians are in close connection with unclean spirits, devils and demons, the magicians themselves and their practices don't mention such relations. They depend radically on the correct conducting of the ritual act and on the power within them, and not on the co-operation of external forces. In many cases prayers for punishment or curses are made in the name of Christian saints and there are no demonic creatures mentioned.[128] Therefore we have a defined folk belief, that Christian saints preserve an image, which helps, but also punishes when it is correctly called. Mainly in these cases saints are called such as St Elijah, St Menas, St Marina and others. The repertoire of the magicians includes knowledge for influencing human relations – for inducing love, hate, but also for influencing health and luck. With the help of their knowledge the magicians could harm a person – take away their health, mind or luck, but they can also do this so that no one could harm them, no matter what evil they inflict. If they are dealing with trade they can increase their number of clients,

---

социална необходимост // Етнографски проблеми на народната култура 5, София 1998).

[126] This used to happen most often during the rituals for stealing the fertility of the fields when their owners guarded them on particular calendar days (St George's Day/Gergyovden, St John's Eve/Enyovden).

[127] One of my acquaintances, whose mother-in-law was taught the magical rituals, used to tell that her mother-in-law was chosen only because her teacher estimated that she was a very bad person and would make a lot of evil deeds. This again proves the belief that the magician works against the community and therefore is rejected by it.

[128] This practice has ancient roots. As far back as the Hittite texts there are examples for that, see Mouton A., *Hittite Witchcraft //* A. Süel (ed.), Acts of the VIIth International Congress of Hittitology, Ankara 2010, 515-528. The Greco-Roman antiquity and the tablets with curses also give evidence for the practice to indispose the deity to someone with the help of prayer or spell, see Gager J., *Curse Tablets and Binding Spells from the Ancient World*, New York/ Oxford 1992.

if they are farmers - their fields to be the most plentiful, if they are stock breeders - their stock to be the most healthy and numerous and so on. In this regard the notion of the magicians as familiar with the ways of influencing the forces in nature could be related also to the fragment which Hesiod dedicates to the goddess Hekate:

"For to this day, whenever anyone of men on earth offers rich sacrifices and prays for favour according to custom, he calls upon Hekate. Great honour comes full easily to him whose prayers the goddess receives favourably, and she bestows wealth upon him; for the power surely is with her. For as many as were born of Earth and Ocean amongst all these she has her due portion. The son of Cronos did her no wrong nor took anything away of all that was her portion among the former Titan gods: but she holds, as the division was at the first from the beginning, privilege both in earth, and in heaven, and in sea. Also, because she is an only child, the goddess receives not less honour, but much more still, for Zeus honours her. Whom she will she greatly aids and advances: she sits by worshipful kings in judgement, and in the assembly whom she will is distinguished among the people. And when men arm themselves for the battle that destroys men, then the goddess is at hand to give victory and grant glory readily to whom she will. Good is she also when men contend at the games, for there too the goddess is with them and profits them: and he who by might and strength gets the victory wins the rich prize easily with joy, and brings glory to his parents. And she is good to stand by horsemen, whom she will: and to those whose business is in the grey discomfortable sea, and who pray to Hekate and the loud-crashing Earth-Shaker, easily the glorious goddess gives great catch, and easily she takes it away as soon as seen, if so she will. She is good in the byre with Hermes to increase the stock. The droves of kine and wide herds of goats and flocks of fleecy sheep, if she will, she increases from a few, or makes many to be less."

In this ancient fragment a great scale is listed of what can be influenced by knowing the magical rites, though in this case it is replaced with veneration of a Goddess, who in late antiquity turned into a guardian of magicians. Impressive in this hymn is the moment that the Goddess *"increases from a few, or makes many to be less"*, i.e. the ones who know the ways for influence can also give and take luck, awaken or destroy love. In this sense the abilities of the magician can be used to work in a positive, as well as in a negative direction, but not to be on one pole and operate with only one side of the power.

One of the most widely spread examples of the belief in the role of magicians is regarding the influence of personal relations. Bulgarian folk songs describe cases of doing magic for hatred, and although they are part of the folklore, they reflect the performing of real practices:

Stoyan's mother,

to Petkana fierce enemy,

where she went, she asked

to find a hatred herb,

hatred and separating,

so Petkana could be hated,

hated and then separated

from her son Stoyan...

...

They gave her hatred herb,

Gave it and bespeak:

- Take the herb to boil it

on Friday before Saturday,

in a deserted house,

in a pot that hasn't been used

with undrank water,

and naked and bareheaded,

then go and pour it on Petkana.[129]

---

[129] Minkov Tsv., *I am loved by a zmey, mother.* Mythical folk songs, Sofia 1956 (Минков Цв., *Мене ме, мамо, змей люби. Митически народни песни, София 1956*). The text in Bulgarian:
Стояновата майчица,
Петкани върла душманка,
къде ходила, питала
да найде биле омразно,
омразно, та па отделно,
да си омрази Петкана,
омрази, та па отдели
от свойго сина Стояна...
...
Дали й биле омразно,
дават й и заръчват й:
- Вземи да вариш билето
във петък спроти събота,
във къща запустеница,
във гърне необжежено
и с вода неначетена,
и гола и гологлава,
та па да полейш Петкана.

The magic for hatred has a lot of variations and is used with a great number of instruments, but the oldest hatred rituals known to Bulgarian culture are those that use special hatred herbs, picked on exact days and prepared in an exact way, just as it is described in the folk song above. Perception is relevant to not only the hatred herb, but also the way it is prepared – it is done preceding Saturday, because Saturday is the day of the dead and just like them should the object of the magic become cold in the heart of the other; the action is performed in an abandoned place, so the object of the magic should also be abandoned; the perpetrator is naked and bareheaded, in order to stop being a part of this world and become a part of the other – the world beyond, and in this way to have the necessary impact. With the potion from the hatred herb is sprinkled the one, who must become hated. Along with other hatred herbs like for instance herb Paris (*Paris quadrifolia*), dog's tooth violet (*Erythronium dens-cans*), valerian (*Valeriana officinalis*), lesser honeywort (*Cerinthe minor*), to which are accredited properties and powers to inflict hatred towards a given person, other means are also used, of which the most popular is the so-called *'dead water'*.

'Dead water' is a name for the water taken from the washing of a dead person. In the past many rites were connected with washing. Usually when the deceased is a man, he is washed by a man, and when it is a woman – she is washed by a woman. Apart for the washing of the deceased with water, soap and basil, in some places there is a practice of washing the body with wine,[130] to which are usually accredited the same properties as to the water from the washing of the dead. In separate regions the bowl, in which the basil is dipped is broken after that, and the vessel with which the water for the washing was brought is turned with its bottom up.

According to different beliefs and local peculiarities, there are also different ways of using *'dead water'*. Some claim that in order to make a man hated – the water must be taken from the washing of a deceased man, and if the object of the magic, i.e. the person who is to become hated is a woman – the water must be taken from the washing of a deceased woman.

Different magical practices have different requirements for the *'preparation'* of *'dead water'*, i.e. its transformation

---

[130] Vakarelski Hr., *Bulgarian burial customs*, Sofia 2008, 105-107 (Вакарелски Хр., *Български погребални обичаи*, София 2008, 105-107).

into a magical instrument. According to some of them it should be left for an exact number of days under the waning moon and after that appropriate spells must be said over it; according to other it must have diverse ingredients placed in it or only the spoken spell over it is considered as sufficient, so that the magic is fulfilled and the sprinkled with *'dead water'* becomes *'dead'*, i.e. cold and isolated.

Similar principles of operation are used for the other different types of water, which are prepared for the same purpose. Most often their ingredients are – soil from a grave, threads from widows, fur from a dog, cat and others. But in every case the obtained liquids should be sprinkled on the person who is to be hated. According to beliefs the liquid prepared in such ways absorbs *"the badness, the wickedness"* from the things that are in it and through sprinkling (of clothing for instance) and through the spell over it, it is transmitted to the object of the magic.

If the basis of magic for hatred is jealousy, then envy is the most common reason for magic for ill success. Their own failures and lack of luck often incite some people towards actions, which aim to disrupt the success of others, who they perceive as enemies and opponents (even if those people have no idea about that). The main method used in this case is the so-called *'binding the luck'*. Even today the expression is widely known, when we say about somebody that their luck was bound and we understand that the undertakings of this person are either unsuccessful or they are realised very hard, often the people with *'bound'* luck also don't succeed in their personal relations – to find a beloved, to get married and so on.

The methods for binding the luck are various, but they have one common magical principle in their basis – closing and fastening. The ritual inventory could include either a thread from the loom of a deceased woman; or thread, which was used to measure the height of the object of the magic and to which knots are tied with the corresponding spells; or thread, that was overstepped by the object of the magic or a thread from a carpet in their house; or thread which was used to measure their bed and others. Along with the types of threads to which knots are tied, other methods are also used like locking a padlock and burying it or throwing it in an inaccessible place.

Other practices, which are part of the knowledge of magicians are spells for illness and death. Bearing in mind the severity of the desired outcome of these spells, their requirements are also reasonably difficult in the complexity of the ritual act. Of course there are some short practices known in this area too, but most of them require serious preparation from the one making them. The most widespread and known attributes in this area are – buried eggs in a grave; buried clothes; soap buried or placed under a river stone, with which the object has bathed; melting an image of the object; burning an item of clothing or part of an item of clothing of the object. All these ritual techniques are known from antiquity.

In order to get a better idea of the technique for this type of magic, I'm going to quote the description of one:

Description of practice 8 SPELL FOR ILLNESS AND DEATH[131]

The step of the person is measured with a black thread from black heddles and to the thread ten knots are tied. Soil is taken from a grave, forty beans of black pepper, three beans of red pepper and baked hedgehog's intestines. All this is put in a pot, and the pot is placed next to the hearth, where every morning a fire is lit to heat it. In another new pot is put a living hedgehog and a *vrana* (the wedge used to plug the spigot) of a barrel is used to cover it, and on top of the *vrana* a *posh* (red cloth) is tied. Tied and covered in this way the pot is buried under the hearth of the one for whom the magic is made, and this person begins to wither and fade, until the spell is broken and the pot is found and brought out.

Along with influencing some completely everyday life things like fertility, success in trade and the changing of human relationships, magicians in the Bulgarian lands were also credited with the ability to draw down the moon, and according to some beliefs even the sun and the stars. Most often this drawing was done, so that the magician could increase their power and obtain an additionally stronger magical inventory, to use in other rituals. The drawn moon tells the magician everything which she knows, and if we consider that the moon lights the night, it was believed that she knows also the secrets of people and nature. Drawing the power of the moon, the sun or the stars in Bulgarian traditional belief is done most often as the celestial body takes the image of a cow and it is milked by the magician,

---

[131] *Collection of Bulgarian Folklore and Folk-Studies*, vol. 1, 172 (СбНУ *m. 1, 172*).

and the milk is the essence of its power. In other cases the drawing is done in a sieve, water with herbs or directly by magicians, who take the power into themselves. This mysterious rite is described in literature, but incompletely, and we cannot be sure as to the veracity of the description, nor do we have the ritual texts. The zeal with which the ritual for drawing down the moon is kept hidden, shows it belongs to the innermost part of the magical tradition. If we bear in mind that the mentioned practice is known from antiquity and is mentioned most often as a part of the knowledge and abilities of the witches of Thessaly, we can suppose that in Bulgarian folk culture this practice also originated in antiquity. According to Bulgarian folk belief the moon can be drawn by a mother and daughter, who breastfeed at the same time,[132] and also by one female magician. There are almost no known cases, when there is a mention of a drawing down the moon performed by a man.

23 - Wall-Painting From The Church In The Village Of Dolno Leshko, Southwestern Bulgaria, Depicting A Magician, Who Didn't Succeed In Drawing Down The Moon And That's Why She Milked The Devil – Personal Archive Of The Author 2011

---

[132] In the magical practices of the Bulgarians, Greeks and Serbs, the strong magical function of mother and daughter who breastfeed at the same time is known. From their mother's milk a round bun is kneaded, which is used for love spells and others. It is quite possible that the explanation of this belief is based on a mythological idea, according to which in this way the two women unify the role of a mother and daughter, but also of a nurse and to impersonate in them the image of the Goddess.

Description of practice 9 DRAWING DOWN THE MOON[133]

Although that there is no full description of the rite, one of the most detailed and trustworthy analyses of the ritual elements is given below.

The woman who performs the rite places a cauldron with water which was poured after midnight in the middle of the threshing floor, and in it she puts special herbs. Next to the cauldron she places her sieve, which she uses for spells.[134] All this is done before midnight. When midnight comes the magician strips naked and with a bunch in her hands goes to the cauldron, says the ritual formula and looks to the moon. She goes back in her house and goes out with a pot in her hands, in which powerful magical instruments are placed, she goes to the cauldron and says a new spell. When she says the words, the magician takes the sieve and goes around the house three times, goes back to the cauldron and says a third spell, after which she places the sieve on the cauldron. Then she dips the bunch in the pot, sprinkles the sieve, the threshing floor on four sides, herself and sprinkles towards the moon.

It is considered that with this the spell is done and the moon, that until that moment has shined on the sky, becomes darker and disappears, and becomes bright as day on the ground at the place where the magician performs her rite. The moon falls in the sieve and from there talks with the magician, who asks for everything and after that releases it to go up in the sky again. There the moon shines weaker, because it is tired from going up and down. The magician gathers the water, the bunch and the herbs, which are transformed into a powerful magical tool. According to folk belief, if someone becomes a witness to the actions of the magician, they become either insane or mute.

There are a number of elements that make an impression in the preserved notion of the rite for drawing down the moon, but my wish is to focus on one of the ritual elements – the sieve. During archaeological excavations of Thracian cult sites parts of objects have been found resembling a sieve or

---

[133] Following the description made by Marinov D., *Living antiquity*, vol. 1, Ruse 1891, 51-52 (*Маринов Д., Жива старина т. 1, Русе 1891. 51-52*).
[134] The sieve is a commonly used instrument in magic and in the Bulgarian tradition it is used as a protective instrument, because its holes can't be counted, as well as in spells for love and taking fertility.

strainer,[135] which until recently were easily related to wine making. According to the latest research and findings these strainers don't have traces of wine, and hypotheses have arisen that it is possible that they were used for producing cheese and not wine.[136] The presence of fragments of such objects in the burial mounds of cult sites shows a possibility, and it is a big one, for a cult function of the strainer, especially the sieve, since Thracian antiquity. In Bulgarian traditional culture the sieve is a ritual instrument, which is present in a different character in different actions – the flour for ritual bread is sieved with an upside down sieve or with three sieves, the ritual offerings are placed in a sieve, a sieve is rolled in rites and divinations are made according to the way it falls, with a sieve the magician steals fertility and others.

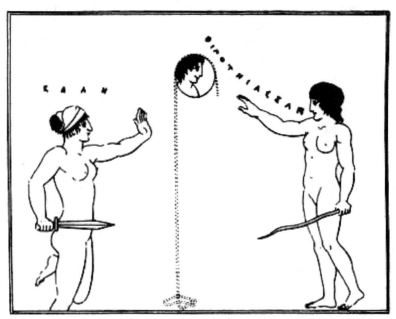

24 - Thessalian Witches Drawing Down The Moon[137]

Another element, which appears as common between the ancient idea of magicians drawing down the moon and their later images in Bulgarian folk culture, is the fact that ritual nudity is a necessary precondition for the act's success. The Thessalian witches who are drawing down the moon are also

---

[135] Similar pot objects are found in the burial inventory of the Thracian priestess Leseskepra, see supra in this chapter.
[136] Hristov Iv., *Temple of the Immortals*, Sofia 2010, 72-76 *(Христов Ив., Храмът на безсмъртните, София 2010, 72-76)*.
[137] www.dressrehearsalrag.tumblr.com<22.06.2011>.

depicted naked.[138] In a number of magical acts, nudity is a requirement for achieving the result of the act.[139] Unlike male nudity, which even today is relatively more accepted in society, female nudity has been regarded as unacceptable from antiquity to the present day. Getting naked, the magician comes out of the profane field, i.e. she is no longer part of human society, she disregards it and unifies with the sacred. A further element is the finds of naked female figurines from prehistoric times. In this case the magician identifies herself with the Goddess and like her, accepts the features of the master of the elements. Therefore she receives the ritual power to unify her forms, i.e. the human form with the celestial, as is the moon and in this manner she receives the knowledge of the initiate, i.e. the one who has unified with the deity.

Although many similarities are noticed between the image of the healer and the magician, the social status of the magician is lower and he is more of a necessary evil, which is tolerated. Unlike the situation in Western Europe, in Bulgaria the magician, even if he was known to the community, did not result in his banishing, burning at the stake etc., i.e. the apparent and strong confrontation has not taken place. Certainly, the main reason for this is the lack of strong church influence and also the superstitious fear among the people which to a certain degree helps for the preservation of many archaic ritual practices in later ages or even to the present day. Along with this, entire magician lines continue their family traditions throughout the centuries.

An intriguing example of the interesting symbiosis between Christian rituals and the people's magical practices is found in an account told to me by a woman,[140] in whose family the magical rituals have their own tradition. Her paternal grandmother was a renowned magician in the community, whilst her father was a Christian priest. The same woman recounts how families which had personal problems appealed to her father for counsel and prayer. In turn the Christian clergyman sought the skills of his mother

---

[138] See also Hristova P., *How to call down the Moon or cultural continuity in Southeastern Europe* // Orpheus. Journal of Indo-European and Thracian Studies, Vol. 7, Sofia 1999, 101-110.

[139] In this connection see also Risteski L., *The Orgiastic Elements in the Rituals Connected With the Cult of the Moon Among the Balkan Slavs* // Studia Mythologica Slavica 5, 2002, 113-129.

[140] Name omitted by her request.

for assistance, who prepared potions from love herbs in order to improve relations in the troubled families.

This account certainly has other parallels, but it also reflects another function of magicians that has been known since ancient times. Despite the fear of them, society accepted them to a certain extent, because in some of life's situation with no alternative, people resorted again to their help and as I already said – oral culture accepts or rejects its members on the basis of their part in the community. The magician and the healer have found their place in traditional Bulgarian society. It is possible to presume that in Thracian antiquity, the attitude towards experts skilled in the properties of nature's materials, by means of which one could affect life's events, was a reason for respect, fear and tolerance towards their carriers.

Separating the two images in the folk idea is also inherited from pre-Christian antiquity and shows that the apprehension even in later times is not because of knowing magical practices, but because of their type and their purpose. The people continued their traditional faith and didn't stop respecting the good magicians, such as the healers, despite every form of magic being criticised by the Christian church. Healing, the power to destroy evil magic and knowledge of the rituals healers acquire during their initiation, i.e. they are taught and initiated in the ritual practices by other healers, but at the same time they are always under the protection of spiritual patrons, which they invoke for help in their healing rituals and to whom they give gratitude on their celebrations. Other types of magic, most often malicious, were considered as a part of the repertoire of the bad magicians, who according to the folk concept are in connection with unclean forces.

In antiquity priests who officiated and knew the rites for worshipping the Gods were separated as an image from magicians. This idea is represented also in ancient literature, as an example we can quote the opinion of the priest Kalasiris from the Ethiopian story (*Aethiopica*) from Heliodorus of Emesa. The rite performed by an old Egyptian magician woman is described like this (Heliod. *Ethiop.* VI):

"The old woman thinking she had now gotten a time wherein she would neither be seen nor troubled of any, first dug a trench, then made a fire on both sides thereof, and in the midst laid her son's body. Then taking an earthen pot from a three-footed stool which stood thereby she poured honey into the trench; out of another pot she poured milk, and from

the third a libation of wine. Lastly she cast into the trench a lump of dough hardened in the fire, which was made like a man and crowned with a garland of laurel and fennel. This done, she took up a sword which lay among the dead men's shields, and behaving herself as if she had been in a Bacchic frenzy, said many prayers to the moon in strange outlandish terms. Then she cut her arm and with a branch of laurel besprinkled the fire with her blood; and after doing many monstrous and strange things beside these, at length bowing down to her dead son's body and saying somewhat in his ear, she awakened him, and by force of her witchcraft made him suddenly to stand. Chariclea, who hitherto had been looking not without fear, trembled with horror and was utterly discomforted by that wonderful sight, so that she awaked Calasiris and caused him also the behold the spectacle. They could not be seen in their dark corner, but they saw easily what she did by the light of the fire, and heard also what she said, for they were not very far off, and the old woman spake very loud to the body."

We understand the position of the ancient priests regarding that scene (Heliod. Ethiop. VI):

"While this was done, Chariclea begged Calasiris earnestly that they might go near and ask the old woman some tidings of Theagenes. But he would not go, saying that the sight was wicked although they were compelled to endure it. It was not becoming for priests either to take delight or be present when such things were doing. Their prescience came from lawful sacrifice and virtuous prayer;"

The words of the priest give us the information that during antiquity magical rituals pertained to the knowledge of priests, but part of those rituals was considered inadmissible, i.e. not to be performed by them. Although the very magical ritual practice was forcing the cosmic powers to fulfill the will of the officiator, only part of the rituals were considered allowable for the priests to perform, who had to make the connection between the people and the immortal gods. In this case it is not only the goal but also the way of accomplishing this goal which must be defined, because the priest and the initiated, as followers of the faith in the divine origin of the human and in the divine will, have to practice rituals consistent with that faith.

Just like healers magicians must pass through a corresponding initiatory rite, in order to receive the secret knowledge. In some cases, when dealing with a carrier of both healing and magical traditions, the transmitting and the beginning of the tuition starts in early childhood from the grandmother or respectively someone else. For the spells in the magical ritual practices there is also a known requirement that they must be transmitted and learned, when the child, who is going to be taught, is ritually clean, i.e. before the first menstrual period for the girls and before the first sexual contact for the boys. As with the healing tuition, the teaching in magic and its techniques is accompanied by the explanation of the properties of different herbs; the time when they have to be picked; the way of their picking and preparation; using different magical instruments – such as the harness from a deceased woman, bone from a dead bastard child and others.

In the folk concept witches are usually old women with no children, widows or women who have had twins several times. The folk notions have also preserved an idea of how a woman who wants to become a magician can achieve her wish. Because the rite reflects a number of archaic views and also has ancient parallels in initiatory ritual practices, it deserves to be discussed as a whole.

Description of practice 10 TO BECOME A WITCH[141]

On Great Thursday she takes the first egg laid by a black hen, but only if it is laid very early, before sunrise. This egg she will carry in her armpit, until it hatches. The chicken must be black just like its mother: if it is white, grey, red – it can't be used. This chicken she butchers at an abandoned hearth, being stripped naked, and with this blood she smears all the joints of her body, i.e. all the places where the body of a person bends: to the feet, to the knees, to the hips, to the hands, to the fingers, elbows, shoulders, neck and so on. After that she dresses in a new, never worn or newly cut and sewed chemise; and she stays in that way with the blood for forty days; then again after midnight she goes to a reversed or left water-mill, in which the water wheel turns contrariwise – to the left; such a water-mill usually has one water wheel. And here, under the water-mill, under the very water wheel she bathes and washes. After that, naked, she goes to the upper part of the water stream or to the millpond of the same water-mill and she pours prepared *samovili* herbs over herself, boiled in a new pot at an abandoned hearth on a fire of Milk Thistle. Here she submits to the devil

---

[141]Marinov D., *Religious folk customs – selected works in 5 volumes*, v. I, part 2, Sofia 2003, 311 (Маринов Д., *Религиозни народни обичаи – избрани произведения в 5 тома, том I, част 1, София 2003, 311*).

and when she pours those *samovili* herbs over herself the devil becomes visible for her. She speaks to him, receives lessons and when the song of the first roosters is heard, she goes back in her house, no longer an ordinary woman, but a witch.

The quoted rite is incomplete, as is clear from its contents. But if we disregard the missed details there are elements which indicate a real basis to this description. In the *Greek Magical Papyri* a typologically similar rite is described, which has the aim of initiation, PGM IV.26-51:

Description of practice 11 INITIATION PGM IV.26-51[142]

Keep yourself pure for seven days beforehand. On the third of the month, go to a place from which the Nile has recently receded, before anyone walks on the area that was flooded - or at any rate, to a place that has been inundated by the Nile. On two bricks standing on their sides, build a fire with olive wood (that is, with a branch of it) when half of the sun is above the horizon; but before the sun appears, dig a trench around the altar. When the disk of the sun is fully above the horizon, cut off the head of an unblemished, solid white cock which [you are to carry] under your left arm (and dig the trench around the altar before the sun appears). When you are beheading the cock, fix it in place [with your knees] and hold it down by yourself. Throw the head into the river and drink up the blood, draining it off into your right hand and putting what is left of the body on the burning altar. Then jump into the river. Immerse yourself in the clothes you have on, walk backwards out of the water, and, after changing into fresh garments, depart without turning round. After this, take bile from an owl, rub some of it over your eyes with the feather of an ibis, and your initiation will be complete. But if you can't get hold of an owl, use an ibis' egg and a falcon's feather. Make a hole in the egg, insert the feather, break it open, and thereby get the fluid to rub on yourself.

---

[142] Betz H., *The Greek Magical Papyri in translation, including the Demotical spells*, Chicago/London 1986, 37.

In original:[144]

Τ]ελετή· προαγνεύσας ζ΄ ἡμέρας ἐλθὼν τῇ τρίτῃ | [τ]ῆς σελήνης εἰς τόπον ἀπο-
γυμνωθέντ[α γε]|ωστὶ ἀπὸ τοῦ Νείλου, πρὶν ἐπιβῇ τις αὐτοῦ τὸ περί|ρυτον (ἢ ἄλ-
30 λως· κατακλυσθέντα ἀπὸ τοῦ Νείλο[υ), ‖ ποίησον ἐπὶ δύο πλίνθων ἐπὶ κροτάφων
ἑστη|κυῖῶν ἐκ ξύλων ἐλαῖνων, τουτέστιν κλημα[τίδ]ος, | πυρὰν ἀνίσχοντος κατὰ
τὸ ἥμισυ τοῦ ἡλίου, πρ[ό]|τερον πρὶν ἀνατείλῃ ὁ ἥλιος, περιγυρεύσας | τὸν βωμόν,
35 πλήρους δὲ ἀνελθόντος τοῦ ἡλιο|δίσκου ἀποτεμὼν τὴν κεφαλὴν ἀλεκτρυόνο[ς |
τελείου ὁλολεύκου, ὃν ἐν τῇ ἀριστερᾷ ἀγκάλῃ <ἔχεις>, | περιγυρεύεις, πρότερον
πρὶν ἥλιος ἀνατ[είλη, τὸν | βωμόν. ἀποτέμνεις δὲ τὸν ἀλεκτρυόνα [τοῖς τό|ναςι
40 συλλαβὼν μηδενὸς ἄλλου αὐτὸν κατέχον‖τος· τὴν μὲν κεφαλὴν εἰς τὸν ποταμὸν
ῥῖψον, | τὸ δὲ αἷμα ἀποδεξάμενος τῇ δεξιᾷ χειρὶ ἔ[κ]|πιε, τὸ λοιπὸν σῶμα τῷ
ἡμμένῳ βωμῷ ἐπιθ[ε]ίς, | καὶ ἐνάλλου τῷ ποταμῷ· μεθ᾽ ἧς ἔχεις ἐςθῆτος | βαπτισά-
45 μενος ἀναποδίζων ἄνελθε καὶ μεθα[μ᾽ φιεσάμενος καινὰ ἄπιθι ἀνεπιστρεπτί. λα-
β[ὼν | δὲ μετὰ ταῦτα νυκτικόρακος χολήν, ἀπ᾽ αὐτῆ[ς] | ἐγχρίου πτερῷ ἴβεως
τοὺς ὀφθαλμούς [σου], | καὶ ἔσει τετελεσμένος. ἐὰν δὲ ἀπορῇς τοῦ [νυκτι]|κ[ό]-
50 ρακος, χρῶ ᾠῶ ἴβεως, πτερῷ δὲ ἱέρακος· ‖ τρήσας τὸ ᾠὸν καὶ ἐνεί[ς] τὸ πτερὸν
κατάρ⟨ρ⟩ηξον | οὕτω ἐγχρισάμενος. |

The first thing we have to say about the described
Bulgarian rite for becoming a witch is that it contains
elements which are opposed to the rite presented above for
becoming a healer. The hearth is abandoned, i.e. this altar
is dedicated to other forces, which do not care about the
welfare of the community. They are elemental and out of the
cultural space. The similarity with the practice described in
the magical papyri can be found in some elements, but we
also see a polarity. There the action takes place at sunrise
and the sacrifice is a white rooster, here the rite is performed
in the evening and the sacrifice is a black chicken. This
black chicken is unusual. The witch-candidate has hatched
it herself, i.e. it appears as her offspring, which she sacrifices
to receive the desired result and to compel the spontaneity of
the wild. The usage of birds in this sense is absolutely
justified bearing in mind that according to the *Derveni
Papyrus*:

*"VI....Therefore the one who desires to make a sacrifice for
the god(s), first (offers) a bird..."*[145]

In the rite from the papyri the candidate-initiate drinks
from the blood of the sacrificial rooster, and the witch
smears her joints with blood from the chicken, which is a
typologically similar action of accepting the divine presence.
After she has smeared with the blood, the woman puts on
new clothing and stays with it forty days, i.e. she keeps a
period of transformation, such as that for women after birth

---

[144] Preisendanz K., *Die griechschen Zauberpapyri*, I, Leipzig 1928, 68.
[145] Yordanova-Aleksieva M., *Hellenic Orphic evidences*, Sofia 2004, 179
(Йорданова-Алексиева М., *Елински орфически свидетелства, София
2004, 179*).

and the soul after death. After the passing of these days she goes to another liminal place, saturated with negative symbolism – a reversed water-mill. There she washes with magical herbs boiled in a special way – in a new pot, on a fire of Milk Thistle and on an abandoned hearth. With that washing she becomes initiated and can communicate with the chthonic forces, which following the Christian example are called devils. The behaviour of the candidate-initiate according to the rite from the papyrus is similar – after he has tasted the blood of the rooster, he goes in the river, after going out he puts on a new clothing and after he rubs with bile from an owl he can communicate with the divine as an initiate. What is interesting in both practices are the similarities in the initiation, which of course have different rationalisations in the different cultural environments.

It is very possible that real practices lay behind that description, which the ethnographic records give as a legend. Did the Thessalian witches and their Thracian parallels remain only in the stories of the ancient authors or do their generations even today enchant the spontaneity of nature's elements...

The idea that the carriers of magical belief are a connection and mediators with the gods, or respectively their Christian correspondences – the saints, leads to the belief that they have divine patrons, whose celebrations they also celebrate. This is the reason why in the folk calendar there are special days filled with magical ritual practices. The calendar celebrations themselves and the rites connected with them, according to some Bulgarian folk beliefs, were established by three mythical female characters, who dressed in their magician clothing, stood on a high mound and determined the days.[146] From a story preserved in a speech of Joseph the Bearded from the Eighteenth century under the name *"Grandmother's celebrations or grandmother's fables"* we learn the following:

"...once there were two old women. The one was called Drusa, she was making incantations against fear by melting lead, and the other was called grandma gorogleda[147] Petka, she was making divinations using wax. They were herbalists and witches and many other cures they knew. At the time

---

[146] Lyubenov P., *Baba Ega: Compendium of different beliefs, folk healings, spells, incantations and customs from the region of Kyustendil*, Tarnovo, 1887, 4 (Любенов П., Баба Ега. Сборник от различни вярвания, народни лекувания, магии, баяния и обичаи от Кюстендилско, Търново 1887, 4).

[147] A word with unclear meaning, it is possible that it means cross-eyed, but the interpretation is disputable.

there were two clergymen, priest Torno and priest Migno. These two old women celebrated twelve Fridays in the year. Grandma Drusa came and said to priest Torno to write those twelve celebrations down, because priest Torno was literate. Grandma Drusa was saying and priest Torno was writing: the first Friday is in March, the second Friday is before Annunciation, the third Friday is before Easter, the fourth Friday is before Mark the Evangelist, the fifth Friday is before Pentecost, the sixth Friday is before Feast of Saints Peter and Paul, the seventh Friday is before Assumption, the eighth Friday is before Beheading of St. John the Baptist, the ninth Friday is before Feast of the Cross, the tenth Friday is after Feast of the Cross, the eleventh Friday is before Saint Andrew the Apostle, the twelfth Friday is before Nativity of Jesus. And priest Torno wrote it down. And grandma gorogleda Petka made a divination with wax and she saw where it was good to write other celebrations. Grandma gorogleda Petka said to priest Migno – let us write the Mrata Saturdays and Thursdays, and Wolf celebrations,[148] and Rusal celebrations,[149] and Hot days,[150] and feast of German[151] and that the women should not spin on Friday[152] and on some Tuesdays. Priest Migno wrote that down and many lies they wrote down, priest Torno and priest Migno and these two old women. They gathered a lot of simple-minded folks and women and men, who were magicians and witches, as well as men, who were promiscuous, atheists, tobacco smokers and drunks, thus a lot of them gathered and they went out on a mound, priest Torno and priest Migno dressed in robes, the lawless and established a law that no one should work on these celebrations..."[153]

These beliefs, recorded and commented by the Christian clergy, reflect the notion that a number of celebrations, as well as rites, are established among the people by the will of the carriers of magical ritual tradition. This folk priesthood, which have continued to perform their ancient functions synchronously with the Christian clergymen, didn't renounce

[148] For the Mrata nights and the Wolf celebrations see chapter *The She-Wolf*.
[149] The Rusal celebrations are days connected with the honour to the rusalki – female mythological character, see in the index *rusalki*.
[150] For the Hot days see chapter *The Virgin Mistress of the Fire*.
[151] For German see chapter *Mother of the Sun*.
[152] See chapter *The She-Wolf* in the section on St Petka and spinning.
[153] Mochulskiy V., *Sermons and teachings against the pagan beliefs and rites. On the traditional history of the Bulgarians*, Odessa 1903, 15-17 (Мочульский В., Слова и поучения, направленные против языческих верований и обрядов. К бытовой истории болгар. Одесса 1903, 15-17) Translation in English by Ekaterina Ilieva on the basis of the Bulgarian translation by Georgi Mishev.

the old celebrations, but gave them a new colouring, so they could fit in the new time. They preserved the knowledge of performing the calendar rituals and the empathy of the cyclic time and non-mortality, which it validates. They gathered and established the laws for celebrating the festivals – says the Christian clergyman, and not from anywhere, but from the top of the mound, which for the ancients symbolised the primordial mountain and was an image of the Goddess.

25 - Depiction Of The Goddess From The Late Bronze Age, From Kličevac, Serbia[154]

---

[154] Farkas A. *Style and Subject Matter in Native Thracian Art* // Metropolitan Museum Journal, Vol. 16 (1981), 46.

CHAPTER 5

THE CONCEPT OF THE GODDESS

When religious feeling begins to form in men, that is to say the idea of forces, which sustain order, look after life, health and well being of people and nature, the necessity to depict them also appears and through their image, symbol and naming, to accomplish a connection with them. The first depiction which man gives to the divine is the concept of the Goddess. Some of her oldest depictions from Europe are dated earlier than 25,000 BCE, which in turn confirms, on the basis of material remains, the presence of this divine idea in the mind of the prehistoric man.

26 - Venus Of Willendorf,
Dated To The Period Between 27,000–19,000 BCE[155]

---

[155]   http://www.zeitreise-zukunft.de/kulturspruenge-der-vorgeschichte/ <01.09.2011>.

I cannot agree that the worship of the Goddess suggests a matriarchal society or that consequently the Goddess became subordinated by the male divinities. In this regard I completely agree with the thesis of prof. Alexander Fol, that the Goddess gathers the male divinities around her in the late ages.[156] In spite of the presence of depictions of the Goddess even from Prehistory, she was worshipped by the Thracians for a long time mostly in aniconic form.

27 - Image Of A Pregnant Goddess Figure With Raised Hands, 8th-7th Millennium BCE, Archaeological Museum Asenovgrad[157]

The Goddess is believed, even from the dawn of human history, to be the Primordial spring, the Universe without motion before the creation, at the same time as being creatrix and mother, beginning and end. She is the one, who gives new beginning after the end of every cycle, and this

---

[156] Fol A., *The Thracian Dionysos. Book three: Naming and faith*, Sofia 2002, 107 (Фол А., *Тракийският Дионис. Книга трета: Назоваване и вяра, София 2002, 107*).
[157] http://www.runitravel.com/wp-content/uploads/2011/01/+Plod_01.jpg <01.07.2011>.

belief is exemplary for the territory where the Thracian ethnicity forms. According to Thracian belief the Great Goddess self-conceives and gives birth to her Divine Son and at the end of the cycle takes him back again in herself and gives him new birth. She is called also the Mountain Mother and is seen by believers as a cave womb, where the flame of the Son is being born. The Great Goddess gives birth to *"Her Son, so She could actuate herself, the Cosmos."*[158] In a non-narrative environment the Goddess remains anonymous, but that is the reason why she receives many namings – Bendis, Cotyto, Hypta, Zerynthia, Hekate and others.

The concept of the Great Goddess is widespread and believed in different ethnic environments; the Thracians maintain her supreme role in their ethnic faith and because of that rationalise her visible manifestation in a different way from the nations around them. Typical of Thracian worship is that the Thracians honour the Goddess through herself. Temples and sanctuaries are not separated or differentiated from nature, on the contrary – they fit in nature around them, in the Goddess. Through the Creation, the Creatrix is honoured.

Ritual practice devoted to the Great Goddess, and that of her Son, have a lot in common and for this literature fragments give evidence, too. For instance Strabo, *X, 3, 15-16*:

"Sabazius also belongs to the Phrygian group and in a way is the child of the Mother, since he too transmitted the rites of Dionysos. Also resembling these rites are the Cotytian and the Bendideian rites practiced among the Thracians, among whom the Orphic rites had their beginning."

Mentioning Phrygian rites and beliefs shouldn't be confusing, as the Phrygians were considered to be Thracians who migrated to Asia Minor, Strabo, *X, 3, 16*:

"For these rites resemble the Phrygian rites, and it is at least not unlikely that, just as the Phrygians themselves were colonists from Thrace, so also their sacred rites were borrowed from there."

The Goddess is worshipped as nature itself, guardian of the hearth, birth, fertility, health and as blessing the sacred union – in its social meaning – marriage, friendship, as well

---

[158] Fol A., *The Thracian Dionysos. Book three: Naming and faith*, Sofia 2002, 107 (Фол А., *Тракийският Дионис. Книга трета: Назоваване и вяра*, София 2002, 107).

as in its abstract meaning – unifying all of the Cosmic elements. The ancient Thracian ethnic belief follows the idea of the immortality of the intellectual energy of the initiated, and thus the Goddess is also believed to be a giver of immortality. She is depicted in some monuments and findings in this function.

28 - Image Of The Goddess Crowning The Deceased Thracian King With The Wreath Of Immortality, Thracian Tomb Of Sveshtari, 3rd Century BCE[159]

Based on the great honour which the Thracians rendered to the Great Goddess, a side of the folk traditions and beliefs has formed connected with a number of female Christian characters such as the Holy Mother of God, St Marina, St Petka, St Nedelya[160] and other female saints, who appear to be a continuation of the belief in the old Great Goddess. Thus until a very late period, and even until today, she has preserved a large part of her ritual tradition. Of course this image has been enriched by the cults of different female

---

[159] http://bgrod.org/galeria/albums/Sveshtari/sborqnovo.jpg <01.07.2011>.

[160] Saint Nedelya (Saint Kyriake, from Greek kyriake κυριακη the day of the Lord, i.e. Sunday, in Bulgarian nedelya неделя) is in the folk notion a guardian of the day Sunday and she often appears only with her sisters saint Sryada (from Bulgarian sryada сряда, i.e. Wednesday) and saint Petka (Saint Paraskeve from Greek paraskevi παρασκευή literally "Preparation" as the day of preparation for Sabbath, i.e. Friday, in Bulgarian petak петък).

divinities worshipped among the other ethnic groups living in the Thracian lands, but the greatest influence is made by the idea of the Goddess, created during Thracian antiquity, on which the rest stratify.

A number of historical and cultural circumstances help the strong preservation of pre-Christian beliefs in Bulgarian spirituality. One of the biggest researchers of Bulgarian traditional faith and ritual practices - prof. Ivanichka Georgieva, writes in her book *Bulgarian folk mythology*:

"With the imposition of Christianity the church has as its primary task to establish the new ideology. Therefore, it adapts to the consciousness of the masses. Without completely rejecting pagan ideological and ritual system, it Christianises and rationalises them in the spirit of the new religion. Later, during the five-century yoke,[161] *the Bulgarian Church, deprived of state support, cannot fight against the pagan notions, because its main task is through the Christian faith to keep the Bulgarian ethnicity. Therefore pagan phenomena remain much longer and too a much larger extent than in other nations."*[162]

The Holy Mother of God, as the ancient Great Goddess, is also called in many magical practices. A part of those ritual acts are performed during the so-called common festivals connected and woven in the cult of the Christian female saints, and another part is performed by healers and magicians.

---

[161] The Second Bulgarian Empire was conquered by the Ottoman Empire in the period 1365-1396. The Bulgarian territories became an Ottoman province, the Rumelia Eyalet. As a result of the Russo-Turkish War (1877–1878), Ottoman was divided into the Principality of Bulgaria, a self-governing Ottoman vassal state, and the vilayet of Eastern Rumelia. Bulgaria was reunified as the independent as the Kingdom of Bulgaria in 1908. See in: http://en.wikipedia.org/wiki/Ottoman_Bulgaria <22.05.2011>.

[162] Georgieva Iv., *Bulgarian folk mythology*, Sofia 1981, 240 (*Георгиева Ив., Българска народна митология. София 1981, 240*).

29 - Mother of the Sun, by Georgi Mishev

THE MOTHER OF THE SUN

As the Goddess is believed by the Thracians to be the Giver of birth to the Son–Sun, so in later ages the Holy Mother of God inherited part of the festive rituals dedicated to the ancient divine Mother. By adopting the pre-Christian celebration of the new birth of the sun, the Christian religion also assimilated a large part of the local pre-Christian, including Thracian, ritual practices. The worship of the divine Mother during Christmas, a time when in antiquity the birth of the Son-Sun was celebrated, is expected for the Thracian faith, where the Mother is initial.[163] Ritual practices connected with these days in Bulgarian traditional culture carry a strong magical character, as in most of the cases the main personages are women and mainly the most elderly women, who officiate and thus adopt the function of the ancient priestesses, servants of the Goddess.

According to folk belief the labour pains of the Goddess start from December 20th, as magical rites begin on the evening of December 19th. One of the performed rites is the so-called *Pazene na kvas* - *'Guarding the sourdough'*.

Description of practice 12 GUARDING THE SOURDOUGH[164]

This rite lasts for twelve nights and it begins on the eve of December 19th preceeding December 20th. Here is its description:

"The rite has magical nature, which is the reason why it is chased by the priests. On December 19th, i.e. the eve before Ignazhden,[165] they gather in some house: unmarried women,

---

[163] The case in Western Europe is analogical, where we have written sources that on Christmas Eve the Goddess was honoured. The ancient concept of the Goddess having her festival in the longest night in the year, i.e. before the new birth of the Sun, is preserved even in late Christian ages, as the different ethnic environments continue her pre-Christian reverence. The festive supper is known as a ritual practice for celebrating this day in Western Europe, but with time it has lost its ritual colouring unlike for instance the sustainability in Bulgarian traditional culture. Proof for those beliefs is a record from 13 century CE: *"In the night of Christ's birth they serve the table for the Heavenly Queen, which people call lady Holda, so she could help them."* ("In nocte nativitatis Christi ponunt regine celi, quam domi-nam Holdam vulgus appelat, ut eas ipsa adiuvet.") in List E., *Is Frau Holda the Virgin Mary?* //The German Quarterly, Vol. 29, No. 2 (Mar., 1956), 81.
[164] *Collection of Bulgarian Folklore and Folk Studies 28*, Marinov D., 276-277 (*СбНУ, 28, Маринов Д., 276-277*).
[165] *Ignazhden* is the day of St. Ignatius of Antioch, which is observed on December 20th and is the first day of the Christmas celebrations.

brides and women, but there are also several elderly women, usually those who are known to be familiar with magic, incantations, divination and others. These unmarried women, brides and women begin to play the horo (line dance); this horo is done either in the room around the bread trough or in the yard. While they play that horo, two unmarried women, of whom one must be the firstborn of her mother, and the other last born – "iztarsak", knead a sourdough, but knead it turned with their backs towards the bread trough. When they begin to mix the flour, the elderly women, under whose guidance all this is being done, put in the sourdough different healing and magical powdered herbs, charcoaled hazel twigs, maple and Turkey oak. The elderly women take this sourdough with those herbs, wrap it and put it in a corner of the room and guard it all night, i.e. a woman or a bride constantly sits awake next to it. The horo is played all night, while the sourdough is being guarded.

This sourdough is guarded in the same way during twelve nights – from December 19th until Vasil,[166] but the ritual mystic horo is played only three times: before Ignazhden, before Christmas and before Vasil. In early morning on Vasil or Survaki[167] all the maidens, brides and women, who had taken part in the "guarding of the sourdough", gather in the house, where the dough has reached before Vasil, i.e. on the twelfth night, and the elderly women tear this dough in as many pieces as people have participated in the rite. None of it is given to any other woman."

The connection between the Goddess and the bread, respectively the sourdough in this case, is significant even from ancient times and so it remains today. The identification of the sourdough with the growing fruit in the womb of the Goddess can be seen in the described rite. In a number of rituals, connected with the worship of the Goddess even from antiquity different kinds of bread are being offered – an example for this is the offering of barley breads by Orpheus to the Goddess in *Argonautica*, and also a number of contemporary ritual practices connected with one of the Christian images that is successor to the ancient Goddess – the Mother of God.[168]

---

[166] *Vasil* is the day of St Basil the Great celebrated on January 1st.

[167] *Survaki* is the folk name of the day of St. Basil the Great, because this is the day when the rite of *"survakane"* is done – patting on the back of a person with a cornel-tree stick decorated with a lot of fruits, coins, colour threads and others, along with saying good wishes.

[168] Example of this rituals inherited in the honour of the Mother of God is for instance the kneading of a bread on the third day of the birth of a child, called *"Bogorodichna pita"* (Mother of God's bread), which *"...must be eaten*

For the inheritance of this ritual practice among the Christianised Thracians we find evidence in one text from Epiphanius (*Panarion, 78.23*):

"For it is related that some women in Arabia, who come from the region of Thrace, put forward this silly idea: they prepare a kind of cake in the name of the ever-Virgin, assemble together, and in the name of the holy Virgin they attempt to undertake a deed that is irreverent and blasphemous beyond measure — in her name they function as priests for women.

...This heresy was once more taken up in Arabia from Thrace and the upper parts of Scythia, and has come to our attention...

The harm is equal in both these heresies, of those who disparage the holy Virgin, and again of those who glorify her beyond what is necessary. Are not those who teach this merely women? The female sex is easily mistaken, fallible, and poor in intelligence. It is apparent that through women the devil has vomited this forth. As previously the teaching associated with Quintilla, Maximilla, and Priscilla was utterly ridiculous, so also is this one. For some women prepare a certain kind of little cake with four indentations, cover it with a fine linen veil on a solemn day of the year, and on certain days they set forth bread and offer it in the name of Mary.

immediately, so Mother of God can go and help other women", Georgieva Iv., *The bread of the Bulgarians: bread without sourdough, bread with sourdough.* // Bulgarian ethnology issue 3, 1993, 15-23 (Георгиева, Ив. *Хлябът на българина: хляб без квас, хляб с квас.* // *Българска етнология № 3, 1993, 15-23*). The idea that the Mother of God is helper of every woman giving birth and stays with her during the birth identifies her with the images of the ancient goddesses of childbirth as Ilithyia. This practice of giving bread away for the birth of a child is known from antiquity and it is criticized by Christian priests in the rules of the Ecumenical councils, as for instance in rule number 79 of the Third Council of Constantinople or also called Trullan Synod from 680-681 is written: *"As we confess the divine birth of the Virgin to be without any childbed, since it came to pass without seed, and as we preach this to the entire flock, so we subject to correction those who through ignorance do anything which is inconsistent therewith. Wherefore since some on the day after the holy Nativity of Christ our God are seen cooking σεμίδαλῖν, and distributing it to each other, on pretext of doing honour to the puerperia of the spotless Virgin Maternity..."* (Source: http://www.ccel.org/ccel/schaff/npnf214.xiv.iii.lxxx.html <09.02.2012>). Also see Pankova Y., *Terminology and ritual functions of bread in South-Slavic folk rites* // Symbolic language of traditional culture. Balkan studies II, 1993, 63-75 (Панкова Ю., *Терминология и ритуальные функции хлеба в южнославянских родинных обрядах* // *Символический язык традиционной културы. Балканские чтения II, 1993, 63-75*). The shown examples again attest the stability of these ritual practices and the connection bread - Goddess.

They all partake of the bread; this is part of what we refuted in the letter written to Arabia."[169]

The text above gives an impression of the great honour that Thracian women pay to the Goddess, even after her Christianisation, who found her successor in the image of the Mother of God. For this great honour the Thracian women were criticised by Christian priests. An interesting moment in the quoted text is also the stable preservation of that belief among the Thracian immigrants, in this case in Arabia. Along with that, one of the most widespread rites connected with the Goddess also makes an impression, namely the making of ritual bread, which is shared and given in her name and which rite, as we are going to see, remains very similar among the population in the Bulgarian lands. Although offering bread to the Goddess is a rite also known and preserved by other Balkan people, the mentioning of this practice as popular among the Thracian women is immediately parallel to the women's rituals in Bulgarian lands.

This faith and ritual practice is confirmed also by the archaeological finds, as grinding stones for grinding grains and preparing of sacrificial breads at the place of the sanctuary are found near many of the ancient sanctuaries.

The bread made from many grains is a symbol of the multiple consistency of the Goddess. It is not by accident that Bulgarian folk belief considers that *"the bread is a soul, and the soul is steam."*[170] The Thracian Goddess, as a source of souls, most often receives as sacrifice exactly this kind of offering and according to the contemporary worship this bread varies – sourdough or not, bread coated with honey, with herbs and magical plants mixed in it (as in the above described rite *'Guarding the sourdough')*, with flour sieved three times with an upside down sieve, with water from three springs, with different bread decorations and in many other variations. Different types of bread and their usage in rites is evidenced even in the Hittite ritual texts, where a lot of bread types are listed, as in different rites a necessity of the usage of different types of bread as a sacrificial offering can be seen – a requirement which we'll also see preserved in Bulgarian folk belief and which can be a reminiscence of antiquity.

---

[169] Kraemer, R., *Women's religions in the Greco-Roman World*, New York/Oxford 2004, 85-86.
[170] Georgieva Iv., *The bread of the Bulgarians: bread without sourdough, bread with sourdough.* // Bulgarian ethnology issue 3, 1993, 15-23 *(Георгиева, Ив. Хлябът на българина: хляб без квас, хляб с квас. // БЕ № 3, 1993, 15-23).*

The described rite *'Guarding the sourdough'* is performed only by women and is part of a type of female magical ritual practice.[171] At the end of the rite every woman participating in it gets a piece of the sourdough which is full of power, is believed to be magical and will assure the blessing of the Goddess during the upcoming year over the family and the home. There it will be used for preparing the bread, because through it the food itself will be blessed and filled with the divine presence. The participation of women only in this rite reminds us again of the text from Epiphanius, who says that in their rites Thracian women function as officiators. In this role we also see the women here as the ones who perform the rite.

Bread is connected with the hearth through the process of its baking. For this reason it is connected both with the image of the Goddess as a keeper of the hearth, and also with her image as the one who helps in its creation. Because of the belief in the Goddess as a giver of blessings over marriage and relationships, this sourdough is believed to have the power of creating love.

After the days of the labour pains of the Mother of God comes the last evening, when it is believed the birth of the Young God occurs, as the divine Son-Sun/Fire is called in folk songs and blessings, dedicated to this day. In Christmas terminology the prevalence of the namelessness of the divine offspring can be seen, who is called the Young God, but not with his Christian appellation of Jesus or Christ. The birth of the Sun is preceded by a worship of the Mother, who also usually remains anonymous and is called in most cases Mother of God and very rarely Mary.

BADNI VECHER (Christmas Eve)

According to folk belief the day before Christmas (December 24th) is the last of the days of labour pains of the Holy Mother of God. In Bulgarian folk culture this is the day filled with most excitement and rites, not Christmas itself. The culmination of this festive day is the ritual supper, but in short the day itself goes like this.

Everything begins with the preparation of a number of different types of bread, the main is a big round bread with plastic decoration – cross, circle and others.[172]

---

[171] Suggested by the symbolism of the number 12, which in this case represents the new twelve solar months that are to come.
[172] On this subject and for information regarding the types of ritual breads prepared during Christmas among other Balkan peoples see Plotnikova A.,

In addition ring-shaped buns are made, which are given to the *koledari* (Christmas carollers).

The women in the family cook the main dishes for the supper, which must be without any animal products and odd in number.

For the feast, men have the duty of preparing a special wood for the fire, which will be lit in the evening and will burn during the whole night. It is most commonly called *badnik*. The wood in most cases is from oak, pear or beech – healthy and plentiful. In its thicker end a hole is made and in it they put frankincense, wine, oil, and after that they close it with a wooden wedge and wind around it white hemp or linen cloth.

The culmination of the festive day is the supper, around which all the members of the household gather. It is believed that the more plentiful and 'big' it is, so too will the household be plentiful and healthy during the year. Therefore there is an inclination to place a part of everything that has been produced in it. In the evening the elder kindles the *badnik* and the supper begins when all of the family members have gathered. The supper is served on straw spread on the floor.

When everyone gathers around the supper, the eldest man or woman fumigates with frankincense and after that goes about fumigating every room and the outbuildings. Once they sit, the members of the family must not get up, and if that is necessary only the elder can get up, but he has to walk bent so the wheat spikes will be heavy and bent, too. The goal is for the supper to begin as soon as possible so the wheat can ripen earlier. After the whole house is fumigated, the elder breaks the bread, the first piece is intended for the Holy Mother of God and is placed in front of her image at the home altar, the second piece is intended for the house, i.e. for the spirits protectors of the house and after that everyone gets a piece of the bread. Only then can the eating begin.

Christmas symbols in the terminology of ritual bread among Serbians // Symbolical language of traditional culture. Balkan studies II, Moscow 1993, 37-62 (*Плотникова А., Рождественская символика в терминологии обрядового хлеба у сербов // Символический язык традиционной културы. Балканские чтения II, Москва 1993, 37-62*), as well as in Yaneva St., *Varieties of Bulgarian Ritual Bread*, Sofia 1989 (*Янева Ст., Български обредни хлябове, София 1989*).

In many regions women put aside a bit of everything and carry it to the graveyard,[173] so they can feed the *stopanin* – the spirit protector of the house.[174]

A number of divinations about the weather, health and fertility are done on the celebration. If the *badnik* burns bright, with sparkles, this means that the year will be plentiful. Part of the ash of the *badnik* is put aside and is kept until autumn, when it is mixed with the wheat for sowing and is put in the field to assure the good growth of the wheat. The marks placed in the bread – silver coin, straw, pumpkin seed, promise good luck to the one they fell to for the area of agricultural activity they have been named for. The one who finds the silver coin will be healthy and happy; his beginnings during the year will be successful.

When the supper is over, all await the arrival of the *koledari*,[175] who enter the house singing special songs, dedicated to the members of the household, beginning with the elder. The songs express wishes for prosperity, health, and marriage. In the end the leader of the *koledari* says their blessing which is recitative and in a fast tempo.

This really short description of the celebration aims to describe the order of the ritual activities, which are

---

[173] Or the food, which has been put aside, is placed somewhere high in the house, so the so-called St Namestnik could eat (Strandzha, region).

[174] The *stopanin* is usually perceived as a spirit of a male ancestor, but this is not always mandatory. The folk belief forms an image of a protector, i.e. a divine master and guardian of the home, but doesn't define its gender. In some cases it is believed that the builder of the house is bound through rites during the building process with the building, and after his death becomes its guardian. In this connection there is a concept that the guardian of a given building is inherited by the newcomers, i.e. they must be accepted by him and offer him appropriate sacrifice (*kurban*). Unlike the Russians, among the Bulgarians the connection of the home cat with the guardian of the home is not familiar and that is the case also with the rite for transferring a *stopanin* from an old home to a new one. The *stopanin*, although it has its parallels with the Slavic people, as for instance the Russian *domovoi*, has inherited a number of pre-Slavic features in its veneration, for which see chapter *The She-wolf* in this book. Among the other non-Slavic speakers the naming of that guardian has the same semantics, for instance the Greek population in the Macedonia region calls the *stopanin* νοικοκυρές, i.e. also a master of the home, see Abbot G., *Macedonian folklore*, Cambridge 1903, 19. This mythological notion has its peculiarities when it comes to a *stopanin* (guardian) of a region, spring, tree or village. The belief about him in a theriomorphic image, i.e. his appearance as an animal, is also known. The usual appearances in those cases are in the guise of a snake (*Colubridae*), bull, eagle. In those animals we see a symbolic relation with the popular male deities from antiquity and their function of guardians as carriers of the male power.

[175] The *Koledari* are boys up to 12-13 years old, carrying bags, who go around the houses of relatives and neighbours with wishes for fertility – both for animals and crops. They are expected as heralds of the desired prosperity and are gifted with dried fruits, nuts, small coins, and ring-shaped buns, which they string on their staffs.

performed by the people, but on a great scale without realizing their ritual function and the antiquity of some ritual elements. In this connection I am going to look at the basic elements separately, so I can try and present them in the meaning of a possible interpretation in the spirit of the ancient Thracian beliefs.

30 - Image Of Ritual Bread, Prepared Especially For Christmas Eve[176]

THE RITUAL BREAD

The bread prepared for the celebration is a bloodless offering given to the Goddess during the night, when she gives birth to her divine Son. It is kneaded by women, who must be dressed in clean festive clothes.[177] Only the finest flour is used for the kneading and it is sieved three times, mixed with *'unspoken'*[178] and *'undrunk'*[179] water, brought in a white cauldron and heated on a living fire.[180] Women sing special songs while kneading the breads. There are three

---

[176] http://augusta-books.com/blog/wp-content/uploads/2011/12/Pogacha2.jpg <02.07.2011>.

[177] The requirement for purity in kneading the ritual breads, which in this case is understood not only in the physical, but also in the ritual plan too, is known from antiquity. The Hittite texts report the duties of the temple staff and for the requirements for the preparation of bread, see Sturtevant E., *A Hittite Text on the Duties of Priests and Temple Servants* // Journal of the American Oriental Society, Vol. 54, No. 4 (Dec., 1934), 365.

[178] *"Unspoken"* is the name given to the water, which is poured while no word is being uttered from going out of the house to coming back, and stepping over the doorstep.

[179] *"Undrunk"* is water which hasn't been drunk, i.e. hasn't entered in another function except ritual.

[180] *"Living"* is a fire started with special ritual and by rubbing two pieces of wood.

types of Christmas breads.[181] The first is named after the celebration itself and bears the names *bogovitsa* (where *'bog'* means god), *bozhia pita* (god's bread), *svetets* (saint). The typical decoration for it is the cross[182] and its varieties – swastika, rosette, flower and others. The second type of bread is dedicated to the house and the farm. Usually the sheep pen, the livestock, the vineyard and so on are depicted on it. The third type of bread is the *'twisted, over twisted buns'* with a hole in the middle, which are given to the *koledari*. A candle is placed over the ritual bread, part of which is also lit during the year and is used in a number of rituals both healing and magical.

Here I'm going to comment only on the bread dedicated to this celebration because there are a great variety of ritual breads and plastic decorations. The symbols of the Son-Sun in this type of ritual bread are very expressive, but along with the solar crosses that mark the sun, the equal-armed cross may be interpreted in another way, namely as a plastic depiction of the Goddess from whom the God is being born. The equal-armed cross with the form of "X" is called a symbol of the World's Soul by Plato,[183] an image of the cosmic order and model of the individual souls. For the combination of this symbol and the circle and its use even by the Egyptians we learn from Proclus who quotes Porphyry:

"As reported by Porphyry, among Egyptians there was a character of this kind, which, surrounding the "x" by a circle, gives the World's Soul symbol."[184]

The ancients identified the World Soul with the idea of the Goddess. Late fragments that bear record and beliefs close to Thracian Orphism reflect some of those ideas:

"Workwoman, she is the bestower of life-bearing fire,

And filling the life-giving womb of Hekate...."[185]

and

---

[181] In this case is commented the most widespread terminology for calling these types of bread among Bulgarians. For detailed information regarding different names among other Balkan peoples see the quoted above article of Plotnikova - Plotnikova A., *Christmas symbols in the terminology of ritual bread among Serbians* // Symbolical language of traditional culture. Balkan studies II, Moscow 1993, 37-62 (Плотникова А., *Рождественская символика в терминологии обрядового хлеба у сербов* // *Символический язык традиционной културы. Балканские чтения II, Москва 1993,37-62*).

[182] The solar equal-armed cross, which is embodiment of the four directions.

[183] Plato, *Timaeus* 36 b-c.

[184] Proclus, In *Tim., III* ed. E Diehl, vol 2, BT, 1904, 247, 1.18-20.

[185] Johnson S., *Hekate Soteira: A Study of Hekate's role in the Chaldean oracles and related literature*. Atlanta 1990, 64.

"[The self-moving Soul] provides life to other things, rather to herself..."[186]

The connection which I'm making here is with one of the hypostases of the Goddess in antiquity, Hekate, is not coincidental because it is only in the Bulgarian lands[187] that we see the Goddess with the theonym Hekate depicted holding a child in her hands.[188]

31 - Image Of The Goddess Hekate[189]

---

[186] Ibid. 67.

[187] At least as far as I know.

[188] Although Hekate is believed as a guardian of children and because of that having the epithet *"Kourotrophos"*, she has not been depicted holding a child or in a combination with children. The only similar image, which depicts children in relation of Hekate worship is also found North from Greece, namely on the scenes of the statue of Hekate situated in Sibiu, Romania, see Köppen P., *Die dreigestaltete Hekate und ihre Rolle in den Mysterien*, Wien 1823.

[189] Mladenova Y., *Images of Hekate in our lands*, Archaeology magazine 1961, b. 3 (Младенова Я., *Паметници на Хеката от нашите земи*, сп. *Археология 1961, кн. 3*).

32 - Statue Of The Goddess Hekate, Situated In Sibiu/Hermannstadt, Romania[190]

33 - Ritual Scene On The Statue Depicting A Child As A Participant In The Rite As Its Role Is Not Clear, But It Possibly Suggests An Initiatory Ritual[191]

---

[190] Köppen P., *Die dreigestaltete Hekate und ihre Rolle in den Mysterien*, Wien 1823.
[191] Ibid.

Other close features can be found in the image of the Holy Mother of God, preserved in magical formulae, of the image of the Goddess who was honoured in antiquity on roads and crossroads and is called with the theonym Hekate, but this connection is going to be examined in detail down below.

Because the ritual materials are believed to be saturated with a specific power from their connection with the divine, which is fulfilled on the celebration, many of them are used in different rituals and magical practices with an apotropaic and purificatory nature. An example for this is the use of the candle which has burned on the Christmas Eve bread for driving a hail cloud away.

Description of practice 13 PROTECTION FROM A HAILSTORM[192]

During summer, when a hail cloud appears, an elderly woman from the village goes to a high place facing the cloud, takes off her clothes, takes with her what's left from the candle which has burned on the ritual bread on Christmas Eve, and some red eggs, painted on Holy Thursday and a sieve, as knocking facing the cloud she says:

"Come back, come back cloud Dzherman

and go where the forest is desolated,

where the beasts are wild,

where no man walks,

where no rooster sings,

where no lamb bleats."[193]

German[194] or *Dzherman* is known as a lord of the hail among other Balkan nations too – including the Romanians, Macedonians,[195] and Serbs. In the western Bulgarian lands

---

[192]Lyubenov P., *Baba Ega: Collection of different beliefs, folk healings, spells, incantations and customs from the region of Kyustendil*, Tarnovo, 1887, 37 (Любенов П., *Баба Ега. Сборник от различни вярвания, народни лекувания, магии, баяния и обичаи от Кюстендилско, Търново, 1887, 37*).
[193] In Bulgarian:
Върни се, върни се облаче Джермане
и иди дека е пуста гора,
дека са диви зверове,
дека човяк не оди,
дека петел не пое,
дека ягне не бляе.
[194] This name has no connection with Germany or the Germans.
[195]About the invocation of the lord of the hailstorms in Macedonia and Romania see in Mihaylova G., *Are the masked ones masked*, Sofia 2002 (Михайлова Г., *Маскирани ли са маскираните, София 2002*), as well as the research of Kaindl R., *Die Wetterzauberei bei den Rutenen und Huzulen*

as well as in Eastern Serbia and Macedonia similar ritual formulae-appeals to *German* are preserved, recognised sometimes as St Germanus.

The incantations among the Serbs which mention Dzherman have a similar structure to the Bulgarian,[196] because they belong to a comparatively similar contact zone which is the territory of West Bulgaria, Macedonia and East Serbia. The difficulty in identifying the mythological character *German* with St Germanus is commented in scholarly literature,[197] and the ritual practice connected with the summer rite for protection against rains or drought called *'German'* among the Bulgarians and *'Skaloyan'* among the Romanians is given as an example. Most likely the mythic lord has gained the name of the Christian saint because of the coincidence in the time of making the rite with the celebration of the saint, namely May 12th. The rite called *German* is performed for calling the rain as well as for stopping the rain, as both rites have similar technique, but different ritual instruments.

// Mittheilungen der kaiserlich-königlichen geographischen Gesellschaft in Wien, XXXVII, Wien 1894, 626.

[196] See incantation Nr. 608 in Radenkovic L., *Folk spells and incantations*, Nis-Pristina-Kragujevats, 1982 *(Раденковић. Љ., Народне басме и бајања. Ниш-Приштина-Крагујевац, 1982)*
"Stop German, this is not your place!
At the mountain is your bedding, German,
The meadows are not mowed German,
The wheat is not reaped, German,
The vineyards are not gathered German,
The boys are not married German!"
(Translation in English by Ekaterina Ilieva on the basis of the Bulgarian translation from Serbian by Georgi Mishev).
[197] Venedikov Iv., *The copper threshing-floor*, Stara Zagora 1995, 322-323 *(Венедиков Ив., Медното гумно, Стара Загора 1995, 322-323).*

34 - Ritual Figurine Of German For Provoking Rain[198]

Description of practice 14 GERMAN FOR CALLING THE RAIN[199]

When there is tough drought the children make a male figure from mud, in the stomach of which they put a recently killed frog with an open mouth. One of the children – a girl, plays the role of a mother to *German*, she covers her head with a black cloth, a second child plays the role of a priest, others are the carriers and arrange themselves like they are at a burial, they mourn *German* and say:

"Oh German, German, cries German from drought for sludge!"[200]

They carry and bury him by a river; they make a small mound like a grave, put over it a cross and go back where they came from. They spread around the village and start to beg the people from different houses with the words:

"Give for the German!"[201]

From what they collect – money, sweets and others, they prepare a commemoration for *German*. They boil wheat and prepare everything else needed for the commemoration of a

---

[198] Archive of Association Ongal. Still from a photo story about the homonymous folklore custom for calling the rain in the village of Gorun, Shabla Municipality. Authors: Konstantin Rangochev and Rosen R. Malchev. Field studies of the University Club UNESCO at "St. Kliment Ohridski" in July 1987.

[199] *Collection of Bulgarian Folklore and Folk Studies 13*, 178 (*СбНУ т. 13, 178*).

[200] In Bulgarian: *"Ой Германе, Германе, плаче Герман от суша за киша!"*

[201] In Bulgarian: *"Дайте за Германа!"*

deceased person. They burn frankincense and the commemoration starts, when it ends all the children go home. While the commemoration lasts all of them must cry, and if a child doesn't cry the others beat it so it cries. If a person is in the way of the performance of the rite, the children say to him:

"Instead of for the German, we should mourn for you!"[202]

Description of practice 15 GERMAN FOR STOPPING THE RAIN[203]

The figure of *German* for stopping the rain is made from a broom instead of mud, which the children steal from a woman pregnant for the first time, they dress the broom as a doll and the rite is performed only by three girls.

The whole rite is just like the *German* from mud, but the mourning this time goes with the words:

"Oh German, German, cries German from sludge for drought!"[204]

There are records from the neighbouring Balkan countries of magical rites connected with mentioning *German* for driving away hail and storms. Their performance is mainly by women, and shows the strong pre-Christian base on which they have developed. In comparison with the Bulgarian rites, those from Serbia contain more Christianised elements, which are only perfunctory – the naming of the ancient lords of natural forces are replaced by names of Christian personages, but a pagan basis can be seen through them. We can't be sure to what extent this basis consists from ancient Thracian, Roman and Greek ideas and how much from Slavic and later, but these ritual practices deserve to be given attention because of their archaism.

---

[202] In Bulgarian: *"Вместо Германа, тебе да оплачем!"*
[203] *Collection of Bulgarian Folklore and Folk Studies 13*, 178 (*СбНУ т. 13, 178*).
[204] In Bulgarian: *"Ой Германе, Германе, плаче Герман от киша за суша!"*

Description of practice 16 CHASING A HAIL CLOUD AWAY – FROM EASTERN SERBIA[205]

In the region of Leskovac, Eastern Serbia, chasing a hail cloud away is performed by the housewife. She takes a plate, which she takes out to a ladder in the centre of the threshing floor, puts salt in the plate and lights a candle from the festival of Mother of God (Golyama Bogoroditsa – Assumption of Mary, August 15th). The woman unbraids her hair, kisses the ground three times and spins the plate three times from left to right. She takes a cloth, waves it above her head and says:

"Let us pray to God

and to saint German,

to Mother of God

and saint Elijah,

saint Peter

and saint Paul.

Go back, go back,

German cloud,

this is not your place.

Your place is in the deserted Galilean woods,

where sun doesn't shine,

where rain doesn't fall,

where wind doesn't blow,

where there are no children,

where there is no livestock,

where there are no kids,

where there are no lambs,

where there are no pigs,

go there to hit,

there should thunder strike!"[206]

---

[205] Tolstye N. I. and S. M., *Protection from hail in Dragacheve and other Serbian regions* // Slavic and Balkan folklore, Moscow 1981, 92 (*Толстые Н.И. и С.М., Защита от града в Драгачеве и других сербских зонах // Славянский и балканский фольклор, Москва 1981, 92*).

[206] The translation in English is made by Ekaterina Ilieva using the Bulgarian translation by G. Mishev from the Russian edition of Tolstye N. I. and S. M., *Protection from hail in Dragacheve and other Serbian regions* // Slavic and Balkan folklore, Moscow 1981, 92 (*Толстые Н.И. и С.М., Защита от града в Драгачеве и других сербских зонах // Славянский и балканский фольклор, Москва 1981, 92*).

Description of practice 17 CHASING A HAIL CLOUD AWAY – FROM THE REGION OF MACEDONIA[207]

The housewife takes the first egg, an axe and a cauldron. She goes out on the yard, puts the cauldron with the bottom up, places the egg and the axe over it and says:

"Lord!

Where roosters don't sing,

where hens don't cluck,

where sheep don't bleat,

where goats don't squeal,

unleash a hail in the mountain, in the woods,

so it won't kill our good harvest!"[208]

The rites shown for protection from hail use a number of objects from calendric ritual practices – candle from the bread for Christmas Eve, egg from Maundy Thursday, candle from the Assumption of Mary and others, showing the belief in their magical power.

Often it is easily accepted that the chasing hail (or diseases in other cases) away formula to a place where *'roosters don't sing'*, *'hens don't cluck'*, *'no man goes'* and so on, is a Slavic motif. I can't agree with that statement, because there are known magical formulae for chasing hail away from the region of Spain, dated Eighth century CE, which according to some scholars continue an old Mediterranean tradition and where the same formula can be seen:

"...[e]diciantur de uila e de 'ilas' auitaciones p(er) montes uada et reuertam ubi neq(ue) galus canta neq(ue) galina cacena, ubi neq(ue) arator e(st) neque seminator semina, ub'i'ui neq(ue) nulla nomina reson'a'."

In translation:

"...let it be driven out from the town and the houses; let it wander the mountains, where neither the cock crows nor the

---

[207] Tolstye N. I. and S. M., *Protection from hail in Dragacheve and other Serbian regions* // Slavic and Balkan folklore, Moscow 1981, 96 (*Толстые Н.И. и С.М., Защита от града в Драгачеве и других сербских зонах // Славянский и балканский фольклор, Москва 1981, 96*).

[208] The translation in English is made by Ekaterina Ilieva using the Bulgarian translation by G. Mishev from the Russian edition of Tolstye N. I. and S. M., *Protection from hail in Dragacheve and other Serbian regions* // Slavic and Balkan folklore, Moscow 1981, 96 (*Толстые Н.И. и С.М., Защита от града в Драгачеве и других сербских зонах // Славянский и балканский фольклор, Москва 1981, 96*).

hen clucks, where neither the ploughman tarries nor the sower sows, where no name resounds.[209]

The notions in the magical formulae are a reflection of the technique of the adjuratory rite. In this case the goal is to drive away a negative influence to outside a given territory. This driving away is not to any location, but to a deserted and uninhabited territory where there will be no consequences from that influence. The opposition is shown between the cultural sacred space and chaos, where the troubling element is being sent. The chronological period between the Latin spell and the ones listed above is about a thousand years. Along with that the shown spells are a part of the culture of different ethnic groups in the Mediterranean, a region of strong cultural interactions. These facts suggest and even confirm the great sustainability of magical texts and the reason why they should be regarded as representatives of the most archaic part of the folklore. Certainly one and the same idea could be seen and perceived in different ways depending on the ethnocultural environment.

BADNIK (Yule log)

The *badnik* is commonly an oak or pear wood log, cut and brought in the house by a young man, and with that wood the fire is kept alight for the whole night. The youngest man in the family, wearing festive clothes, goes into the forest. He chooses a healthy and fertile tree for a *badnik* – oak, elm, pear or other. Before he cuts the tree down, he begs for forgiveness. The wood shouldn't touch the ground and is carried to the house on the right shoulder.[210] Everybody at home awaits him with eagerness. The young man asks: *"Do you praise the Young God?"*,[211] and the women answer - *"We praise him, we praise him, welcome!"*[212] after which the man adds: *"I go in the house and the God comes with me!"*[213] Carrying the wood-*badnik* in the house in some places is accompanied by the following blessing:

---

[209] Nieto F., *Visogothic charm from Asturias and the classic tradition of phylacteries against hail* // Magical Practice in the Latin West, Leiden-Boston 2010, 552-553.

[210] Carrying on the right shoulder is a requirement also in the carrying of the icons of the *nestinari*, as they carry the image facing it, i.e. they think of it as something alive and that is the case with the wood-*badnik*. See Fol V., Neykova R., *Fire and music*, Sofia 2000, 128-129 (Фол В., Нейкова Р., Огън и музика, *София 2000, 128-129*).

[211] In Bulgarian: *"Славите ли Млада Бога?"*

[212] In Bulgarian: *"Славим, славим, добре си ни дошъл!"*

[213] In Bulgarian: *"Аз в къщи и Бог с мене!"*

"Good evening, Christmas eve has come, year has come with children, with piglets, with foals, with calves, with young lambs, kids and chicks – here, here grandma's chicks – walk around the village, but at home lay eggs."[214]

The wood is placed next to the hearth, where it is blessed - a hole is made in its thicker end and wine, olive oil and frankincense are put in it, the hole is closed and is wound with white linen cloth. While the *badnik* is being anointed the women sing:

-Oh you, tree, straight tree,
where you grew so thin,
so thin and so high?
Thin tree answers:
-Oh you little woman,
little woman krivoperka,[215]
I have grew up there,
up there in the mountain,
in the mountain, in the forest mead,
by the lake of the samovili[216]
a black-eyed shepherd cut me down,
brought me here to plant me
near the hearth, near the supper!
I am, little woman, golden tree,
golden tree that is fertile:
I will grow to the sky,
branch will drop to the ground,
leaf will leave like small pearls,
blossoms will bloom like pure silver,
fruit will bear like dry gold!
On me the Young God will come down,
and will give good gift:
to the unmarried woman – small pearl,
to the mother – pure silver,
to the father – dry gold,
dry gold, full house

---

[214] Lybenov P., *Baba Ega: Collection of various beliefs, folk healings, spells and traditions from the region of Kyustendil*, Tarnovo 1887, 27 (Любенов П., *Баба Ега. Сборник от различни вярвания, народни лекувания, магии, баяния и обичаи от Кюстендилско*, Търново, 1887, 27). In Bulgarian: „Добър вечер, дошла е бъдни вечер, повалила се година с дечица, с прасенца, с жребчета, с телета, с млади агънца, яренца и пиленца – тъкъ тъкъ бабини пиленца – по село ходили, а в къщи носили."
[215] *Krivoperka* – the meaning of that word is not clear.
[216] *Samovila* with plural form *samovili* are mythological female forces similar to the ancient nymphs.

with little children, with lambs,
with calves, with foals,
with kids, with piglets,
with lightly winged bees,
life, health, joy!![217]

After putting the *badnik* in the hearth the oldest woman scatters wheat in the fire so the upcoming year will be plentiful. Scattering wheat on the altar is a practice attested from antiquity and is a part of the sacrificial rite. With the scattering of wheat in one hand an offering is made and in the other a marking of the altar fire, which has to burn during the whole night. According to folk belief this is done so that it could be bright for the Mother of God and the deceased ancestors, who are also believed to participate at the festal supper. According to belief the *badnik* has magical and healing power. The ash from it is used for healing, but is also put on fields, vineyards and meadows, so they can be productive.

---

[217] *Collection of Bulgarian Folklore and Folk Studies 28,* 280, village of Litakovo, Botevgrad region *(СбНУ 28, 280, село Литаково, Ботевградско).* In some places they sing that song while the *badnik* is carried in the house. In Bulgarian:
- Ой те, дръвце, право дръвце,
де си расло толко тънко,
толко тънко, та високо?
Отговаря тънко дръвце:
- Ой те тебе, малка моме,
малка моме кривоперка,
я съм расло тамо горе,
тамо горе на планина,
на планина, на рудина,
край езеро самовилско,
отсече ме вакъл овчар,
донесе ме да ме сади
край огнище, край трапези!
Я съм, моме, златно дръвце,
златно дръвце плодовито:
ще порасна дор до небо,
клон ще пусна дор до земля,
лист ще листна дребен бисер,
цвят ще цъфна чисто сребро,
род ще родя сухо злато!
Слез ще по мен Млада бога,
ще дарува добра дарба:
на момата - дребен бисер,
на майката - чисто сребро,
на бащата - сухо злато,
сухо злато, пълна къща
със дечица, със ягънца,
със теленца, със конченца,
със яренца, със прасенца,
със пчелици лекокрилки,
живот, здраве, веселие!

While the *badnik* burns protective rites are performed too.

Description of practice 18 FOR PROTECTING THE HOUSE FROM EVIL SPELLS[218]

A child or a girl takes millet and goes in a circle around the house sprinkling it and says:

"The one who will be able to count those grains, this one will be able to cast a spell on us!"[219]

Although placing such a tree in the fire during that night is a ritual practice known to western and eastern European peoples, the rationalisation and symbolism of this act in Bulgarian traditional culture has different hues. Mainly the *badnik* as an ethnolinguistic term is known among the South Slavs[220] and most of the research is made on the basis of materials from Serbians and Bulgarians. An impression of the abundance of ritual acts is namely among the Bulgarians, as well as the poor Christian element in them. The main ritual actions are:

- cutting the tree for *badnik*, which is accompanied by some ritual requirements – to beg for forgiveness and that the *badnik* shouldn't touch the ground;

- carrying – moving the sacred object through space is a sacred act and in this case the requirement to carry the wood on the right shoulder is preserved;

- carrying in the home – bringing in the sacred object is accompanied by the uttering of ritual formulae, which again validate it as a carrier of the divine presence;

- anointing – a first sacrificial rite through placing sacred liquids and incense;

- lighting – lighting the *badnik* actuates the ritual and gives a start to the celebration;

- second sacrificial rite – scattering wheat in the fire by the eldest woman;

---

[218] Lybenov P., *Baba Ega: Collection of various beliefs, folk healings, spells and traditions from the region of Kyustendil*, Tarnovo 1887, 28 (Любенов П., *Баба Ега. Сборник от различни вярвания, народни лекувания, магии, баяния и обичаи от Кюстендилско, Търново, 1887, 28).*

[219] In Bulgarian: *"Който може да изброи тези зърна, той ще може да ни направи и магия!"*

[220] See Tolstoy N., *Balkan-Slavic badnik in a pan-Slavic perspective //* Balkans in the context of the Mediterranean, Moscow 1986, 128 (Толстой Н., *Балкано-славянския бадняк в общеславянской перспективе //* Балканы в контексте Средиземноморья, Москва 1986, 128).

- keeping the ash – the ash from the *badnik* is kept and with it a number of magical actions are made, of which the most common is the dusting of the fields with it for fertility and protection;

The wood transforms into a living figure and into a ladder, on which the deity goes down to the mortals *"...On me the Young God will come down, and will give good gift...".* For the ladder and its symbolism among the Thracians Mircea Eliade writes:

"Polyaenus (Stratagematon, VII, 22) talks about Kosingas, a priest-king of several Thracian peoples, who threatened his people that he will leave them climbing up a wooden ladder to the goddess Hera; this proves that similar ritual ladder really existed and it was believed that with climbing it up the priest-king could actually go to the Sky. Rising to the sky with a ritual climbing on a ladder probably was part of orphic initiation."[221]

In our case the *badnik* is exactly that ladder and connection with the divine and as such must be ritually clean. That is why the wood is consecrated through contact with the sacred liquids – wine and olive oil, which in this case marks both the chthonic and solar manifestation of the God who is born again. The wine appears as a symbol of the blood and the connection with earth, and the oil as an indication of the solar hypostasis of the dual Son God - Sun and Fire.

Of interest and deserving attention is the interpretation of the naming of the wood *'badnik'*, which according to some scholars derives from the Indo-European root **bhudh* meaning *'depths'*, *'basis'*, but in this way is also etymologically connected with the *'serpent of the Deep'*[222] (Ahi Budhnya). The similar etymology only confirms the earthly, fiery and chthonic hypostasis of the divine, which is conjured through the *badnik* and its role as a mediator, i.e. to connect the foundations and namely the earth with the high sky and to realise the descent and the unification of the divine and human.

Nowhere in the rite itself there is any mention of the Christian naming – Jesus or Christ. All of the time the Young God is mentioned who stays anonymous and is called in his manifestations through the ritual acts. This god is not

---

[221] Eliade M., *Images and symbols: studies in religious symbolism*, Princeton, 1999, 48.
[222] In this connection see: Watkins C., *How to kill a dragon : aspects of Indo-European poetics*, New York 1995, 461.

perceived as an abstract idea; he is present during the rite and is brought into the house through the wood, through the fire, which is his earthly image. From it during that night will be born the celestial fire – one magnificent depiction and co-experience of the ancient Thracian belief in the Son-Sun, who is a child of the Great Mother Goddess.[223]

THE SUPPER ON CHRISTMAS EVE

The culmination of the ritual practices privy to this day is the ritual supper. According to folk belief it must begin early, so the crops can ripen early, no one should get up from the table so the hens shouldn't get up early from the laying-place, but if that is necessary the one who gets up has to walk bent so the wheat spikes will also be bent and heavy. This belief supports the idea of magical acts aiming to stimulate fertility during the upcoming year. The supper must be arranged around the hearth, so everyone is facing it, because it is believed that the hearth is the sacred place in the house. The sacredness of the hearth comes from its ancient ritual function as an altar and a place for sacrifice, evidence for which are the numerous altar hearths known from publications of archaeological research in ancient Thrace.[224] The supper is served on straw and in it different seeds are placed as a symbol of fertility, a sack or a piece of cloth is put on top of it. The meals must be uneven and mustn't have any animal products in them. The elder of the house (male or female) – acting as an officiator, invites the God at the supper with the words: *"Come God, let us have supper!"*,[225] this calling of the God in some regions has another meaning and transforms into calling of the God who is lord of the clouds, storms and hails:

"Come you cloud let us have supper, we brought you a supper, now we call you to have it, and during summer your eyes shall not be seen, go in a desolate forest with wild beasts, where no rooster sings, where no lamb bleats."[226]

---

[223] See also Nikolova M., *Pagan and Christian motifs in the Christmas song about the birth of the "Young God"* // Crypto-Christianity and religious syncretism on the Balkans, Sofia 2002, 69-76 *(Николова М., Езически и християнски мотиви в коледните песни за раждането на "Млада Бога" // Криптохристиянство и религиозен синкретизъм на Балканите, София 2002, 69-76).*

[224] Example for this are the researches of Seuthopolis, see in Seuthopolis, Vol. 1, Sofia, 1984 *(Севтополис. т. 1. София, 1984).*

[225] In Bulgarian: *"Ела Боже да вечеряме!"*

[226] Lybenov P., *Baba Ega: Collection of various beliefs, folk healings, spells and traditions from the region of Kyustendil*, Tarnovo 1887, 28 *(Любенов П., Баба Ега. Сборник от различни вярвания, народни лекувания, магии, баяния и обичаи от Кюстендилско, Търново, 1887, 28)* In Bulgarian: *Ела*

This same God of Thunder can be seen this time named and is known to us – *German* or Djerman:

"German, German, you cloud! Come to have a supper with us. Come now, but in summer your eyes shall not be seen neither on a field, nor in a meadow. Now we've prepared bread, stewed dried fruit, beans, seeds, white onion, everything is full, but mostly the rakia[227]!"[228]

After calling the God for supper the table is fumigated with frankincense, which is actually a continuation of the calling. The burning of incense itself, along with the cleansing effect, believed by the people, has a pure sacrificial function which is part of the ritual prayer calling. After the supper is fumigated, the burner with the incense is taken by the eldest woman in the house and she fumigates all the rooms and buildings in the yard one by one. In this case we see a shared officiation between the man and the woman who are the eldest of the house, which reflects the ancient notion, that everyone is an officiator in his own house and in the performing of their house rites. After the prayer the bread, in which a coin has been put symbolising the lucky lot, is broken as it is, rose facing upwards, so the wheat should grow higher. The first piece is devoted to the Holy Mother of God and is placed in front of her image at the home altar, where it is kept until next Christmas. This represents the bloodless offering which is left to the ancient Goddess, keeper of the house and giver of prosperity. The next piece of the bread is for the house, i.e. for the spirits protectors of the house and the family guardians. The supper itself should not be cleared, because it is believed that during the night the deceased ancestors come to have supper. Feeding with the Gods is of great importance, because in Christian tradition it is forbidden and its continuity follows an ancient religious ritual practice.[229]

и ти облаче да вечеряме, донесли сме ти вечеря, сега те викаме да вечеряш, а през лятото очите ти да не видим, иди в пуста гора при диви зверове, където петел не пее, където агне не блее.

[227] Rakia is an alcoholic beverage that is produced by distillation of fermented fruit, mainly grapes.

[228] Stareva L., *Bulgarian spells and divination methods*, Sofia 2007, 39 (Старева Л., *Български магии и гадания. София 2007, 39)* In Bulgarian: Джермане, Джермане, облаче! Дойди да вечеряме. Сега да дойдеш, а летоска очи да не ти видим, ни на нива, ни на ливада. Сега сме приготвили хляб, ошав, боб, семе, бял лук, всичко е пълно, а на ракия най-вече!

[229]For the prohibitions of the so called brother suppers in the Christian canonic literature and their continuity in the folklore environment see with cited literature Fol V., *The Forgotten Saint*, Sofia 1996, 131-136 (Фол В., *Забравената светица, София 1996, 131-136)*.

According to folk belief this night is also appropriate for making a number of divinations about the weather and fertility during the upcoming year, for marriage and prosperity. The next ritual element privy to this day is the arrival of the koledari.

KOLEDUVANE[230]

The *koleduvane* begins after midnight, i.e. with the coming of the birth of the new sun, the Young God. The groups of the *koledari* consist of young men, who perform Christmas songs and make blessings, with every group having a leader. Going around the houses the *koledari* receive gifts from the eldest woman of every house and then the leader of the group lifts up the ring-shaped bun and says a long blessing for health, happiness and prosperity.

In some places this blessing has kept a lot of archaic features, which have preserved the image of the ancient Great Goddess. Particular interest is provoked by one text that describes the divine Mother in her Thracian image:

"So the Mother of God reached,

to a road, to a crossroad,

on a high mound

at the scarlet guelder rose.

With her right hand she was resting

on a golden torch,

With her left hand

a great fortune divided:

to which brother a bowl,

to which brother a spoon,

And to our old householder

and to him She divided a share –

Old kilo from Tarnovo,[231]

kilo and a half.

He was happy and more happy,

so he puffed up like a well fed horse

and jumped like a lamb[232] on St George's Day,

as a chicken[233] on St Peter's Day."[234]

---

[230] *Koleduvane* is a type of Christmas caroling
[231] Old measure.
[232] The lamb and chicken mentioned here are the usual sacrifices for both celebrations, lamb for the day of St George and rooster for the day of St Peter. The comparison between the blessed man and the sacred animal gives an additional sacred status. The sacrifice, which has been prepared for the deity (resp. in the Christian context for the saint) is desired and loved by it.

35 - Image Of Hekate With A Child In Her Arms,

---

[233] See previous note.
[234] *Collection of Bulgarian Folklore and Folk Studies* 35, Nr. 68 (*СбНУ т. 35, № 68*).
In Bulgarian:
*Най си стигна божа майка
на път, на кръстопът,
на висока могилка
при алена калина.
С дясната ръка се подпираше
на златна главничка,
с лявата ръка
тежко имане делеше:
кому, брат, паничка,
кому, брат, лъжичка,
а на този наш стар станеник
и на него делба отдели —
старо търновско кило,
кило и половина.
Той се радва и обрадва,
та се наежи като хранен кон
и подскочи като агне гергьовско,
като пиле петровско*

National Archaeological Museum Sofia[235]

The divine Mother in this fragment is presented standing on a crossroad, moreover on a mound, which is also the image of the sacred mountain, next to the Guelder rose tree and in her right hand holding a golden torch, on which she rests, and with her left hand she gives prosperity.[236] The image described here is of the Goddess honoured and appearing on the road and crossroad and called in antiquity by Thracians and Greeks with different theonyms, but most often Hekate.[237] The connection of the Mother of God with the crossroad can also be seen in other Christmas blessings, for instance:

"She has set, oh Kolade, my Kolade,
Mother of God, my Good one, oh Kolade,
in the middle of the road, of the crossroad,
to await her son.
She didn't meet her son,
but she met a group of young men..."[238]

And also in another song:

"...at last reached a road, a crossroad
where St. John with the Mother of God –
were sitting on a golden table,
barbell fish were eating,

---

[235] Mladenova Y. *Monuments of Hekate in our lands*, Archaeology magazine, 1961, book 3 *(Младенова Я., Паметници на Хеката от нашите земи, сп. Археология 1961, кн. 3)*.

[236] For the same interpretation see in Venedikov Iv., *The golden pillar of the proto-Bulgarians*, Sofia 1987, 314 *(Венедиков Ив., Златният стожер на прабългарите, София 1987, 314)*.

[237] Many scholars comment and suppose an explanation for the Thraco-Phrygian origin of the cult to Hekate, because she is perceived by the Hellenes as a foreign deity, bearing strange features and rituals and was perceived as a barbarian goddess, see Zeleny K., *Die Göttin Hekate in den Historiae Deorum Gentilium des Lilius Gregorius Gyraldus (Basel 1548) unter besonderer Berücksichtigung der Rezeption Hekates in humanistischen Handbüchern und Kommentaren des 16. Jahrhunderts*, Wien, 1999, 12; Ronan St., *The Goddess Hekate: Studies in Ancient Pagan and Christian Religion & Philosophy, Vol. 1*, Hastings 1992, 23-24.

[238] In *Bulgarian folklore motifs. Vol. I. Ritual songs*, compiled by Mollov T., Varna LiterNet, 2006-2010: http://liternet.bg/folklor/motivi/maika_diri_sina_si/vabel_3.htm <29.12.2011> *(Български фолклорни мотиви. Т. I. Обредни песни Съст. Тодор Моллов. Варна: LiterNet, 2006-2010)*.
In Bulgarian:
"Седнала ми, Коладе ле, мой Коладе,
Божа майка, мой Добро ле, Коладе ле,
на сред пътя, кръстопътя
да си чака своего сина.
Не дочака своего сина,
най дочака отбор момци..."

red wine were drinking,
heavy wealth of God were dividing.
Amen, group!"[239]

The crossroad as a place where the Goddess stops to perform the act of blessing, shows the proximity of the Goddess of the Roads among the Thracians with the idea of her, who was described by Hesiod in *Theogony*[240] - as a giver of prosperity. In this blessing the crossroad is also a place where the Goddess feeds and there is the place where her table is situated, a parallel reminding of the ritual practice of leaving the so-called Hekate's supper.[241] The torch in the hand of the Goddess identifies her as a bearer of light and the known epithet of the Goddess among Thracians – Phosphoros, who in some places has separate sanctuaries recorded as for instance the Phosphorion in the Thracian settlement Kabyle (today near the town of Yambol).[242] The depiction and the idea of the Thracian Mother Goddess as Hekate, i.e. as the one who gives birth to the divine son, shouldn't seem strange to us because of the images found in the territory of Bulgaria of Hekate with a little child in her hands,[243] again accompanied by her sacred dogs-wolves,

---

[239] In *Bulgarian Christmas blessings*. Compiled and edited by Mollov T., Varna: LiterNet, 2005-2009
http://liternet.bg/folklor/sbornici/blagoslovii/nova_kamena.htm
<29.12.2011> *(Български коледни благословии. Съставителство и редакция Тодор Моллов. Варна: LiterNet, 2005-2009).*
In Bulgarian:
"...най стигна на път на кръстопът
свети Иван с Божа майка -
на златна трапеза седяха,
мряна риба ядяха,
руйно вино пиеха,
Божи тежко имане деляха.
Амин, дружина!"
[240] For the connection of the description of Hekate in the *Theogony* of Hesiod with the Thracian concept, a possible explanation is the Boeotian origin of Hesiod.
[241] See in Aristoph. Pl. 595 in Aristophanes. *Wealth. The Complete Greek Drama*, vol. 2. Eugene O'Neill, Jr. New York. Random House. 1938:
Chremylus: ...Ask Hekate [595] whether it is better to be rich or starving; she will tell you that the rich send her a meal every month and that the poor make it disappear before it is even served.
[242] Chichikova M., *New discovered epigraphic evidence for the cult of Phosphoros in northeast Thrace* - *Terra Antiqua Balcanica IV*, Sofia 1990, 82-92 *(Чичикова М., Новооткрит епиграфски паметник за култа на Фосфорос в Североизточна Тракия – ТАВ,4, София 1990, 82 – 92).*
[243] The image of Hekate as nurse of the young, called Κουροτρόφος is to be seen in the *Theogony* of Hesiod:
[450] And the son of Cronos made her a nurse of the young who after that day saw with their eyes the light of all-seeing Dawn. So from the beginning she is a nurse of the young (Κουροτρόφος).

which are a second naming of the divine son in his winter hypostasis, at the time of his birth.[244]

The connection of the Mother of God with the crossroad is significant for Bulgarian ritual texts. Along with the Christmas blessings it is also in the incantation formulae where the crossroad is seen as a place where the Mother of God, i.e. the Goddess is situated, there she can be met, there she feeds or there the ill person stands and calls her. Similar parallels cannot be found in the ritual texts of Serbs, Russians and others summarised as 'Slavic peoples'. The crossroad in their traditions is a place inhabited by unclean forces, a place where a person is attacked by them and where they harm him, after which he could turn to the Mother of God for help, but not to go there and call her. An example for this is one of the few Serbian incantations where the image of the Mother of God and the crossroad are connected:

"A man went on a big road,

He got to a crossroad,

But he came across vilas and halas.[245]

The halas grabbed him by the head,

And hit him in the ground:

His bones they broke,

His brain they sucked,

His blood they drank.

He cried with a loud voice.

Mother of God heard him..."[246]

---

[244] About the wolf-dog and the winter image of the Son see in Fol V. *The wolf/the dog and the North as the direction of wisdom.* – In: *Studia archeologiae et historiae antiquae.* Doctissimo viro Scientiarum Archeologiae et Historiae Ion Nikuliță, anno septuagesimo aetatis suae, dedicator. Chişinău, 2009, 149–158.

[245] The *vili* (plural form of *vila*, i.e. *samovila*) are female mythological creatures among the Serbs which cause illness, but are called as healers and experts on healing rituals and plants. They are close to the Bulgarian *samodiva* and to the ancient notion of the nymphs. The *hala* is believed as a mistress of the wind, who brings diseases.

[246] Radenkovic L. *Folk spells and incantations,* Nis-Pristina-Kragujevats, 1982, Nr. 418, 251 *(Раденковић Љ. Народне басме и бајања. Ниш-Приштина-Крагујевац, 1982, № 418, 251).* The translation in English is made by Ekaterina Ilieva using the Bulgarian translation from Serbian by Georgi Mishev.

In Russian[247] and Serbian texts the Mother of God often sits on a white stone or throne, but not on a crossroad and in addition the possibility for her table to be situated there is absent. The rock Alatyr or the idea *"in a blue sea on a white stone"* can be perceived as a Slavic element in the ritual texts, but is rarely seen in the Bulgarian incantation formulae for example:

"Mother of God has sat,

in the Danube river on a white rock..."[248]

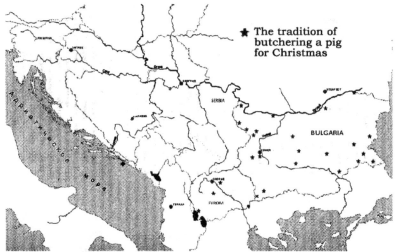

36 – Christmas offering amongst the Balkan Peoples.[249]
Tradition of butchering a pig at Christmas – *it can be seen that this tradition is spread mostly in the Bulgarian ethnic territory*

---

[247] There is a lot of literature about Russian magic formulae, but in this book the following books are mostly used: Zabyilin M., *Russian people: their customs, rituals, legends, superstitions and poetics. In four books.*, Moscow, 1880 (Забылин М. Русский народ: *Его обычаи, обряды, предания, суеверия и поэзия. В четырех частях., Москва, 1880*); *Russian erotic folklore. Songs. Rituals and ritual folklore. Folk theater. Spells. Riddles.* Chastushki. Compiled and edited by A. L. Toporkova, Moscow, 1995 (*Русский эротический фольклор. Песни. Обряды и обрядовый фольклор. Народный театр. Заговоры. Загадки. Частушки. Составление и научное редактирование А. Л. Топоркова. Москва. 1995*); Maykov L., *Great Russian spells*, Saint Petersburg, 1994 (Майков Л., *Великорусские заклинания, Санкт Петербург, 1994*); Vetuhov A., *Charms, spells, amulets*, 1907 (Ветухов А. Заговоры, заклинания, обереги., *1907*).
[248] Pirgova I., *Traditional healing rituals and magical practices*, Sofia, 2003, 148 (Пиргова И., Баяния и магии, София, 2003, 148). In Bulgarian: *"Седнала е Божа майка, на Дунава на бял камък..."*
[249] The map is from Plotnikova A., Ethnolinguistic geography of the Balkan // Blood sacrifice. Transformation of one ritual, Belgrade 2008, 249 (*Плотникова А., Етнолингвистичка географија Балкана // Крвна жртва. Трансформације једног ритуала, Београд 2008, 249*).

In her honouring on Christmas Eve the Mother of God embodies a lot of features and rites from the ancient Goddess in both her function as a mother and as the one who gives birth to her Son-Sun. After the ritual honouring during the night of the Birth, on the next day in the Bulgarian lands another sacrificial rite is performed, namely the butchering of a pig, which in the past (and even today) was accompanied by a lot of ritual acts.

According to Bulgarian custom the blood of the butchered pig must run into the earth. In some places the youngest child is placed to sit on the pig as a rider and says a blessing formula for fertility:

"Penda and Perenda, next year hundred kilos of bacon!"[250]

It is not hard in the appeal *Penda*[251] to find one of the theonyms of the Thracian Great Goddess, namely Bendis. The pig as a sacred animal to Bendis is known from antiquity and evidence for the connection of this hypostasis of the Goddess with the pig are preserved until later times, as for instance in the hagiography of St Hypatius in Bithynia where he encounters the Goddess as a woman as tall as ten men, who at the same time knits and pastures pigs.[252]

The next word in this short blessing formula – *Perenda*, also raises interest because it is possible its etymology and connection come from the Thraco-Illyrian theonym Perendi/Perendy,[253] meaning god of the sky and rock god, i.e. born from the rock (which is a naming of the Goddess). If this interpretation is correct we see a preserved prayer to the Goddess, and her companion, for ensuring fertility in the upcoming year. A child pronouncing the prayer formula is not surprising because in antiquity there was a practice for divinities to be invoked by children (virgins[254] or boys who still haven't *'known'* a woman).

---

[250] For this evidence I have to thank my mother Sonya Misheva (born 1952) who as a child has performed this very rite. In Bulgarian: *"Пенда, че Перенда – догодина сто кила сланина!"*

[251] For Penda as a naming of the female image from the *martenitsa* see chapter *The Mountain mother*.

[252] Popov D., *The Thracian goddess Bendis*, Sofia, 1981, 29 (Попов Д., *Тракийската богиня Бендида, София 1981, 29*)

[253] Gamkrelidze, Ivanov, *Indo-European and the Indo-Europeans*, Berlin/New York, 1995, 528, as well as Fol Al., Jordanov K., Porozhanov K., Fol V., Ancient Thrace, Sofia 2000, 76.

[254] Examples of this practice are found in Hittite ritual texts, for instance in the ritual of Anniwiyani for the Lamma-gods, D. Bawanypeck, (ed.), hethiter.net/: CTH 393 (TRde 2008-10-30) в: http://www.hethport.uni-wuerzburg.de/txhet_besrit/translatio.php?xst=CTH%20393&expl=&lg=DE&ed= <29.12.2011>.

The Goddess as a Mother of the Sun is one of the hypostases which have been preserved in traditional folk culture, as her functions are inherited by the Christian image of the protector of motherhood – St Mother of God. From the quoted folk texts and beliefs it can be seen that St Mother of God in Bulgarian folk culture and especially in the ritual practices has a strong connection with the crossroad, which is a significant element connected with her image. In this connection the following rites, in which the Goddess is called in a Christian manner the Mother of God, is shown at a crossroad.

Description of practice 19 INCANTATION AGAINST EVIL EYE[255]

Three lumps of sea salt are taken. The healer (female or male) stands in front of the ill person. The salt is taken with the right hand and whirled around the head of the person while saying:

God's mother sat on a crossroad,

tucked up her white sleeves,

began to knit a black tow and said:

-Wild samodivi,

pass across nine forests,

across nine cold waters –

to our child bring a cure.

If it's from a male –

from male the evil eye curse should burst.

If it's from a female –

from female the evil eye curse should burst.

If it's a male –

his left ball should burst;

if it's a female –

her left bosom should burst.

As the people

scatter from church,

so should scatter

its evil eye

from the waist,

from the heart,

from the little nails.

As the line dance scatters,

so should scatter

its evil eye

from the waist,

from the heart,

from the little nails.

Yesterday three brothers were born,

yesterday were born,

---

[255] Pirgova I., *Traditional healing rituals and magical practices*, Sofia, 2003, 139-140 (Пиргова И., Баяния и магии, София 2003, 139-140).

yesterday they began to walk,

yesterday they began to speak

and they took fast horses,

and went in a Tililean woods

to cut a tree –

top down,

roots up.

When it comes

this child to sit

under that tree,

only then it can

be cursed by evil eye.[256]

---

[256] The text of the incantation in Bulgarian:
Божа мале седнала на кръстомпът,
запретнала бели ръкави,
запрела църна къдела и рекла:
- Диви самодиви,
през девет гори да минете,
през девет води студени –
на нашто дяте ляк да донете.
Ако е от мъжко –
от мъжко да са пръснат уроките.
Ако е от женско –
от женско да са пръснат уроките.
Ако е мъжко –
да му са пръсне лявото мъдо;
ако е женско –
да й са пръсне лявата бизка.
Къкто са хората
от черква разтурят,
така да са разтурят
неговите ураки
по снагата,
по сърцето,
по некътчетата.
Къкто са хоро пръска,
така да са пръскат
неговите ураки
по снагата,
по сърцето,
по некътчетата.
Снощa са родили трима братя,
снощи са родили,
снощa проходили,
снощa продумали
и отзели бърза коня,
и отишли в гора тилилейска
дърво да отчат –
върха надолу,
корена нагоре.
Кога дойде
да седне тва дяте
под тва дърво,
тогава нега

37 - The Healer And The Magician
Carriers Of The Ancient Sacred Knowledge
Image by Georgi Mishev

ураки да фанат.

In this healing rite, that aims to remove the influence of the evil eye, the ancient Goddess is described, who is invoked and makes her divine appearance on the crossroad. The Goddess is invoked by one of her signs – the salt, which in Ancient Rome was honoured also as a separate Goddess called Salus. In the incantation the dual nature of the Goddess is named through the white and black and thus she is made closer to the image of Bendis, who was called δίλογχος – *'the one with the double spear'*, explained by the lexicographers by the meaning that the Goddess accepts honour both from earth and sky. The Goddess is invoked to reorganize the Cosmos both in the horizontal – represented by the crossroad, and in the vertical – represented by the knitting. The knitting itself again directs us to the image of Bendis in the case, where she is described as a knitter.[257] With her knitting the Goddess creates the connections and threads in the Cosmos, i.e. she connects[258] it and generates its unity, unifying the vertical and the horizontal.

In the healing incantation-charm the Goddess gathers around her the *samodivi*, these successors of the Thracian nymphs, which in folklore are believed to also be healers. The *samodivi* as manifestations of the Great Goddess are being sent to pass across the nine steps of the ten-level cycle of the building of the Cosmos according to Thracian Orphism, i.e. to perform the rite of passage and passing through the nine forests and the nine waters to create again the created, i.e. to give new birth and purification. The new birth is a notion left from mystery tradition ritual practice, but it has been preserved as a relic and in a number of healing rites as the passing under a root of a tree, hole in a rock and others.

After the calling of the healer nymphs (the *samodivi*) in the incantation follows a part which is based on the principle of associative magic – *'as-so'*. The spoken destruction of the sex characteristics of the person causing the illness has the goal of also destroying the effect of his deeds. The sex characteristics in this case represent the power of the person causing the illness – the testicles of the man, the breasts of the woman.

---

[257] As a whole the image of the Goddess in her function of a Mistress of Fate is commonly connected with knitting. This image is known from the Hittite ritual texts, see Bossert H., *Die Schicksalsgöttinnen der Hethiter* // Die Welt des Orients, Bd. 2, H. 4 (1957), 349-359.

[258] It is likely that the name Bendis can be interpreted as originating from the Indo-European bhendh, *"to connect"* exactly in this sense as the One, who connects and unifies the elements and the cosmic forces.

In the next element the three brother riders appear, who are sent to the world beyond with the charm to bring a tree, under which the ill person should sit and only then could he be harmed again, i.e. the last part of the incantation is for the future protection of the patient.

Description of practice 20 INCANTATION AGAINST EVIL EYE[259]

The healer sits next to the ill person, with their thumb rubs him or her on the forehead between the brows and says:

(The name of the ill person) sat,

on a road, on a crossroad,

he cried, he wept.

The Holy Mother of God passed and

asked him (her):

-Why do you sit (the name),

on a road, on a crossroad,

why you cry, why you weep?

-How could I not cry, not weep,

when my waist is taken.

The Holy Mother of God said:

-Get up (the name), from here,

go to (the name of the healer) healer!

Her charm catches

as a grafted pear,

as a planted field.

Shake off,

cleanse,

as a light feather,

as pure silver![260]

---

[259] Pirgova I., *Traditional healing rituals and magical practices*, Sofia, 2003, 156 (*Пиргова И., Баяния и магии, София 2003, 156*).
[260] In Bulgarian:
Седнал (името на болния)
на път, на кръстопът,
та вика, та плака.
Минала св. Богородица и
я (го) пита:
- Що стоиш (името),
на път, на кръстопът,
що викаш, що плакаш?
- Как да не викам, не плача,

After this the healer spits three times and washes the eyes of the patient with water that was used to wash the image of the Mother of God. Finally the healer gives him or her the same water to drink from three times and the rest of it is poured by a fence or wall, so no one could step on it.

The scene described in the rite presents the one who calls the Goddess standing on a crossroad and sending his prayer to her. Interesting in this case is the direction to the relevant healer, which the Goddess gives to the ill person. The Goddess declares and guarantees the ritual power and knowledge possessed by the healer. With this the healer, who is identified by the deity as a carrier of sacred knowledge is recognised also as her officiator. This idea comes from the remote past, when the priestess was identified with the Goddess. The priestess perceives herself as a carrier of a divine power and the relevant knowledge through which she actuates the divine forces. In the incantation the Goddess herself validates this ritual position of the healer and assures of the power of their words. According to folk belief it is not enough only to know the ritual words, they have to 'catch', i.e. to succeed to actuate the divine.

The next stage in the rite itself is the role of the saliva in the ritual healing that is a known element from antiquity.[261] The contact of the saliva with the tongue and by that with the spoken words of the incantation fills it with power and its next impact with the body of the patient aims to transfer that power to them.[262]

An interesting element of the ritual act is the washing of the image of the deity (the icon) and the usage of the water from that washing as consecrated. This practice shows the belief in the impregnation of the divine power into the image of the deity. The icon in Bulgarian folk belief completely replaces the antique xoanon. The wood image of the deity is

като ми е земена снагата.
Па рекла св. Богородица:
- Стани (името), оттука,
иди при (името на лечителя) баснарка!
Нейната басня фаща
като круша присадена,
като нива засадена.
Да се отърсиш,
да се очистиш,
като леко перо,
като чисто сребро.
[261] For the healing effect of the sacred snakes of Asklepius see Angeletti L., Agrimi A., French D, Curia C., Mariani-Costantini R., *Healing rituals and sacred serpents* // The Lancet Volume 340, Issue 8813, 1992, 223-225.
[262] See in Selare R., *A Collection of Saliva Superstitions* // Folklore, Vol. 50, No. 4 (Dec., 1939), 349-366.

considered also as a vessel for the divine power and because of that it consecrates by contact. It is the place of the divine appearance, which we know from antiquity with the name xoanon. The widespread belief about the sanctity of icons long transmitted in the community is another example of the continuity of ancient beliefs and their inheritance by the Christian tradition.

The water left from the rite is poured next to a fence or wall, because it should not be stepped on or to have contact with a human, as it has given its sacredness to the person and has taken his or her ritual impurity. This transfer and cleansing is exactly the point of the rite, which is shown in the incantation text where in a symbolic way the cleansing is shown with the silver and the feather. The silver is considered a metal connected with the feminine principle and the Great Goddess, and the feather, besides being associated with lightness, is connected to the celestial as the bird which is also a ritual presence of the Goddess, as many of her ancient images give evidence.

Like the ancient Goddess, the Mother of God is believed by the people to be a giver of fertility and is honoured in cases of childlessness, as in this connection a number of magical rites for conception are made. Some of these magical rites are believed to have been revealed to the people by the Mother of God herself.

Examples for such rites are seen in the practices performed in the region of Asenovgrad, Plovdiv region. In the church situated in the village of Gorni Voden a special homage is paid to an icon of the Mother of God, called 'Golden apple'.

Description of practice 21 MOTHER OF GOD GOLDEN APPLE[263]

According to local custom on the fifth Saturday from Lent the image is decorated with apple wreaths, which stay there five weeks and are given away on the celebration to the infertile women. According to the belief, in order for her wish to obtain a child to come true, a woman must eat the whole apple. The explanation of the local people for this custom is the appearance of the Mother of God herself, who gave a golden apple to a woman wishing to conceive in her sleep.

---

[263] Bozhinova V., Southwestern university *"Neofit Rilski"* - Report on subject: *St Mother of God – golden apple*, Blagoevgrad 2009, online: http://satrae.swu.bg/media/5366/st.%20virgin.pdf <29.12.2011> (Божинова В., Югозападен университет *"Неофит Рилски"* – Доклад на тема: *Света Богородица-златна ябълка, Благоевград 2009*).

Actually the dream doesn't explain why it is exactly on this day and why the whole apple must be eaten, but the explanation is absolutely clear if we bear in mind the ancient beliefs where the eating, i.e. taking the divine power, leads to unification of the human with the divine, i.e. through the fertility of the Mother, the woman also obtains such fertility. The apple as a fruit with a meaning of carrier of fertility could hardly be explained through Christianity, because the apple is the fruit of the Original sin and in this connection is definitely not the most appropriate decoration for the image of the Mother of God. But in the context of ancient beliefs the apple is right where it should be, because in antiquity it is considered as a ritual attribute and sacred fruit of the Goddess. A number of examples for this can be found in mythology, as well as in folklore, where the apple is a carrier of wealth and fertility. We only need to remember that the Mother Goddess in one of her names as Gaia gifted the tree with golden apples on the wedding of Zeus and Hera, i.e. the Earth blessed the union of the divine couple so it could be fertile.

Another magical rite in the same region is the weaving of a special belt.

Description of practice 22 BELT FOR CONCEIVING[264]

According to local legend – in 1919 the Mother of God appeared in the dream of a woman, who was spending the night in the church. During her appearance she said to the woman to go out early in the morning at the door of the church, where another woman with three white reels would meet her, and with the threads of those reels they should walk around the church and with them a belt should be woven, which the one who wanted to conceive must wear.

Weaving the belt with threads with which the temple has been circled is a magical act, which aims to bind the divine presence in it, so the wish of the one who performs the rite could come true. The weaving itself is a magical operation that represents an act of forming and creating an idea, which must be realised through the doing of the physical act. An interesting element, which is neglected in most cases, is the appearance of the Mother of God. During her appearance she

---

[264] Bozhinova V., Southwestern university *"Neofit Rilski" - Report on subject: St Mother of God – golden apple*, Blagoevgrad 2009, online: http://satrae.swu.bg/media/5366/st.%20virgin.pdf <29.12.2011> (Божинова В., Югозападен университет "Неофит Рилски" – Доклад на тема: Света Богородица-златна ябълка, Благоевград 2009).

doesn't guide the supplicant to making rites that are part of the Christian tradition and to acts dictated by the canon, but to operations that are completely magical in their identity. We could only suggest what the explanation for this is, but it can be assumed that among the people and in folk belief, the Mother of God as a successor to the image of the Goddess is a protector of different magical rites, which aim to stimulate fertility and which are considered sacred acts, prescribed by the deity itself, practices that were known and spread in antiquity too. The next element is the way of receiving the revelation, namely by sleeping in the temple, i.e. through performing so-called incubation, which is also a widespread practice in antiquity that has remained as a relic in Christian ritual.[265]

Weaving a belt for conceiving and the connection of this practice with the image of the Mother of God is known also in other parts of the Bulgarian ethnic territory. Finding a correspondence in the apocryphal moment for the handing down of the belt of the Mother of God to Thomas the Apostle[266] on her Assumption has given the folk belief a chance to attach a magical practice to the Christian legend. This fact is clear, because in many places this practice is performed without making any relation to the belt of St Mother of God. Providing fertility through the contact with a blessed material (which has been in contact with a cult object or image) is a practice known from antiquity, but what is interesting in this case is that we see the sustainability of this practice attached to the image of the Mother of God. There are some variations in the practice, but a lot of common features are seen in them. In the city of Melnik, South-western Bulgaria[267] the ritual for obtaining a child is known as the wearing of a red thread around the waist for forty days, which thread must have stayed one night on the image of the Mother of God, on the local celebration (August 31st).[268] Besides the connection to the Mother of God, these

---

[265] On the subject see Hamilton M., *Incubation or the Cure of Disease in Pagan Temples and Christian Churches*, London 1906.

[266] See Miltenova A., Toncheva I., Barlieva Sl., *The speech of Thomas the Apostle for exaltation of the Holy Panagia: textological observations – Marina Yordanova* in *Pyati dostoit. Collection in the memory of Stefan Kozhuharov. Sofia 2003, 275-285* (Милтенова А., Тончева И., Бърлиева Сл., *Словото на апостол Тома за въздвижение на Светата Панагия: текстологически наблюдения - Марина Йорданова в Пяти достоитъ. Сборник в памет на Стефан Кожухаров, София 2003, 275-285*).

[267] Melnik is a village which began from Thracian times, as during excavations of the oldest church in the town *"St Nicholas"* votive plates of the goddess Bendis have been found.

[268] Baeva V., *Holy Zona: a specific local cult in the region of Melnik//* Ideas and terrenes in ethnology, folkloristics and anthropology 2010 (*Баева В.,*

rites for weaving a belt for conceiving and its wearing are known as being connected with the day of St George and performed on Thracian rock sanctuaries.[269] Except for conceiving, there is a known practice for weaving a similar belt, but with another purpose.

Description of practice 23 A BELT FOR MARRIAGE[270]

This practice is also from the region of Melnik, South-western Bulgaria. The requirement is that the temple be walked around with white and red thread and after that to use the white thread for making candles, i.e. to use it as a wick, and the red thread to be worn by the person, who wishes to start a family, after which it is placed by the altar lamp near the home icon of Mother of God.

In the case of Melnik an impression is made by the fact that the oldest church in town, of St Nicholas, is build over a sanctuary of the goddess Bendis,[271] where the idea of replacing the ancient Goddess as a protector of the village was unsuccessful, because in folk belief she has taken her place by receiving her Christian mask, but preserved a part of her ritual tradition.

The ritual practices of weaving and knotting as connected to the worship of the Mother of God can be related to the Bendis cult, because the very name of the Goddess has been derived from the Indo-European *bhendh – 'tie', 'connect', and if the goal for the weaving and knotting is traced, then the associations with the Thracian Great Goddess are even clearer. The usage of knots and threads in a ritual binding is a widespread practice, but what is seen here is the connection between the knot, the weaving and the feminine principle. A number of magical rites are connected with the use of knots, thread, spindles and loom accessories, all of which are elements related to the feminine principle and the Goddess. According to some ancient notions the Universe is

---

"Света Зона: един специфичен местен култ от Мелнишко", ИТЕФА 2010).

[269] Markov V., Cultural heritage and succession. Heritage from the ancient pagan holy places in Bulgarian folk culture, Blagoevgrad 2007, 132 (Марков В., Културно наследство и приемственост. Наследство от древноезическите свети места в българската народна култура, Благоевград 2007, 132).

[270] Baeva V., "Holy Zona: a specific local cult in the region of Melnik" // Ideas and terrenes in ethnology, folkloristics and anthropology 2010 (Баева В., "Света Зона: един специфичен местен култ от Мелнишко", ИТЕФА 2010). The name Zona is a Bulgarian form of the Greek αγιας ζονις, i.e. holy belt.

[271] Nesheva V., Melnik – the town build by god, Sofia 2008 (Нешева В., Мелник – богозиданият град, София 2008).

a cloth sheet and the Goddess is the one who weaves it. On a social level the woman executes that function, and the objects used in the weaving also become magical instruments, because they impersonate this same idea. An interesting magical ritual is the use of the knot as a way of protection.

Description of practice 24 FOR HEALTH AND PROTECTION[272]

One should take a thread from deserted harnesses (i.e. harnesses from the loom of a deceased woman), stand in the middle of the yard and double the thread (on two-ply) and watch that it is absolutely quiet around. If it is not an absolutely quiet time, one could not make the binding. As long as nothing makes a sound the knots are made, but if something makes a noise the rite is performed again, because it hasn't caught. While knotting one must say:

"As I bind this knot on the thread from the deserted harnesses,

so should be bound all the diseases,

that are to come this year to (the name).

Fever should not catch him/her, jaundice, blisters and rashes,

plague, heavy disease, prickling and wounds on the eyes and no other magic!"

This is called for all of the people in the house and this thread is placed under the doorstep, so it won't let the diseases in.

During excavations of Thracian sanctuaries loom weights and spindle whorls are common finds,[273] which suggests their cult function and their usage in ritual practices which later remains in magic. Related from ancient times with the idea of the divinities of fate, the weaving and knitting accessories have an immutable place in magic. The presence of practices in Bulgarian folklore, connected to the local worship of the Mother of God and other Christian characters

---

[272] *Collection of Bulgarian Folklore and Folk Studies 4*, 93 *(СбНУ m. 4, 93).*
[273] See the reports of the excavation of the sanctuary of Babyashka chuka on http://www.eufunds.bg/uploads/belica/babyak.html <29.12.2011>, as well as in Chohadzhiev A., *Weights and/or Spools: Distribution and interpretation of the Neolithic "cocoon-like loom-weights". Prehistoric Thrace,* Sofia/Stara Zagora, 227-230, 236-238 *(Чохаджиев А., Макари и/или тежести: разпространение и интерпретация на неолитните "пашкуловидни тежести за стан". Праисторическа Тракия, София/Стара Загора, 227-230, 236-238).*

in the context of the archaeological finds at Thracian sanctuaries, and even their performance in those sanctuaries, is a reason to assume the likelihood of such types of practices in Thracian antiquity. If we bear in mind the resistance of these practices it is quite possible the ritual activities seen today are relics of those made in antiquity. Of course with time they must have changed, but they have preserved some really archaic notions and rituals.

The cultural synthesis of the Christian image of the Mother of God in Bulgarian folk belief is unquestionably built on the basis of plenty of elements and components, brought in by different ethnic groups in the way of linear time. The Mother of God in her worship during Christmas is recognised in her function of a giver of birth to the Young God, who is the Son-Sun and thus we see the so-called Sun Mother, who separates also as an image in fairy and song Bulgarian folklore. The notion that the Sun has a mother, but no father, wonderfully illustrates the Thracian ethnic belief in which the Goddess self-conceives, carries and gives birth to her Son-Sun/Fire.

THE MOUNTAIN MOTHER

After the passing of the cold winter months the Bulgarian people, along with their neighbours from the Balkan Peninsula, mark the coming of spring. The ritual festive cycle that starts on March 1st was probably formed as far back as Thracian antiquity. We can judge the antiquity of this festival from the definitions against its celebration in the rules of the first Ecumenical councils, as for instance in rule number 62 from the Fifth-Sixth Ecumenical Council known also as the council of Constantinople or Trullan Synod from 680-681 CE:

"The so-called Calends, and what are called Bota and Brumalia, and the full assembly which takes place on the first of March, we wish to be abolished from the life of the faithful..."[274]

From this record we can be sure that this day was traditionally marked by the people even in the Seventh century CE, but unfortunately we don't get any more information about the form of its celebration. Even without such details it is clear that the beginning of March was believed to be a moment of passage and was accompanied by festive rituals from antiquity to later times and even today.

The beginning of March is dedicated to the welcoming of the mythical mistress of the month. The first days of spring are connected with the notion of the grandmother. The distribution range of beliefs for this period spreads all over the Mediterranean and the Balkans. But the ritual system and the completeness of the actions and legends are preserved mostly in the region of the Bulgarian ethnic territory, which suggests this region as its most likely origin.[275] The mistress of the month is called Baba Marta (Grandmother Marta) by the Bulgarians and Baba Dokia (Grandmother Dokia) by the Romanians. It is possible that her old age as a life sign reflects the connection with the end of winter, but in Bulgarian folk belief Baba Marta as a mythological character is connected also with the idea of the

---

[274]

http://www.ccel.org/ccel/schaff/npnf214.xiv.iii.lxiii.html?highlight=canon,lxii#highlight <16.02.2011>.

[275] Concerning the area of diffusion and the arguments for most probable Eastern Mediterranean origin of beliefs and rituals connected with this festive cycle see Kabakova G., *Structure and geography of the legends for Baba Dokia //* Balkans in the Mediterranean context, Moscow 1986, 146 (Кабакова Г., *Структура и география легенды о Бабе Докии //* Балканы в контексте Средиземноморья, Москва 1986, 146).

giver of the forthcoming spring, who must be propitiated and made benevolent.

An interesting moment in the beliefs connected with this day is the notion of an elderly woman who goes out in the mountain to pasture goats. While going she says an offensive formula which is directed either to the month February or to another mythical character or is a manifestation of arrogance and human self-confidence: *"Marta is a woman and I am a woman, tsuts*[276] *goats on a mountain!"* For such actions the mortal woman is punished with petrifaction. The woman is turned into stone from which water sprang. The legend of the petrified goatherd can be found mainly in the Balkan regions. According to some variations of the legend this woman is called Marta and the month is named after her, and according to other legends separate mountain tops and rock formations bear her name. It is interesting that some of these rock formations have been proved by archaeologists to be Thracian sanctuaries.[277] This mythical female character has preserved in folk legends a main characteristic of the ancient Goddess – from the nonliving (the rock) she begins to give life (the water).[278] For the belief in the Goddess called the Mountain Mother among the Thracians we get evidence from the inscriptions-dedications of the Thracian kings, for instance ΚΟΤΕΟΥΣ ΜΗΤΡΟΣ ΟΡΕΑΣ – *"Kotes, (offspring, servant) of the Mountain Mother"*.[279]

The Bulgarian traditional faith keeps a lot of archaic rituals connected with the welcoming of Baba Marta, the elderly mistress of the elements. These always come from the unassimilated, the wild, from the mountain and enter the city, the cultural. In order to ensure her propitiation a number of rites are performed. According to folk belief this mythical character is carrier of both positive and negative features – she punishes and gives prosperity.

---

[276] Untranslatable onomatopoeic word.

[277] See for instance the Thracian sanctuary on the summit Kozi gramadi and the connected with its name legend in Mishev G., *Cultural memory in the region of Thracian cult centre Starosel //* The Bulletin of the National Museum of Bulgarian History, XXII, Veliko Tarnovo 2010, 192 (*Мишев Г., Културна памет в района на тракийски култов център Старосел // Известия на националния исторически музей, XXII, Велико Търново 2010, 192*).

[278] Very interesting in this case is the seeming coincidence of the Marta with the possible Thracian etymology of *mar- as "the big water", see Fol A., *The Thracian Orphism*, Sofia 1986, 41 (*Фол Ал., Тракийският орфизъм, София 1986, 41*).

[279] See Fol Al., *The Thracian Dionysos. Book three: Naming and faith*, Sofia 2002, 48 (*Фол Ал., Тракийският Дионис. Книга трета: Назоваване и вяра, София 2002, 48*), as well as Theodossiev N. *"Κοτεους ΗΛΙΟΥ and Κοτεους Μητρος Ορεας" //* Hermes, Vol. 129, No. 2, 2001, 279-283.

Significant in the ritual practices dedicated to this day is the presence of the colour red as symbolically bound with the propitiation of the Goddess, replaced in later times with the name Baba Marta. The rituals have a completely magical nature and therefore deserve attention, because ancient mythological notions are strongly outlined in them.

Description of practice 25 RITUALS BEFORE FIRST OF MARCH

The rites for the first of March begin the day before it. The home and the yard are cleaned up and the collected dust is burned on the eve of the first of March. Usually the lighting up is made either by children or by a woman, for whom there is a prohibition on going to the toilet just before that. While lighting up the fire the following formula is pronounced:

"Grandmother Marta, I warm you today, you warm me tomorrow!"[280]

An old broom is also kindled and it is walked around the house, while saying:

"Fleas outside, Marta inside!"[281]

The so called *'singeing of Marta"* is also known, and is done when the new moon appears during March. Then the junk from the yard and straw are gathered, kindled and the entire household leaps over the fire with the words:

"We should singe baba Marta, rather than she singes us!"[282]

The night before the first of March a red cloth is placed on the fence of the house or on a fruit tree in the yard, because according to folk belief that will propitiate Baba Marta on her arrival. This piece of cloth is usually left outside for nine days, i.e. until March 9th.

Significant and most widespread is the practice of weaving the so called *martenitsa* – twisted white and red thread.[283]

---

[280] In Bulgarian: *"Бабо Марто, аз те грея днеска, а ти мене утре!"* in Mikov L., *First of March rituality*, Sofia 1985, 15 (Миков Л., *Първомартенска обредност*, София 1985, 15) .
[281] Ibid. 19, in Bulgarian: *"Вън бълхи, вътре Марта!"*
[282] Ibid. 19, in Bulgarian: *"Ние да опърлим баба Марта, а не тя нас да опърли!"*
[283] In some regions to the white and red are added other colours like green etc.

*38 - Martenitsa – The Female Figure Is Red And The Male Is White,
Depicting The Goddess And The God[284]*

Description of practice 26 PREPARING OF MARTENITSA[285]

Martenitsa are prepared for the whole family, including the livestock, even for the trees as well as for some instruments like the loom, plough and so on.[286] The *martenitsi* are made by the grandmother in the family, i.e. the elderly woman, who has given birth most times, possesses most life experience, has gone through the menopause and because of that is already ritually clean. For the preparation of *martenitsi*, wool is used that was gathered during the summer from bushes in the field, i.e. it shouldn't be sheared from the sheep, but should have fallen by itself, stayed in the open on the bushes and absorbed the magical power of the field herbs and the stars. A part of this wool is dyed in red, and the other part is left white. The elderly woman, preparing the *martenitsi* should be clean and in

---

[284] http://dariknews.bg/view_article.php?article_id=673508 <06.09.2011>.

[285] The description follows the one given by Mikov L., *Rituals on the First of March*, Sofia 1985 (Миков Л., *Първомартенска обредност, София 1985*), as well as from personal observations.

[286] These instruments also have strong ritual functions in other rites and in this way through their decoration with martenitsi is stimulated their fertile power and they are protected from outer negative influence.

clean clothes, and there is a ritual prohibition that she shouldn't have touched fire just before that. Weaving the *martenitsa* is made leftward, as the woman closes her eyes, so that just like that the eyes of snakes, those of wolves will be closed, i.e. the eyes of enemies and foes, so they won't attack the person who is going to wear the *martenitsa*. When the two ends of the *martenitsa* are knotted it is said in the same way that just like that the mouths of snakes should be tied up, so respectively the wolves (enemies) won't attack. After the threads are twisted the *martenitsa* is hung to stay overnight on a rose (*Rosa multiflora*), so it could be additionally saturated with purifying and protecting power.[287] The morning on the first of March everyone ties them on their wrist or decorates their clothes with *martenitsi* for health and luck in the upcoming year, because the first of March itself is a new beginning.

Some *martenitsi* are made in the form of two figures – male and female. The female is red and is called Penda, and the male is white and is called Pizho. It doesn't take a lot of efforts to recognize in this figure image the depiction of the primordial divine couple – the Goddess and the God. The very name Penda has a very possible etymology from Benda, i.e. Bendis. This naming of the Great goddess of the ancient Thracians continues to be present nowadays and moreover in a very overt way. This is noticed in the ritual formula connected with the pig sacrifice on Christmas – *"Penda and Perenda, next year hundred kilos of bacon!"*, and here in the naming of the red hued figure of the *martenitsa*. The male figure bears the name Pizho, which as far as it is known is used for an unbaptised male child.[288] In this way the folk beliefs have preserved the traditional faith in the Great Goddess and her Son. By wearing their votive depictions or their colour the people aim to entreat their blessing and the coming of the fertile power of the sun, i.e. the Spring Equinox. The *martenitsi* are worn either until seeing the first signs of spring – stork, swallow, blooming tree or until March 25th. After this period they shouldn't be thrown under any circumstances, but have to be hung on a blooming tree or placed under a stone. Both practices aim to unify on one side the man and the awakening life in the plants and on the

---

[287] Thorny plants are considered to be powerful apotropaic symbols, because of their thorns, which protect them from contact.

[288] *"...they call this way a little child, not baptised yet."* – Gerov N., *Dictionary of the Bulgarian language*, Sofia 1977, 29 (Геров Н., *Речник на българския език*, София 1977, 29).

other – with the power of the earth and the Goddess, symbolised by the stone.

The March ritual cycle as a whole is strongly connected with the awakening of the Mistress of the wild, of the Mountain mother, who once she has been welcomed in the homes, has a red cloth spread out in her honour, so she can give her blessing over those who worship her. Additionally March 25th is believed by the Bulgarian people to be the date on which the samodivi come into the human world.

The samodiva are characters who haven't lost their magic and enchantment even today. The beautiful mistresses of springs, dressed in white finery, dancing during the night in the mountains and shadowy oak forests, mistresses of the wild beasts and experts in herbs. They form the whirlwinds and become angry when the prohibitions connected with them have been violated. The samodivi are the most vivid representatives of the ancient Goddesses, who are whole in their perception by mortals and represent life and death, sickness and health, laughter and sorrow. The synthesis of these beliefs has formed the notion of the samodiva in traditional Bulgarian culture.

The notion of the samodiva varies in different geographical regions, but as the most complete we can describe the image of a beautiful middle aged female figure – neither a child, nor an adult woman; with long white finery; girded with a belt (called *zunitsa*) in the colours of the rainbow, but most of all green; with long red hair; wearing a veil called a *syanka* ('shadow'); with wings on her back; riding a deer; the deer has golden antlers, on his chest shines the moon and on his forehead – the sun; with snakes for bridles; holding a snake in her hands for a whip. The village of the samodivi is at the end of the world, next to the home of the God-Sun, where they go on chariots drawn by eagles.

We see an image of a divine power unifying solar and chthonic features, which are reflected also in the functions accredited to it – the samodiva is a healer, a giver of fertility, she awakens new life with the coming of the longer day (after the Spring Equinox, because March 25th is the date of the coming of the samodivi to the world of mortal people), rules over places of passage, rules over wild nature and the beasts submit to her, she punishes but also gives rewards. Separate elements make an impression – her description as a rider of a deer resembles the many votive tablets of the Thracian hypostasis of Artemis.

39 - Votive Plate Of Artemis From Sadina, Popovo Region[289]

The deer which the samodiva rides possesses a number of divine features – it has golden antlers, on its forehead shines the sun and on its chest the moon. The deer as a solar symbol and hypostasis of the Sun is known from antiquity, but this image makes the clear connection that the samodiva rides such a divine deer, which is her companion and in this meaning also appears as her servant. This connection of the deer with the Goddess in antiquity and in the later idea of the samodiva can be seen, except on the votive plates, in the text of the *Orphic Hymn to Hekate*, where the Goddess is described as ἀγαλλομένην ἐλάφοισιν – *"honoured by deer"*.[290] The deer as an image of the God Sun and perceived also as his sacrificial animal - going to the altar by itself, is known from antiquity and is preserved until today in the beliefs of the Balkan peoples.

---

[289] Venedikov Iv., *The golden pillar of the proto-Bulgarians*, Sofia 1987 (Венедиков Ив., *Златният стожер на прабългарите, София 1987*).
[290] Fol A., *The Hymns of Orpheus*, Sofia 1995, 186 (Фол Ал., *Химните на Орфей, София 1995, 186*).

There is another element from the hymn to Hekate, which connects the image of the Orphic Hekate with that of the samodiva and that is the fact that the Goddess is described as φιλέρημον – *'lover of solitude'* and οὐρεσιφοῖτιν – *'mountain wanderer'*. There is a belief that the samodiva should not be disturbed[291] in her forest habitat, because it is said that she seeks the solitude of the forest shadows and oak forests, of the cold springs and wells, and she is the one that wanders through the mountains, away from people and their world.

The cosmic function of the samodiva is expressed in the unification of the solar and uranic symbols, i.e. the deer, eagles and magpies, with the chthonic elements, presented through snakes and lizards. The role of the snake as a whip held in the hands of female deities is recorded for the whole Mediterranean, and in a number of Hekate's images she is also depicted in that way.

---

[291] Direct parallel with this belief is the legend for Actaeon and Artemis, see Georgieva Iv., *Bulgarian folk mythology*, Sofia 1981, 51 (*Георгиева Ив., Българска народна митология, София 1981, 51*).

*40 - Image Of The Goddess Hekate Holding Snakes In Her Hands,
Severus Alexander As Caesar, 221-222 CE, Pamphylia, Aspendos,
Dr. Stephen Gerson Collection [292]*

*41 - Image Of The Goddess Hekate Holding A Snake In Her Hands,
Gordian III. 238-244 CE, Pamphylia, Aspendos Dr. Stephen Gerson
Collection [293]*

---

[292] Severus Alexander as Caesar. 221-222 CE, Pamphylia, Aspendos, Dr. Stephen Gerson Collection, online: http://www.wildwinds.com/coins/ric/severus_alexander/_aspendos_SNGv A_4591v.jpg <29.12.2011>.

The lizard is depicted in some votive images of the Thraco-Phrygian deity Sabazios – hypostasis of the Son of the Great Goddess. In this train of thought the idea of the samodiva depicts the Goddess together with the manifestations of her consort – the solar-chthonic God Sun/Fire.

42 - Image Showing The Hand Of Sabazius And On Its Right Side Can Be Seen A Lizard, Climbing Up And Headed Towards The Pinecone On The Thumb, Pompeii[294]

---

[293] Gordian III. 238-244 CE, Pamphylia, Aspendos Dr. Stephen Gerson Collection, online: http://www.asiaminorcoins.com/gallery/displayimage.php?album=264&pid=4909#top_display_media <29.12.2011>.
[294]http://centuriespast.tumblr.com/post/1173522576/dressrehearsalrag-hand-of-sabazius-bronze-house <29.12.2011>.

The Bulgarian samodiva, howsoever enriched by different ethnic concepts through the ages, is visibly very strongly influenced by the antique tradition and especially by the ancient Thracians notions of the Goddess.

The names by which this mythological female character is known deserves attention, because hidden in them lies a large part of the essence of the beliefs dedicated to her. Different collective names[295] are found in different parts of the Bulgarian ethnic territory – *diva, samodiva; vila, samovila; yuda, samoyuda.*

Unlike the names most commonly used by Bulgarians – *samodiva* and *yuda,* among the neighbouring Balkan peoples, belonging to the Slavic languages group – Serbians, Croatians, the name *vila* occurs most often. This is one of the oldest names documented in writing, because it can be seen in written sources from the Eleventh century CE.

The etymology of the appellation *vila* is derived from **vi-ti* – *'whirl',*[296] because according to the folk belief the vili create whirlwinds. This type of wind is a common mythological character among the Indo-European peoples, for instance the German Windsbraut – *"'bride of the wind'.*[297] In Greek beliefs the whirlwind is made by the dance of the nereids - χορεύουνε ἡ Ἀνεράϊδες.[298]

The appellation *samodiva"* is spread mostly in the Bulgarian lands and is rarely seen in other Slavic languages, as its etymology is derived from the Proto-Slavic **divā,* which is connected also with the Lithuanian *deive – 'a goddess'.*[299] In Lithuanian, rock sanctuaries are called *dejwa akminau,* and in Turkish they are *peri bacalar,*[300] as in this way they are connected with ancient beliefs and with these female mythological characters that are the Lithuanian nymphs and the Turkish *peri* (*peris*).

---

[295] Along with common names there are a number of known personal names of samodivi – *Gyurgya, Dena, Magda, Stana, Vida, Dimna, Gelmeruda* (or *Germeruda*).

[296] See Dukova U., *Die Bezeichnung der Dämonen im Bulgarischen,* München 1997, 15.

[297] Ibid.

298 See Schmidt B., *Das Volksleben der Neugriechen und das hellenische Alterthum,* Leipzig 1871, 124, where the spell is quoted that is pronounced by elderly women on seeing a whirlwind, they bow their heads to the ground and say: Μέλι καὶ γάλα στὸν δρόμο σας (Milk and honey on your way!). Milk and honey are known as sacred liquids for libation in the Eastern Mediterranean from antiquity.

[299] See Dukova U., *Die Bezeichnung der Dämonen im Bulgarischen,* München 1997, 19.

[300] Ibid. 19.

The composite words *samo-diva* and *samo-vila* are made on the same principle from the root *div* and the prefix *sam*, which can be connected with some Thracian divine names (theonyms) as for instance Ζαμα-ζις = Αὒτο-ζευς, which is translated as *"The one, who alone is God"*[301] and on this principle can be supposed a possible meaning of *samodiva*, as *"The one, who alone is Goddess"*.

The third appellation of this character from folk belief is the word *yuda*, as it is most frequently used in the Rhodope Mountains and in South-western Bulgaria. The origin of this name, in spite of its sound which misleads to a connection with the Christian tradition and the image of Judas Iscariot, is derived from *Podyuzhdam* meaning 'awake', 'revive' from the Indo-European root **youdho* – 'excitation', 'revival'.[302] Bearing in mind the belief that the yudi come after the Spring Equinox – on March 25th, their name fits perfectly with the notion of them as awakening new life and growth.

Common places believed to be inhabited by samodivi are mountains, lakes, springs, wells, during the day they inhabit the clouds and create whirlwinds; also they appear in places like water-mills, flour-mills, eaves and crossroads.

All of those places, along with the apprehension of being haunted by ghosts or as a place where ghosts appear, also have a sacred function. All of them are liminal – eaves, crossroads; others are additionally connected with the water element which is also a limit – well, spring, lake.

The forest connection with the samodiva brought the creation of a number of names, she is called – forest *vila*, *samovila* - *samogorka*, *nagorkinya*[303] and so she is brought typologically closer to the image of the mountain nymphs from classic antiquity, that are called Ὀρεάδες and are connected with the Goddess Ὄρεια – the Mountain Mother.[304]

The Mountain Mother is named and worshipped in the whole Thracian area, including Asia Minor, but what also brings the Bulgarian samodiva closer to her image is an appellation to the samodivi with the word *'mother'*, which is specific to the Bulgarian ethnic territory. This is a specific feature of the Bulgarian rites connected with the samodivi, which shows one possible connection with the image of that Mountain Mother worshipped by the ancient Thracians. The

---

[301] Ibid. 24.
[302] Ibid. 43.
[303] From the Bulgarian **ropa* (*gora*) - forest.
[304] See Dukova U., *Die Bezeichnung der Dämonen im Bulgarischen*, München 1997, 17.

multiplicity of the image, i.e. that from one image of one Goddess, she is perceived also as many doesn't contradict such hypotheses – in some regions the samodivi are even, and in others uneven, because image multiplicity is common for antiquity and is perceived as different appearances, i.e. different hypostases of the same deity.

As an image-successor of the Mountain Mother the samodivi have remained in Bulgarian folk belief as a symbol of freedom which doesn't subordinate to standards and human order. This is why during the five-century Ottoman yoke the samodiva was perceived as a helper and protector of the Bulgarian revolutionary, i.e. the guardian of the lands impersonates the function of the ancient Goddess who gives power to the kings over their lands. In Bulgarian revolutionary literature there are a number of poetic descriptions of samodivi, who give assistance and aid to the revolutionaries, but undoubtedly the most famous among them is that from Hristo Botev[305] in his poem *Hadzhi Dimitar*:

"And samodivi in white finery,
wonderful, beautiful, take up a song, -
silently wade in the green grass
and by the hero come to sit down.

One binds his wound with herbs,
another sprinkles him with cold water,
and third quickly kisses his mouth –
and he watches her – kind, smiling!"[306]

We can see from these verses that in the folk notion the image of the samodiva is preserved as that divine female hypostasis, which supports and responds to the hero, just like in Thracian antiquity the king after passing his value trials could receive the favour of the Great Goddess.

One feature that significantly differs with the Bulgarian samodiva and similar female mythological characters of

---

[305] Hristo Botev was a Bulgarian poet , national revolutionary, symbolic historical figure and national hero.
[306] In Bulgarian:
"И самодиви в бяла премена,
чудни, прекрасни, песен поемнат, -
тихо нагазят трева зелена
и при юнакът дойдат та седнат.

Една му с билки раната върже,
друга го пръсне с вода студена,
третя го в уста целуне бърже -
и той я гледа, - мила, зесмена!"

other peoples and brings her closer to the ancient goddesses, is her highly expressed healing function, which is preserved in literature such as the poetic works, but is most clearly expressed in the ritual practices dedicated to the samodivi.

The rite is an expression of faith, as through it the connection between human and divine is made. The samodivi rites are one very interesting part of Bulgarian traditional culture because they preserve many highly archaic features; they are bound to sacred areas, worshipped since antiquity – from the Thracians until today. The very rites in later times are called *'devilish'*, because under the influence of Christian religion they were realised as belonging to a completely different faith from the official faith and ritual tradition, which faith was secretly followed by the people.

The samodiva as a bringer of illness and health is an expression of the ancient perception of the deities as a whole. They adopt in them all kinds of qualities – they build and demolish simultaneously, but are not defined as good or bad, because these concepts are determined by human standards and ethics and not by the divine. Ancient faith doesn't define the deity as bad, when an illness connected with it has been aroused, but seeks for the reason that the illness arose. Most often the reason was indicated and still is indicated to be the breaking of a sacred prohibition, which has led to the illness arising. At the same time the ancients believed that through ritual practice and the spiritual change realised by it, a recovery could be achieved. For this we find evidence in the written sources:

"But that it [the soul] may not wander, and that when it does so, proper remedies may be applied, and it may be restored, many things have been produced by the gods; for arts and sciences, virtues and prayers, sacrifices and initiations, laws and polities, judgements and punishments, were invented for the purpose of preventing souls from falling into guilt..."[307]

For exactly that reason we find in the ancient texts the idea of the Inevitable Ananke, who shows that irrevocable rules and laws exist among mortals and immortals, the consequences of which are binding for both sides – for the gods and for the people. Breaking the relevant unwritten prohibitions is considered a reason for the arising of different misfortunes – illnesses and other.

---

[307] Sallust: *On the Gods and the World*, London 1793, Chap. XII, transl. Taylor Th.

According to folk beliefs there is a whole group of so-called "*samodivi's illnesses*", which in most cases are nervous illnesses of various nature – fainting, paresis, acquired epilepsy, nervosity, insomnia and others. People believe that insanity or other mental illnesses can be induced by breaking ritual prohibitions connected with the samodivi. These include stepping on their meal, around which they gather at night, because it is believed that mortals can't see it; stepping on the place where they play the line dance – their ritual dance; staying or sleeping under a briar; urinating in an old hearth, under an eave and others.

The notion that the proximity to a number of deities leads to such conditions is attested in ancient sources. In Euripides' *Hippolytus*" (Eur. Hipp. 141) the choir asks from where this condition comes:

"Has some god possessed you, dear girl?

Do your wits wander under the spell of Pan or Hekate, the august Corybantes or Cybele, the mountain mother?"

Those illnesses which are induced by samodivi bear the name *'from outer'*, i.e. the reason for the illness comes from an outer influence of spiritual powers. Those spirits are also known by the name *'outer'* among the Greeks, as they are called ἐξωτικά (ξωτικιά, ζωθιά). Other names of this type of illnesses are *urama, ogradisvane, 'trampled', 'waded'*.

An effect produces the direct influence caused by the breaking of the ritual rules. A result of this, according to folk belief, is imbalance in human spirituality and this reflects on the physical condition – appearance of fainting, physiological problems as paresis, muscle pains, swellings.

One of the main rites which are connected with the propitiation of the samodivi and is a sacrificial rite, is the so-called '*blazhene*' (meaning – '*to sweeten*'). This rite is known by the same term among the Greeks (γλυκαίνω) and among the Albanians (*amëlsimë*), which suggests a deeper antiquity of the practice and its possible source in the culture of the ancient Mediterranean. The sacred liquids for libation in the ritual practices there are: water, milk, wine, honey, and olive oil. They are libated either together or separately depending on the type of the ritual act.

The '*blazhene*' itself is a sacrificial rite, which aims to ensure the propitiation of the samodivi and to obtain their healing intervention by entreaties. Even the name of the rite implies that something sweet is used in it. The sweet thing in antiquity was honey and today in many places sugar is used as a substitute. The use of honey and particularly its use in combination with water is a well known practice connected with the cult of the chthonic deities, but not only with them. In most of the scholarly research this nocturnal and chthonic side of the rite used is always emphasised, but in fact a number of cults in antiquity are known to have had a requirement for making sacrifices without wine, the so-called *nephalia* νηφάλια, made in some places with honey and water and connected with the worship of deities that are not only of a chthonic nature. An example for this is the information from *Schol. Ad Oed.* Col. 100:

"The Athenians were careful in these matters and scrupulously pious (ὅσιοι) in the things that pertain to the gods, and they made wineless sacrifices to Mnemosyne the Muse, to Eos, to Helios, to Selene, to the Nymphs, to Aphrodite Ourania."

With this information it becomes clear that for ancient people libations without wine were not made only for the chthonic deities, but also for a number of other deities, who had this speciality in their cults. The listed deities in the above evidence have more of a uranic nature, but also have another special feature – they are mediators between the realms, a role attributed also to the samodivi, because they inhabit and influence both realms.

The use of water and honey as a libation is also mentioned by Pausanias in his *Description of Greece* (Paus. II, 11.4):

"At a distance along it, in my opinion, of twenty stades, to the left on the other side of the Asopus, is a grove of holm oaks and a temple of the goddesses named by the Athenians the August, and by the Sicyonians the Kindly Ones. On one day in each year they celebrate a festival to them and offer sheep big with young as a burnt offering, and they are accustomed to use a libation of honey and water, and flowers instead of garlands. They practise similar rites at the altar of the Fates; it is in an open space in the grove."[308]

This information is interesting, because it contains a connection between the libation of honey and water with the Goddesses called the Kindly Ones, and the appellation 'sweet and honey' is known to be used for the samodivi, i.e. we can see the same euphemistic appellation. As the Goddesses of punishment have a tabooed appellation, so the

---

[308] Pausanias, *Description of Greece*, tr. W.H.S. Jones and H.A. Ormerod (1918), 305.

samodivi typologically have the same, because their name should not be mentioned in order to avoid their wrath.

This connection of the samodivi and the rites privy to them, with a number of antique Goddesses of the circle of the Eumenídes (Kindly ones) is significant, because the cult of these three Goddesses and the ritual tradition connected with it is very archaic. In this connection it is possible to suggest that among the Thracians similar rites dedicated to the Thracian correspondences of these Hellenic divinities have existed and it is very possible that part of their ritual tradition was inherited in the magical practices connected with the samodivi.

We could also suggest similar beliefs in an Orphic context on the basis of the hymn to one of the Orphic hypostases of the Great Goddess – Melinoe.

Μηλινόης[309]

Θυμίαμα ἀρώματα

Μηλινόην καλέω, νύμφην χθονίαν, κροκόπεπλον,
ἣν παρὰ Κωκυτοῦ προχοαῖς ἐλοχεύσατο σεμνὴ
Φερσεφόνη λέκτροις ἱεροῖς Ζηνὸς Κρονίοιο,
ἧι ψευσθεὶς Πλούτων' ἐμίγη δολίαις ἀπάταισι,
θυμῶι Φερσεφόνης δὲ δισώματον ἔσπασε χροιήν,
ἣ θνητοὺς μαίνει φαντάσμασιν ἠερίοισιν,
ἀλλοκότοις ἰδέαις μορφῆς τύπον ἐκπροφαίνουσα,
ἄλλοτε μὲν προφανής, ποτὲ δὲ σκοτόεσσα, νυχαυγής,
ἀνταίαις ἐφόδοισι κατὰ ζοφοειδέα νύκτα.
ἀλλά, θεά, λίτομαί σε, καταχθονίων βασίλεια,
ψυχῆς ἐκπέμπειν οἶστρον ἐπὶ τέρματα γαίης,
εὐμενὲς εὐίερον μύσταις φαίνουσα πρόσωπον.

---

[309] Abel E., *Orphica*, Leipzig 1885, 95.

HYMN TO MELINOE [310]

Fumigation from aromatics

Melinoe I call, chthonic nymph, saffron-veil'd,

born near where Cocytus' mournful river flows;

conceived by Persephone in the sacred bed of Zeus Kronion,

deceiving and luring her in the semblance of Pluto,

but the wrath of Persephone gave birth to a two-bodied child, who leads the mortals to madness through aerial phantasms,

after showing with strange images the changing form:

sometimes visible, other times invisible,

you shine through darkness

or through the dark nights turn up for a hostile attack.

But I beg you, Goddess, mistress of the world underneath,

lead away the wrath of the soul away to the end of the earth

and show to the mystes your propitious face.

The description of the Goddess, which we find in this hymn, is identical in many respects to the features of the Bulgarian samodiva, which of course could be coincidental, but also could lead to one common Mediterranean basis and notion.

She is called *"terrene"* νύμφην χθονίαν, and as it became clear from the description of the samodiva, she could be determined as terrene or an *earthly nymph* too, because she comes to the world of the living with the awakening of nature.

The goddess Melinoe is born near a river by the Chthonic Mistress – Persephone, and is a child of the celestial and chthonic Zeus and that is why she has two bodies, i.e. has two natures. This also reminds us a lot of the samodiva, who

---

[310] Because of differences between the original text in Ancient Greek and the English translation in the edition of Taylor Th., *The hymns of Orpheus*, London 1792, 202, the present translation is made by Ekaterina Ilieva according to the corrections by Georgi Mishev on the basis of the Ancient Greek text in the edition of Abel E., *Orphica*, Leipzig 1885, 95; Fol Al., *The Hymns of Orpheus*, Sofia 1995, 131 (Фол Ал., *Химните на Орфей, София 1995, 131*) and the Bulgarian translation of Batakliev G., *Orpheus. Hymns. Argonautica*, Plovdiv 1989, 132 (Батаклиев Г., *Орфей. Химни. Аргонавтика, Пловдив 1989, 132*); Russian translation of Taho-Godi A., *Antique hymns*, Moscow 1988, 251 (Тахо-Годи А., *Античные гимны, Москва 1988, 251*) and the notes in the edition of Fol Al., *The Hymns of Orpheus*, Sofia 1995, 132-133 (Фол Ал., *Химните на Орфей, София 1995, 132-133*).

often appears near water – spring, river, lake and also has two natures – she inhabits the shadowy forests (as a symbol of the chthonic), but flies in the clouds and causes whirlwinds.

In the next lines the ability to lead mortals to insanity is accredited to the Goddess, as in traditional culture this illness is accredited to the *'outers'*, i.e. to the samodivi. This insanity is caused by the changing image of the divinity that once is like a ghost, and at other times shines in the darkness, i.e. she is brought closer both to the moon and to the torch-bearing Goddess. It is described in folk songs how the samodiva flies to the moon which is her home.

At the end of the hymn the Goddess is called to change her face, (her *prosopon*) and to *"lead away the wrath of the soul"*.

43 - Image Of The Plate, Showing The Three Hypostases Of The Goddess Hekate From The Magical Device From Pergamon, Where In The Invocation Of The Goddess She Is Called Also Melinoe - Ἰω Μελινόη[311]

---

[311] On the publication of Wünsch R., *Antikes Zaubergerät aus Pergamon*, Berlin 1909.

The name Melinoe is known not only from this Orphic hymn, but also from a magical device, found during excavations in Pergamon, where it is mentioned in a magical formula to the goddess Hekate, which proves the thesis of scholars that Melinoe is an Orphic title of Hekate.[312]

The connection of the name Melinoe with the purificational-expiatory rites called μείλιγμα[313] performed in antiquity and her described image, as well as her connection with the Goddess Hekate, give a number of reasons to assume that it is possible that ancient features have been preserved in the basis of the rites called 'blazhene'.

For this purpose let us examine some variations of the 'blazhene' rite among Bulgarians, Greeks and Serbs.

Description of practice 27 *BLAZHENE* FROM GREECE[314]

Among the Greeks, when someone has slept under a tree and has become ill from the nereids (by which understand the samodivi) a white table cloth is spread on that place and over it is placed a plate with bread, honey and other sweets, a bottle of wine, a knife and fork, an empty glass, unlit candle and censer. This is left by an elderly woman, who on leaving it pronounces magical words, which are probably similar to those written in Chios spells in the same context, which mothers pronounce for the healing of their children:

"Καλημέρα σας, καλαὶς ἀρχόντισσαις
φᾶτε σεῖς τὰ κουλουράκια καὶ γιάνετε τὸ παιδί μου."

"Good day to you, good mistresses,
eat these sweets and heal my child!"

---

[312] See Fol Al., *The Hymns of Orpheus*, Sofia 1995, 132 (Фол Ал., *Химните на Орфей, София 1995, 132*).

[313] Fol A., *The Thracian Dionysos. Book three: Naming and faith*, Sofia 2002, 104 (Фол А., *Тракийският Дионис. Книга трета: Назоваване и вяра, София 2002, 104*).

[314] Lawson J., *Modern Greek folklore and ancient Greek religion*, Cambridge 1910, 145.

Description of practice 28 *BLAZHENE* FROM SERBIA[315]

In Eastern Serbia the healer pours wine and water in a clay bowl and after that adds honey, stirs that and goes to the place where the person has *'ogradisal'* (become ill). She dips basil in the water and sprinkles with it, while saying the spell:

"If you are young men, be brothers,

if you are old, be fathers.

I give you sweet,

you give us sweet.

If you are young women, be sisters,

if you are middle-aged, be mothers,

if you are old, be grandmothers.

I give you sweet,

you give us sweet!"

In Bulgaria the rites have some similar features, but are saturated with even more magical elements.

Description of practice 29 *BLAZHENE* FROM BULGARIA[316]

'Unspoken' water[317] is poured in a clay bowl with green hues, taken from three springs, and in it a bunch of basil with red thread, nine grains of barley, an ox shoe and a spoon of honey are placed and the following incantation is said:

I sweeten you,

yudi and samodivi,

if you are female –

be sisters of X,

if you are male –

be brothers of X.

I bring you barley to feed

your horses with it,

I bring you water to water them,

I bring you rope to tie them,

---

[315] Radenkovic L., *Folk spells and incantations*, Nis-Pristina-Kragujevats, 1982, 244, 416 *(Раденковић Љ., Народне басме и бајања, Ниш-Приштина-Крагујевац, 1982, 244, 416)*.
[316] Georgieva Iv., *Bulgarian folk mythology*, Sofia 1993, 179 *(Георгиева Ив., Българска народна митология, София 1993, 179)*.
[317] See footnote 173.

I bring you a stake to spike them,
I bring you honey to sweeten you.
Go and stray
the earth in a cross,
and the sky you stray
bring a remedy and cure for X.[318]

After the incantation is finished the basil and the red thread are thrown at a crossroad, and the bowl is turned upside down on the ground.

Description of practice 30 *BLAZHENE* FROM BULGARIA[319]

At the place where the patient got ill, three ring-shaped buns are left, with a bowl with honey, unspoken water (taken by a woman alone, without speaking, from three springs, before sunrise in a new vessel, in which there is a bunch of basil tied with a red thread), a live cockerel and clothes belonging to the patient.

Early in the morning the healer carries all that there and sprinkles the place with water using basil, saying three times:

Sweet and honey ones
until now you have eaten from the ill X (the name)
now I bring you here to eat,
here to drink
and to X a cure to bring.
As the sun spreads,
so the illness
of X should spread,

---

[318] In Bulgarian:
Подсладявам ви,
юди и самодиви,
ако сте женски —
сестри да сте на X,
ако сте мъжки —
братя да сте на X.
Нося ви ечемик да ви назобя
с него конете ви,
нося ви вода да ги напоя,
нося ви петала да ги завържа,
нося ви кол да ги забия,
нося ви мед да ви подслада.
Ходете и бродете
на кръст земята,
и небето пребродете
ляк и цяр на X да донесете.
[319] Georgieva Iv., *Bulgarian folk mythology*, Sofia 1993, 179 (Георгиева Ив., *Българска народна митология, София 1993, 179*).

as this water spreads,
so the illness
of X should spread.[320]

This is performed on three consecutive days early in the morning or after sunset.

In a comparative analysis of the listed rituals, there are a number of elements which clearly belong to pre-Christian practices and in their identity are antique sacrificial rites.

In the Greek and Serbian ritual there is usage of wine, which is not present in the Bulgarian 'blazhene', because according to Bulgarian folk belief the samodiva drinks only water, though in some sources the use of other liquids for libation, such as milk, is mentioned.[321]

In the Serbian and Bulgarian rites, which are typologically very similar, there is an element that is basic for the 'blazhene' rite, which is the sprinkling with honey water, i.e. the libation in drops, which is achieved with the use of basil for sprinkling. This libation in drops is absolutely reasonable in the context of the Thracian Orphic belief, but hardly finds its basis in the later ritual practices so it can be viewed as a preserved relic. A similar way of making a libation is mentioned in a number of literary sources that are records of Orphic ritual practice – in the *Orphic Argonautica* Orpheus also makes a libation of water around the altar pit when he calls the Goddess:

"I poured water and made a libation around the pit..."[322]

The libation in drops is mentioned also in the Orphic *Derweni Papyrus*:

"...sacrifices of wine in small drops..."[323]

---

[320] In Bulgarian:
Сладки и медени
До сега сте яли от болния X
(името му)
Сега ви нося тука да ядете,
тука да пиете
и на X ляк да донесете.
Както се пръска слънцето,
тъй да се пръска
болестта от X,
както се пръска таз вода,
тъй да се пръска
болестта от X.

[321] Pirgova I., *Traditional healing rituals and magical practices*, Sofia 2003, 295 (Пиргова И., *Баяния и магии*, София 2003, 295).

[322] Batakliev G., *Orpheus. Hymns. Argonautica.*, Plovdiv 1989, 177 (Батаклиев Г., *Орфей, Химни, Аргонавтика. Пловдив 1989, 177*).

[323] Aleksieva M., *Hellenic orphic sources*, Sofia 2004, 177 (Алексиева М., *Елински орфически свидетелства*, София 2004, 177).

Another feature that makes an impression in the Bulgarian rites is their more complex structure and the more preserved ritual requirements, which in turn indicates their stronger resistance and more preserved archaic features.

All of the elements in the rite are subordinate to a strict symbolism. The water must be unspoken, i.e. ritually clean. It is obligatory to use a clay bowl, i.e. made from earth but not from metal. For the pattern of the bowl there is the same requirement as for the bowl of the healers – to be decorated with green hues, because that is the colour of health and awakening nature, with which the samodivi are connected. The breads, which are prepared as a gift for the samodivi, play a significant role because sometimes they are the centre of the ritual in rites for healing the samodivi's diseases.

Description of practice 31 *BLAZHENE* FOR STEPPING ON A UNCLEAN PLACE[324]

Two round breads are made and covered with honey, one small and one big. The small bread is placed somewhere high on a wall and is left there on the roof-tiles to spend the night under the stars, and for the other big bread three widows are called and they break it and eat it over the chopping log so the disease can be scattered away.

More detailed variants of this rite are described for the region of Strandzha.

Description of practice 32 HEALING OF *URAMA*[325,326]

One or three *'clean'* elderly women go silently after dusk to fill water from three fords. The water is called *'malcheshna'* (unspoken). With part of it the women knead small round bread, called *kaniska* or *tselenik*, which they bake directly in the ash of the hearth and spread honey on top of it. The remaining water is poured in a green clay bowl and is left for a night outside under the stars. In the morning the ill person washes his or her face with some of the water and drinks from it. In the evening the healer wraps the bread in a new cloth, takes the bowl with the water and goes silently to the place where the samovili have made the person ill. The healer spreads the cloth, arranges on top of it

---

[324] Personal archive of the author from field researches in the region of the Thracian cult centre Starosel, informant Maria Kabadzhova, 2011.
[325] Strandzha. *Material and spiritual culture.*, Sofia 1996, 231-232 (Странджа. *Материална и духовна култура.*, София 1996, 231-232).
[326] Disease with different symptoms considered as being caused from the breaking of a ritual prohibition connected with the samodivi.

the bread, walnut kernels, three nails, a clout-nail, a horse shoe, three lumps of sugar and fifty-one grains of wheat, barley and corn. The healer sprinkles the place – east, north and west with a basil bunch tied with a red wool thread, dipping it in honeyed water in the green bowl. After that the healer breaks the bowl and says:

"Yudi, samovili/ samoyudi,

we beg you, we invite you,

wherever you are to come,

to bring the health of (the name).

If you are women, you are our sworn sisters,

if you are men, you are our sworn brothers!

With meal we will feast you,

with water we will water your horses,

with barley we will feed them,

with horse shoe we will nail them!"[327]

The healer leaves a belt or other clothes belonging to the ill person at the place. The sprinkling is made one or three times in the evenings preceding Wednesday and Friday. Another way is taken to return home.

Description of practice 33 THE LITTLE INVITATION[328]

The rite is performed the preceding Wednesday or Friday, when it is forbidden to do any kind of female activity – no spinning and no sewing. The actions are made by three women that have already passed the menopause, i.e. they are considered to be ritually clean. During the day, one of them kneads sourdough bread and brings it into the house of the ill person. When everybody in his or her house goes to sleep, the three women place the bread on the table where the family eats, and over it they put a bowl with honey. Then all three break a piece of the bread, dip it in honey and eat it. Meanwhile the ill person lies next to them and they don't bother him or her for anything. After that one of the women

---

[327] In Bulgarian:

Юди, самовили / самоюди,

молим ви, каним ви,

където сте, да дойдете,

да донесете здравето на (името).

Ако сте жени, сте ни посестрими,

ако сте мъже, сте ни побратими!

С гозба ще ви гостим,

с вода конате ще ви напоим,

с ечемик ще ги назобим,

с подкова ще ги подковем!

[328] Gorov G., *Strandzha folklore*, Sofia 1983, 932 (*Горов Г., Странджански фолклор, София 1983, 932*).

takes three pieces of bread, dips them in honey, goes outside and throws them on the roof of the house. All this is done in absolute silence and not a word is spoken. The bread is thrown so the samodivi could be sweetened, i.e. so they could be propitiated. The women stay awake next to the ill person the whole night, as this breaking and tasting the bread by them and the throwing of three pieces of bread on the roof is repeated three times during the night. Meanwhile the condition of the ill person is watched, i.e. is the sacrifice accepted and will there be healing given or will the patient continue to be so restless, which means that more healing procedures must be made.

If there is no relief after the first time, the rite is repeated two more times, i.e. three consecutive times again preceding Wednesday or Friday, as each time a new bread is kneaded and new honey is used. The remaining bread is taken by the women so it doesn't stay in the house of the ill person.

Description of practice 34 THE BIG INVITATION[329]

The rite is performed by an elderly woman who is considered ritually clean, or if there is no such woman it is possible for a younger woman to do it, but she also must take all of the precautions for purification – to wash all her clothes, not to wear clothing with which she has lied next to a man. The rite is again performed preceding Wednesday or Friday.

For the rite the woman must sieve flour three times through a sieve turned upside down. With this flour and water poured from three fords dough is made, but exactly nine spoons of flour and nine spoons of water are measured and some salt. All is done in complete silence. From the dough she takes only what separates from the vessel in which it is kneaded. The dough that sticks should not be removed and is not used. From this dough nine small breads (kolacheta) are made, and as they are kneaded they are twisted and in their middle a dimple, little hollow, is made. They are decorated with basil and are baked either on the fire or directly in the ash, and are watched to ensure that they do not parch.

When the small breads are ready they are placed on a piece of the ill person's shirt, which is ripped while the baking is done. This is placed on a tray or on a small round table, as a sprig of basil is stuck on each of the breads. The

---

[329] Ibid. 932-934.

tops of the basil sprigs are gathered in the middle and are tied with red thread. In every dimple of the breads the following are placed:

- three grains of barley;

- one walnut kernel;

- a coin;

- three balls (pieces) red wool;

- three red threads;

- Honey is spread on top of each of the breads, and next to each of them are placed an onion scale leaf and a horseshoe nail.

The symbolism of these things is as follows:

- barley – so the samodivi could feed their horses;

- coin – so they could pay their debts;

- red wool and thread – so they could sew or knit something;

- honey – so they could be propitiated;

- onion scale leaf – to be their spoon;

- horseshoe nail – to shoe their horses;

When the table for the samodivi is ready the woman waits for everybody in the village and in the house of the ill person to fall asleep, takes the table in her hands and goes around the ill person three times while saying:

"Samodivki-kaloti,[330] *wherever you are – in sea, in field, in green forest, come here to eat, to drink, to feed and shoe your horses and to (the name) to give health!"*[331]

The table is then left next to the head of the ill person to stay for a while until it is midnight. In the dead of the night, the woman takes someone to accompany her, takes a knife with a black handle, puts a garlic bulb in her bosom, takes the table with the breads on it, makes the sign of the cross

---

[330] The possible meaning of the word *"kaloti"* is interesting, it is untranslatable in Bulgarian, but bearing in mind the spread archaic Greek dialect in the region of Strandzha, where this rite has been recorded, it could be derived from Greek and in this case *"kaloti"* could come from καλω τι. This phrase in Ancient Greek has the meaning – call, i.e. *"call you all"*, which in turn confirms the following words of the invocation – *"...Wherever you are – in sea, in field, in green forest"*. This in turn indicates, except for the strictly conservative nature of the ritual practice itself, the preservation in such rituals of archaic language forms, which in particular moments transform into unintelligible words for the one pronouncing them and at some stage become part of the so called *nomina barbara*.

[331] In Bulgarian: *Самодивки-калоти, дето да сте - в море, в поле, в зелена гора, тука елате да ядете, да пиете, конето да си назобите и да ги ковете и на (името на болния) здравье да дадете!"*

189

and goes outside the village in the dark. The spot where the table is going to be left must be picked during the day, and it must be where the ill person has walked the most and where they probably got ill. The woman goes to a crossroad, next to a cornel-tree (believed to be a tree of the samodivi), to a deserted place, where few people go, leans down to leave the table and says out loud:

"Brothers-sworn brothers, sisters-samodivki! Wherever you are – in sea, in field, in green forest, come here to eat, to drink, to feed and shoe your horses and to (the name) to give health!"[332]

This rite is repeated three times, but some time must be left to pass between them. When it is done for the third time, the woman that leaves the table on the ground will lean and grab with a hand in the dark anything by chance – chops, leaves or other, and moving backwards fast, without speaking, she will walk away and leave the breads. When she is forty steps away she will turn around and go to her village, but will continue to carry in her hand what has taken from the place. If there were companions with the woman, they must stay away from the place, where the table is being left the whole time. When they are going the woman walks in front, but on returning the companions walk ahead and the woman after them.

When they come back home the first thing that the woman must do is to take the iron hearth shovel, to put some coals in it and spill over them all that she has taken from the ground, where she has left the table. If there is soil in that substance, the forehead of the ill person is covered with it. The ill part of the body is fumigated with the shovel and with the things in it.

When she comes back to the house of the ill person, the woman locks the front door, which is not unlocked until cock-crow. After that the healer performs a watch next to the ill person, she doesn't sleep, but carefully listens to hear if there is any sound on the roof or elsewhere. Before going to sleep the ill person is warned to remember the dream they have during that night. If they dream that someone takes something from them, that means that the samodivi will take away their illness. Nothing is eaten until the morning, from

---

[332] In Bulgarian: *"Бракье-побратимье, сестри-самодивки! Дето и да сте - в море, в поле, в зелена гора - тука елате: да ядете, да пиете, конето да си назобите и да ги ковете и на (името на болния) здравье да дадете!"*

the coming back from the forest to the house where the ill person is.

These rites from the region of Strandzha show a particular richness of ritual actions and elements. The concept is very clear for the perpetrators that such a practice is performed rarely, because it is considered as *'devilish'*, i.e. it belongs to the unofficial belief. In the rite itself some elements can be seen that remind of the ancient suppers that were left to the goddess Hekate, to win her favour. The cathartic rationalisation of the rite is shown also with the ritual requirements for the one performing it not to turn back, the companion to stay away and so on.

The seeking of help for healing from the samodivi is carried out when special attention is required, i.e. they are healers who the people address in hopeless situations and in that sense they can't be reckoned among the unclean forces. This makes them severe mistresses of the wild, but as such they also know the ways to heal, and if the ritual requirements are done correctly help could be received from them both for physical and psychological recovery. All this gets them closer to the ancient nymphs, but knowing the Bulgarian traditional rites connected with them makes it possible to outline the Thracian-specific distinguishing features in their Thracian worship.

The healers also come to the aid of the samodivi in some cases, evidence for which is given in the following healings for fear and evil eye.

Description of practice 35 INCANTATION AGAINST FEAR[333]

Early in the morning the healer takes the ill person to a meadow near a spring and makes them lay on the grass. Then the healer marks the place which the patient has covered with his body, with a hoe. After that the patient gets up and the healer hoes the whole upper layer of the marked place like a turf. The turf is called *'uplasa'*. While hoeing the *uplasa* the healer makes this incantation:

"As this uplasa is hoed, so the fear of this person should come out!"[334]

After it is hoed the healer says:

---

[333] *Collection of Bulgarian Folklore and Folk Studies*, v. 12, 148 (СбНУ – m. 12, 148) .

[334] In Bulgarian: *"Както тази упласа се копа, така и уплахата от този човек да излезе!"*

"As the uplasa came out, so the fear should come out!"[335]

After this the healer turns the uplasa upside down and places it on the same spot and says:

"When this uplasa turns the way it was,

then the fear should come back in this person."[336]

The healer takes the patient from the meadow to a spring where after their arrival she starts an incantation over the water:

"You, dear water, come from mountains.

From mountains, from high grounds,

where the samovili gather;

where they eat, where they have dinner.

You will say, dear water,

of this person,

from what is the fear.

Hurry sooner, dear water!

Say to the sea,

so it could tell the samovili,

to take out this fear from this person."[337]

After the healer finishes this incantation, the patient turns his body facing east. The healer takes a handful of water from the spring with their right hand and passes it over the patient, while saying:

"As this water is being passed over, so the fear should be passed.

As this water can't return, so the fear should not return."[338]

---

[335] In Bulgarian: *"Както упласата излезе, така и уплахата да излезе!"*

[336] In Bulgarian: *"Когато тая упласа се обърне как е била, тогава и уплахата да се върне в този човек."*

[337] In Bulgarian:

"Ти, водице, идеш от планини.

От планини, от вишини,

където се събират самовилите;

където ядат, където вечерят.

Ти ще кажеш, водице,

на този човек,

от какво му е тази уплаха.

Бързай по-скоро, водице!

Да кажеш на морето,

да каже то на самовилите,

да изведат тази уплаха от този човек."

[338] In Bulgarian: *"Както се прехвърля тази вода, така да се прехвърли и уплахата. Както не може тази вода повече да се върне, така и уплахата да не се връща."*

Description of practice 36 AGAINST EVIL EYE[339]

The healer chants the text below, makes a cross sign with a knife over a glass of water, and washes with their hand the forehead, hands and feet of the child with the words:

"As you shake off,

so the illness shakes off from (the name)"[340]

(In the region of Valche pole the text is):

"Wild samovili come from the forest on white horses.

From the forest, to the villages, to the children,

to take away their illnesses,

to take the illness in desolated forests, in desolated valleys.

From the valleys to the rivers,

from the rivers in the sea.

(The name) has sat in the sea on a white marble stone[341]

– half crying, half wondering.

From where heard him Saint Mother of God

and went to him, and said him a word:

"Don't you cry, don't you wonder.

Your kind mother will come and give you aid.

And she will say:

"If the evil eye is from a male – let his eyes leak out;

if the evil eye is from a female – let their bosoms scatter."[342]

---

[339] *The Rhodopes. Traditional Folk Spiritual and Socio-Normative Culture,* Sofia 1994, 70 (*Родопи. Традиционна народна духовна и социалнонормативна култура, София 1994, 70*).

[340] In Bulgarian: *"Как са изтърсваш ти, тъй да са изтърси болестта от (името)".*

[341] This is one of the rare examples in which the Mother of God is represented in the ritual text, following the example of the ritual texts of the Eastern Slavs, sitting in the sea on a white stone.

[342] In Bulgarian:

"Диви самовили идат от гората с бели коне.

От гората, по селата, по децата,

да хми сбират болестите,

да я носят в пусти гори, в пусти долини.

От долините в реките,

от реките в морето.

Седнал ми е (името) сред морето на бял мермер камък

– ем си плаче, ем се чуди.

От де го зачу Света Богородица

и при него отиде, и му дума дума:

„Недей плака, недей се чуди.

Ще дойде твойта мила майка и ще ти помощ даде.

И ще ти каже:

"Ако от мъжки урчаса – да му изтечат очите;

ако от женски урчаса – да им са разпръснат нянките."

The mistresses of the forests and mountains have a number of plants, considered to be dedicated to them and which are used in magical and healing practices. Such plants for instance are: dog rose (*Rosa canina*), 'borisii' (Avens) (*Geum coccineum*), small meadow rue (*Thalictrum minus*), German iris (*Iris germanica*), yellow melilot (*Melilotus officinalis*), false helleborine (*Veratrum lobelianum*), cross gentian (*Gentiana cruciata*), common wormwood (*Artemisia vulgaris*), maidenhair spleenwort (*Asplenium trichomanes*), horse tongue lily (*Ruscus hypoglossum*), ivy (*Hedera helix*), dog's tooth violet (*Erythronium dens-canis*) and others. A number of rites are connected with these herbs, and in some cases they are used to drive away, i.e. free some place from the presence of the samodivi and other supernatural creatures.

Description of practice 37 BUILDING A NEW HOUSE[343]

Unspoken water and undrank water are taken and herbs gathered on St John's Eve (*Enyovden*) – common primrose, tansy, yellow melilot, false helleborine, German iris, burning-bush and cross gentian, are put in it.

The water in the cauldron is covered with a new cloth (used for wrapping the bread) and left in the middle of the new threshing floor. During the night a naked elderly woman pours water from the cauldron in the dugs as a fence and swears samodivi, yudi, zmeyove:

> *Samodivi, samovili,*
> *and you, bad yudi,*
> *and you, white rusalki,*[344]
> *grey colourful zmey!*[345]

---

[343] Georgieva Iv., *Bulgarian folk mythology*, Sofia 1993, 229 (*Георгиева Ив.,Българска народна митология, София 1993, 229*).

[344] The *rusalki* are a type of mythological character that are closely connected with the image of the samodiva, but unlike her they don't have a divine origin. The rusalki are believed to be spirits of drowned people (Northern Bulgaria) or women deceased during childbirth. They are also known as an appearance of the samodivi during the Rusal week (the week before Pentecost). In this sense they are viewed and honoured as healers, and in ethnographic literature there are descriptions of cult societies of men, which during this period go around the villages, healing the so-called rusal illnesses. These male cult societies are also known among other Balkan countries (Serbia and Romania), as they continue to exist until today in Romania (and probably in Serbia, but I don't have actual data on the matter). Of course in the separate regions there are local peculiarities and because the subject is vast and complex it won't be discussed here.

[345] The *zmey* is a mythological character, who although it has been related to the concept of the dragon, differs from it in the Balkan folklore. In a number of cases he is known as guardian of a village or place, and the motifs for a woman abducted and loved by him are popular. In this

If you have sat here,
if here was your yard,
now run to a desolated woods,
desolate Tililean woods![346]

This swearing is repeated at every dig, and in the place where the pit of the house is going to be, she pours water with the same swearing, too. After that she digs a deeper pit and buries in it the herbs – this place is going to be a chopping log and there nobody dares to sleep. When they place the four stones, they sprinkle them with water and the oldest man sits on them.

On the place where the hearth is going to be after sprinkling with undrank water with herbs a flat stone is buried. After sprinkling the herbs are buried under the flat stone and the hearth is considered to be inaccessible for the spirits. After that two boys bring fire and ash from two houses of relatives, and the oldest woman sprinkles the flat stone with undrank water, starts a fire and makes a blessing. According to the colour and the direction of the flame they make a prediction for the future.

Undoubtedly the favourite and sacred plant of the samodivi is the burning-bush (*Dictamnus albus*). The burning-bush is connected with the samodivi and their function as healers both in Bulgaria and in Serbia.[347] A

---

connection in Balkan folklore he is symbolically close to the supreme male deities of storms and the elements in antiquity – Zeus, Boreas and others. There is a known notion of his female correspondence – *zmeitsa*, which continues the idea from antiquity of couples of deities, i.e. their paredria (helpers). Because the image of the zmey is multilayered and many ritual actions and beliefs are connected with him, he will be given special attention in future publications connected with the male deities of the ancient Thracians.

[346] In Bulgarian:
Самодиви, самовили,
и вие, лоши юди,
и вие, бели русалки,
сиви шарени змейове!
Ако сте тук седели,
ако сте тук дворили,
съг си бежте пусто горо,
пусто горо тилилейско!

[347] For the description of the rite in Serbia see Chaykanovich V., *On magic and religion*, Belgrade 1985, 52-59 (Чајкановић В., *О магији и религији*, Београд 1985, 52-59). He probably didn't know that this rite is known in almost the whole Bulgarian ethnic territory and claims that sleeping under a burning-bush is *"specially ours"*, i.e. Serbian practice. These rites, as was mentioned above exceed national borders, because they descend from and belong to an ethnic belief and ritual practice, and the ethnic borders often don't coincide with the political. It is possible this practice is also found among other Balkan peoples, which of course should be examined by the scholars in order to achieve a clearer idea of this rite, which is largely no longer practiced and in some places is even completely forgotten.

number of scholars make a mistake and confuse the burning-bush (*Dictamnus albus*) with another plant, mentioned by the ancient authors and which is an endemic for the island of Crete - *Origanum dictamnus*. This confusion begins from the Middle Ages and unfortunately continues even today. According to ancient authors the Cretan plant is sacred to Artemis and animals wounded by arrows turn to its aid,[348] as it helps to even throw the arrows out of their bodies. The proximity of the samodivi image to the image of Artemis, results in the misperception that this plant is the burning-bush, but this is wrong, because the ancient authors mention the other plant. Of course this fact doesn't reject the possibility that during antiquity the burning-bush was also considered to be sacred, but for the present moment we don't have such information from antiquity and this could be claimed only on the basis of legends and rites connected with it preserved until now. According to some Bulgarian legends the burning-bush was left to the people by the *'heavenly inhabitants'*. This is made by them for the purpose that when mortals become ill from contact with immortals, to be able to seek healing with the help of the burning-bush.[349] As was already mentioned a number of neuro-psychological disorders were considered in the past to be inflicted by such contact. In this connection healing with burning-bush was also performed mostly in such cases, but also for infertility.

Description of practice 38 HEALING AT A BURNING-BUSH[350]

"*Two hours southwest from Plovdiv, above the village of Dermendere (today Parvenets) there is a place called Rosin. It is surrounded by a small forest and there grows a flower with nice, but heavy smell, high up to two spans. This place was favourite to the samodivi, that is why they used to visit it and bathe in the "samodivi's spring" in the ravine.*

All the sick from the Plovdiv region go to this place with the hope to be cured, and this is done only once in the year, during the night preceding Spasovden (Feast of the Ascension). A day before that people with all kinds of

---

[348] See Aristotle, *The History of Animals* (612a4): "*Wild goats in Crete are said, when wounded by arrow, to go in search of dittany, which is supposed to have the property of ejecting arrows in the body.*"

[349] Georgieva Iv., *Bulgarian folk mythology*, Sofiá 1993, 180 (Георгиева Ив.,*Българска народна митология, София 1993, 180*).

[350] Nachov D., *Vili and samovili.* / Chitalishte, 1871, №7, 310 (Начов Д., *Вили и самовили.* / Читалище, 1871, №7, 310).

diseases come, accompanied by healthy people, and everyone tries to grab at least a root of the mentioned plant, next to which they spread a small carpet, then place next to the root a bowl with honey, covered with a small round bread. After everyone has spread their carpet, the ill go down to the samodivi's spring to wash and to place some sign, after that they come back silently to the reserved spot and lay, covered with white cloth by the healthy ones, that lie next to them. Deep silence falls, not a single sigh can be heard in this multitude. In the middle of the night a tempest brews, then second and third; the samodivi have come and will throw on the white cloth a sign for healing or death. When the storm goes away, the healthy gather the cloths and suddenly all the ill disperse quietly in the darkness, so that the dawn doesn't catch them at Rosin. Having arrived at their homes, everyone opens the cloth to see what the samodivi have dropped for them. If it is a green grass, they will heal, if it is dry or some soil – they will die. In order to be absolutely assured, the ill person must visit Rosin three times during the exact time of the year."

From the listed practices and rituals the conclusion could be drawn that the Mistress of the Mountains is called in the cultural space and is welcomed with the hope of awakening the earth's fertility, when the God Sun again retrieves his fertilising power, i.e. after the Spring Equinox. Nevertheless the Mountain Mother remains worshipped far beyond human reach, there her suppers are left, there help is asked from her and thus she continues to be an image of the unassimilated elements, which called with honour and faith give health and power to the deserving.

THE VIRGIN MISTRESS OF FIRE

During the time when the Sun burns the ground the most in the lands of the Thracians, Bulgarian people, as well as the neighbouring peoples in the Balkans, mark a period connected with the performing of a number of rites related with fire. One part of these actions aims to protect from the sky fire – the lightnings, another from the fires on earth, and a third part is related to performing actions focused on love. The earthly fire, the power over snakes, the protection of children, the rites of passage of unmarried men and women are connected with the worship of a Christian saint, who bears a lot of archaic features and continues the ancient worship of the Virgin Mistress of fire. This saint is called

Fiery Marina and Fiery Maria among the Balkan peoples, as in some cases similar elements in the ritual practices have been transferred to other Christian characters, for instance to the Mother of God.

Generally this period could be defined as the range from the end of July to the middle of August. This period was called in antiquity *'dog days'*, because it is marked by the heliacal rising of Sirius the *'Dog Star'*. It is not accidental that in the folk notion the three days July 15th, 16th and 17th are called *Goreshtnitsi* (Hot days). Although this period begins with the dog-days, so its continuation and end could be considered the celebration of the Assumption of the Mother of God and the lighting of the fire of the *sedyanka* (work party), i.e. lighting the fires, around which the celebrations begin.[351]

The historical sources which mention a festival during this period in the cultural borders of the Mediterranean, and according to me are connected with Thracian ritual practices, are from the Roman historians. They give accounts of the sanctuary of Diana in Aricia and for a celebration of the Goddess in August. Regarding the celebration Statius (Statius, *Silvae* 3.1.52-60) writes:

"It is the season when the most scorching region of the heavens takes over the land and the keen dog-star Sirius, so often struck by Hyperion's sun, burns the gasping fields. Now is the day when Trivia's Arician grove, convenient for fugitive kings, grows smoky, ant the lake, having guilty knowledge of Hippolytus, glitters with the reflection of a multitude of torches; Diana herself garlands the deserving hunting dogs and polishes the arrowheads and allows the wild animals to go in safety, and at virtuous hearths all Italy celebrates the Hecatean Ides."[352]

---

[351] The fire of the sedyanki has been lit in places exactly on the day of St Marina, i.e. July 17th, but the most detailed written rite is connected to the celebration of Assumption of the Mother of God, see Popov R., *Calendar folk celebrations and customs from the region of Troyan* // Cultural-historical heritage of the region of Troyan, Sofia 1991, 77-78 (Попов Р., *Народни календарни празници и обичаи в троянския Край* // *Културно-историческото наследство на Троянския край, София 1991, 77-78*).

[352] Green C., *Roman Religion and the Cult of Diana at Aricia*, Cambridge 2007, 60-61.

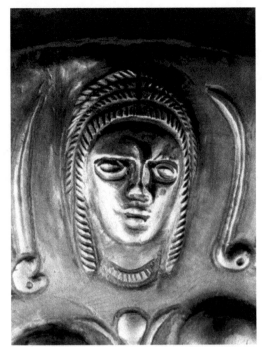

*44 - Image Of The Goddess On A Phiale
From The Findings From Rogozen*[353]

45- Mistress of Fire by Georgi Mishev

---

[353]   http://www.runitravel.com/wp-content/uploads/2010/12/14-1.jpg
<29.12.2011>.

46 - Denarius From 43 BCE
With An Image Of Diana Nemorensis[354]

From the information of Statius several things become clear, that are confirmed by other authors too. Diana as worshipped in Aricia is called Trivia and this is the Latin name of the Goddess who the Hellenes called Hekate Trioditis, i.e. of three roads. On the basis of archaeological research it becomes clear that actually the sacred area the Goddess had for a primarily centre was the sacred cave, where it is possible that subsequently a cult image was placed and the temple built.

In addition we read the information of Strabo (*Geography*, 5.3.12):

"The temple of the Arician, they say, is a copy of that of the Tauropolos. And in fact a barbaric, and Scythian, element predominates in the sacred usages."

With this information, which is also confirmed by other authors, the notion of Diana in Aricia binds itself with one ideological perception of Artemis which, regardless of its nuances, shares some similar features and is spread in the Mediterranean, as well as in the North Black Sea regions. In this way, in spite of the huge geographical territory and the many differences in the ritual cult, some basic features form in the image of the Goddess connected with this period.

She is perceived as a virginal hypostasis – even in some local cults this is her official epiclesis – in Chersonese she is

---

[354] http://wildwinds.com/coins/rsc/accoleia/accoleia1a.jpg <29.12.2011>.

called the Tauric Virgin - Ταυρική Παρθένος,[355] in the Latin regions she is called sometimes only the Virgin – Virgo.[356] The Tauric Virgin has a number of features which reckon her among the great chthonic Goddesses of antiquity. This hypostasis of the Goddess is also compared and even absolutely identified by some with Artemis Tauropolos and is approximated to the Thracian Bendis. She shares a lot of common features of her worship with the Goddess Hekate, who also bears this epithet in the Orphic hymn dedicated to her. The worship of Tauropolos in Amphipolis[357] is under strong Thracian religious influence.[358]

47 - Coin From Amphipolis, 41-54 CE,
Depicting The Goddess Tauropolos[359]

---

[355] Moore C., *On the Origin of the Taurobolium*, Harvard Studies in Classical Philology, Vol. 17 (1906), 45.

[356] Grattius, transl. J. W. Duff and A. M. Duff, *Minor Latin Poets*, Loeb Classical Library, Cambridge 1934, 493-496.

[357] For the founding of Amphipolis see Thucydides, *History of the Peloponnesian War 4.* 102-108. In this connection additional interest is seen in the information about the successful founding of the city after the transfer of the bones of the Thracian hero Rhesus, for a commentary see Fol V., *Rock-cut topoi of faith in Southeastern Europe and Asia Minor during Antiquity*, Sofia 2007, 232-233 (Фол В. Скални топоси на вяра в Югоизточна Европа и в Мала Азия през древността, София 2007, 232-233). Regarding the mixed population of the city see Lazaridis, D.I., *Amphipolis, Archaeological Receipts Fund*, Athens. 1997, 14-20.

[358] In this connection see Isaac B., *The Greek Settlements in Thrace until the Macedonian Conquest*, Leiden 1986, 55.

[359] http://www.coinarchives.com/a/lotviewer.php?LotID=428144&AucID=775&Lot=791&Val=f1794b2d42d5afd82b4b179900d52fc5 <18.08.2011>.

In the description of Statius quoted above there are elements of great importance, because they are present in the rituals preserved until today, connected with this period of the year and with the notion of this great Virgin that rules over the days of the most scorching sun.

From the information of Statius we understand the following:

- this is the most scorching period in the year;
- the sacred place is the cave of the Goddess, as well as the lake;
- the rite is connected with nocturnal worship, marked by torches;
- the rites are performed on a hearth and are connected with fire;
- Bulgarian traditional ritual practice in connection with this period of the year consists of the following similar elements:
- the calling of the days defines them as the most scorching period of the year - *Goreshtnitsi* (Hot days);
- the saint worshipped in the period of the hot days – St Marina is called Fiery and has two known sacred caves in the territory of Bulgaria,[360] which are situated in fords, near springs or rivers and as a whole the sacred places of this saint are connected with water;
- the rites and the pilgrimage, which is made in honour of the saint have nocturnal character. Her sacred places are visited in dark on the eve of the celebration and candles are lit, that symbolically replace the torches of antiquity;
- even though the hearth doesn't have a part in the celebration today, in the past on the first of the *Goreshtnitsi* (July 15th) all hearths in the village were put out and on July 17th the new living fire was lit, which was accompanied with special rites and to which great sacred power was attributed;

The similarity in the performed ritual practice in the same period of the year makes the hypothesis of inheritance of the ancient tradition among the Christianised Balkan population very possible. The fact that the rites from this

[360] Such a sacred cave of St Marina is known in Athens, Greece. For its description see Lalonde G., *Pagan Cult to Christian Ritual: The Case of Agia Marina Theseiou*, Greek, Roman, and Byzantine Studies 45, 2005, 91–125.

period of the year are preserved in connection with the character of a virgin, who is worshipped as a mistress of fire and snakes, has her sacred caves and is worshipped next to water – river or sacred springs, gives the opportunity by examining the folk notions and rituals to shed more light on the ancient perception of the Virgin, mistress of fire and snakes in the lands of the Thracians.

The virgin saint that is considered to be a mistress of this period of the year is St Marina. Her folk naming is Fiery Marina,[361] and she is one of the most honoured saints in the Balkans. She bears this epithet because of the folk belief that she is a mistress of fire, and her celebration is the third day of the so called Goreshtnitsi – July 15th, 16th and 17th. A lot of pre-Christian features can be seen in her worship.[362]

According to folk beliefs the saint is a mistress of snakes which she keeps closed in a cave. She lets outside only the smallest and the largest and the most dangerous snakes stay inside. When a snake bites a man they must go to a healer and it is believed that this snake is not allowed back in the cave by the saint and so it dies from cold.[363]

The healing of a snake bite is a very interesting rite, but unfortunately there is very little written documenting healing rituals from the Bulgarian ethnic territory on this. In this connection I'm going to quote one such description, to get an idea of the types of the related practices with such an orientation.

---

[361] The same is known in Western Europe with the name Margaret of Antioch.
[362] The subject of the pre-Christian antiquity of the worship of St Marina in Bulgarian traditional culture and her relation with Artemis-Bendis has been commented by such great experts in Bulgarian traditional culture as prof. Ivanichka Georgieva, see Georgieva Iv., *Bulgarian folk mythology*, Sofia 1981, 238 (Георгиева Ив., *Българска народна митология, София 1981, 238*); Georgieva Iv., *An ancient cult in the Rhodopes, Strandzha and Nestos //* Rhodopes collection, vol. 3, Sofia 1972, 159-174 (Георгиева Ив., *Един старинен култ в Родопите, Странджа и Места // Родопски сб., Т. 3. София 1972, 159-174*), as well as from the Thracologist prof. Valeria Fol, see Fol V., *The worship of St Marina in Strandzha //* Myth-Art-Folklore, 1, Sofia 1985, 128-130 (Фол В., *Почитането на св. Марина в Странджа.// Мит-изкуство-фолклор, 1, София 1985, 128—130*) and in Fol V., *The Forgotten Saint*, Sofia 1996 (Фол В., *Забравената светица, София 1996*).
[363] Fol V., *The Forgotten Saint*, Sofia 1996 (Фол В., *Забравената светица, София 1996*).

48 - St Margaret Of Antioch, France Around 1200 CE[364]

[364] http://spiralupward.com/?author=1&paged=8 <01.09.2011>.

Description of practice 39 HEALING A SNAKE BITE[365]

The healing of a person bitten by a snake is a patent to very few *'magicians'* and mostly men from *'another faith'*. When *magyuvaneto* (the making of the magic) is done from *'faith to faith'*, it is not believed to be healing. The purpose of the deed is to call the spirit of the snake, which has bitten the patient, to take its venom back and to live again, because it is believed that when a snake bites a human it dies immediately. The séance of the healing is performed only on the good days of the week, before noon and on a sunny day. If the bite is on the hand, *'the healer'* strips the whole arm and exposes the bitten place to the sunlight. With the right hand he makes some kind of movements over the bitten place, as if he is pulling out the venom and drops it next to his feet, where *magyuvaniyat* (the patient) must believe that the snake has come to take it back and to continue its life. During the first séance the following spells are pronounced:

Chick, chick, chicken,

to me a mild lamb,

many-coloured, even embroidered,

come and take your little tear,

come and take your little spittle,

come and take your little teeth,

come and take your little eyes,

you be healthy and alive,

so you could adorn the field,

so you could protect the forest,

to protect from mice the wheat,

so you could be a star in the grass,

an eagle to go blind, when it sees you,

a hedgehog to become crippled, when it steps on you![366]

---

[365] Koshov S., *Spells from Razlog region* // Bulgarian folklore, Sofia 1980, № 4, 105-106 (Кошов С., Магии от Разложко // *Български фолклор, София 1980, № 4, 105-106*).

[366] In Bulgarian:

Пѝли, пѝли, пѝленце,

на мене кротко ягненце,

пѝсано, та везано,

явди си земи съзѝцата,

явди си земи слюнчицата,

явди си земи зъбѝците,

явди си земи очѝците,

да ми си жѝво и здраво,

да ми красиш полето,

да ми пазиш гората,

от мѝше да пазиш житата,

да ми си звездѝца в тревата,

орел да ослепее, кога те вѝди,

The sun is left to warm the bitten place and after that it is pronounced again:

Chick, chick, chicken,
here is, chick, your little tear,
here is, chick, your little spittle,
here is, chick, your little soul,
come to me to pet you,
to tell you a little tale,
so big and small should envy you,
everything living, little chick![367]

He leaves the bitten place once more in the sunlight, covers it three times with his hand and makes movements, as if he is pulling out the venom from the wound and drops it next to his feet in the mouth of the arrived snake:

Chick, chick, chicken,
did you take what you need,
now go safe and sound,
go to the forest,
so you could go on the grass,
so you could go in the field,
so the eagle doesn't show up,
so the hedgehog doesn't come,
to crunch your head,
now go with health,
so the human could be at ease![368]

After he finishes with the incantations, he sucks with his mouth up to three times, makes a cross with the right hand

---

еж да осакатее, кога те настапи!
[367]In Bulgarian:
Пѝли, пѝли, пѝленце,
еле ти, пиле, съзѝцата,
еле ти, пиле, слюнчицата,
еле ти, пиле, душицата,
явди да си те погала,
да си ти кажа приказчица,
да ти завиди мало и големо,
целата, пиленце, живина!
[368]In Bulgarian:
Пѝли, пѝли, пѝленце,
зе ле си що ти требува,
айда сега по живо и по здраво,
иди си ми в гората,
да си ми одиш по тревата,
да си ми одиш по полето,
да се не яви орлето,
да се не довлече ежо,
да ти сруска главата,
айда сега суздраве,
да улекне на човеко!

over the bitten place and covers it with red cloth. In this way the wound is protected from the unclean forces that could be present during the séance and could spoil the work, could have heard the spells and tried to enervate them. The healer leaves and doesn't turn back. The healed person goes home, without looking to the spot where it is supposed that the evil doer was standing.

A number of elements in the presented rite make an impression. First of all this is the exposure of the bitten place to the sunlight, which in this case appears to be the healer, the healing should be received by it. The other moment is the covering of the bitten place with a red cloth, i.e. the help of the Great Goddess is also called with her colour code. This incantation for healing a snake bite reflects the idea that the snake shouldn't be killed, but has to be left alive and through incantations to give its venom back into it. In this sense the saint herself as *'visia'*, i.e. mistress of snakes, can't be assumed as a dragon slayer image, as some scholars claim[369] going by her hagiology where she is swallowed by the devil in his guise of dragon and comes out from his abdomen with the aid of the cross sign. The saint is their mistress but they are also under her protection, i.e. she is looking after them. In this sense the folk belief preserves in honour of St Marina the pre-Christian tradition connected with the worship of the virginal female deity related with the fire and the snake, and doesn't adapt the hagiological image, which anyway was already known mostly to the Christian clergy and not to the folk masses.

In most of the regions in Bulgaria the saint is called with a diminutive name – Marinka. This is done with the clear idea to emphasise her age – of a young girl. In the region of Strandzha she has also another nickname – Pobarinka.[370]

This epithet of the saint bears erotic characteristic, such as some rituals connected with her have, too. The people have assigned to the saint the last day of the so called *Goreshtnitsi*, when the new living fire and the fire of the sedyanka are being lit. In this sense she is believed as a mistress also of the Cosmic, i.e. the fire above the world, and of the home fire, i.e. the fire in the human community.

---

[369]See Petrova M., *For the cult and hagiographic tradition of St Marina* // Christian hagiology and folk beliefs, Sofia 2008, 144 (Петрова М., *За култа и агиографската традиция на св Марина* // Християнска агиология и народни вярвания, София 2008, 144).

[370] Epithet which comes from the verb to touch, to feel, and has an erotic meaning.

49 - Mural Painting From A Church In Leshko Village, Southwestern Bulgaria, Depicting St Marina Beating The Devil – Personal Archive Of The Author 2011

If the ritual practice dedicated to this Virgin with many faces is described consequently, the following picture emerges.

The three days called *Goreshtnitsi* are honoured for protection from fire. On the first day of the *Goreshtnitsi* (July 15th), all the fires in all the hearths of the village are extinguished, on the second day no fire is lit, and on the third day a living fire is kindled. From the living fire the home hearths are lit again. The prohibition for working is strictly followed during these three days. Especially strong are the prohibitions for performing female activities – sewing, spinning, and weaving.[371] It is believed that if someone works during this time Fiery Marina will send them fire and burn their property. The honour given to the divine during this period reflects the belief that this is the time when the Fire is being born. There are some elements that bring this time closer to the Christmas period, when the Sun is being born. The birth of its earthly projection, the lighting of the new, living, divine fire,[372] is done again on the day dedicated to a Virgin, i.e. the idea for the self-conceiving is preserved. The dual image is again manifested and here we see the fire as an earthly projection of the luminary. And on this birth the main honour is given to the source, i.e. in this case to Fiery Marina, the Virgin, who rules over the fire and snakes.

---

[371] According to folk belief the snakes will bite a person who wears cloths that were worked on during that time.
[372] The acquiring of a living fire is a process that reflects the new creation of the Fire on a human level.

50 - The Interior Of The Chapel Of St Marina In Bratsigovo. The Altar Stone Called "The Pebble Of St Marenka" Can Be Seen, Which Has A Hollow On Top (Now Filled With Cement And Covered With A Marble Plate) And Has Ancient Origins.
Photograph Iglika Mishkova – 2009

Description of practice 40 FESTIVE RITUAL PRACTICE FOR THE DAY OF THE FIERY VIRGIN[373]

The period before the celebration of the saint is dedicated to temperance that aims at acquiring ritual purity. Because the saint is believed to be the protectress of the *lefteri* (unmarried), girls and boys in the premarital age must take part in the celebration. They must be incorporated into the rites in order to make the passage.[374] The requirements for

---

[373] The given description refers to the festive ritual practice in the region of Strandzha, but in general it is similar with the ones in other regions, see Fol V., *The Forgotten Saint*, Sofia 1996, 167, 184-185 (Фол В., *Забравената светица*, София 1996, 167, 184-185). In this connection I would like to mention a chapel of St Marina, situated in my native city Bratsigovo, Rhodope Mountains. It is next to the oldest school in town, but in contiguity to the river, i.e. the closeness with water and the liminal place is kept. The chapel has been moved three times, but there is one element in it that is constant and has been moved from the old to the new building and that is the altar stone. The local population calls the altar – the pebble of saint Marenka. According to the stories told by the elderly women from my childhood the saint has been dreamt and seen as a young girl, with blond hair like gold (informant Margarita Hristova Toshkova 11.06.1924 - 25.09.2000). At night she goes around the stone and sits on it. That is the reason why the stone is considered as the centre of the chapel. In local folk belief St Marina is honoured as a protectress of the children. Her chapel is visited after dark in the evening (July 16/17) and offerings are left – flowers, clothes, breads. On the next day a kurban (animal sacrifice) is made. There is no practice for the kurban to be given away raw, but it is boiled at the place and is given like that. The care for the chapel of St Marina is in the hands of certain women, which only after a dream and upon the request of the saint receive the key of the chapel and undertake the care of it. Their duties consist of its regular cleansing, unlocking in festive days and organising the celebration of the saint. From the description so far it can be seen clearly that the traditional ritual practice has an extremely enduring nature and has modified in its own way the Christian ritual practice, as it has adapted it to its own requirements. In spite of the church canons and laws the people follow traditional rules from thousands of years ago. The story of the current keeper of the chapel, Elena Petrova Kupanova (born 16.10.1926), is a very interesting one. It recounts that after being very ill, while sleeping, a girl appeared who gave her a key so she could be healed. Subsequently the woman recovered from the illness and recognised the same key in the hands of her neighbour woman and that turned out to be the key for the chapel of St Marina. That is how she started her service to the saint, who continued to appear in her dreams. In one of those dreams, the divine girl demanded that her servant learn the saint's songs and sing them to her. This moment makes an impression because ancient fragments give evidence for the belief of the ancients that the deities love songs to be sung in their honour, in this connection see Kowalzig B., *Singing for the Gods*, New York 2007.

[374] Regarding this there are preserved folk songs in which a single man is mentioned who didn't follow the requirement and didn't visit the celebration. This led to the impossibility of passing the liminal state, i.e. premarital. In this way he stays at that limit and doesn't integrate to society, see Fol V., *The Forgotten Saint*, Sofia 1996, 95 (Фол В., *Забравената светица*, София 1996, 95). In this case the connection between the rites of St Marina and the etymology of the epiclesis of the Thracian Goddess Bendis – to bind, becomes even clearer. The Goddess realises not only the connections in the Cosmos, but she also unifies society as it is not by accident that in Hellenic

married women are especially strict. According to folk belief they shouldn't have slept with their husbands before the celebration, and they shouldn't be in their menstrual period. The requirements are less for the men, but they are also expected to be clean, dressed in new clean clothes and to be shaved.

During the day of the saint, in some places immediately before it and in others a week before it, young girls under the direction of an elderly woman clean the sacred space – a cave or a chapel, and if there is a spring they clean it too.

People usually go to the sacred place after dark on the evening before the celebration. The gifts they prepare are ritual breads, which are offered only by women. Also flowers, money, cloths are left, candles are lit and in a number of cases people sleep near the sacred place, which could be done by everyone regardless of sex and age. On the day of the celebration (July 17th), a *kurban* (animal sacrifice) is made. The butchering is always done only by a man. For the kurban in some regions (for instance in Strandzha mountain) there is the requirement for it to be a black male lamb. Today even if the requirement for the colour is not always followed, it is obligatory that the lamb is male. In some places a prohibition is known for the man who has dedicated the kurban to eat from its meat. This is regarding the individual kurban, but everyone eats from the common meat. Usually the butchering of the sacrificial animal is done early in the morning. For this purpose it is decorated with a wreath and a lit candle is placed on its right horn. Before the butchering, fumigation with frankincense is made while walking around the lamb three times from left to right. The candle is unstuck from it and is placed on a stone in front of the saint's icon. The lamb is turned so its head points east and is butchered. Before the butcher kills it he says:

"God, give us health and life! I shed its blood for health!"[375]

The blood is not collected and is not buried.[376] The severed head is thrown in the forest, the lamb is skinned and the skin is hung on a tree near the sacred area. The money from the sale of skins is bestowed on the church.

---

ritual practice and faith Demeter is called also Thesmodoteira, i.e. giver of rules, which aims to do the same – to regulate society.

[375] In Bulgarian: *"Боже, дай хи здраве и живот! Проливам кръвта му за здраве!"*

[376] According to the description made by V. Fol the blood of one of the lambs is left to flow in the water of the sacred spring, see Fol V., *The Forgotten Saint*, Sofia 1996, 186 (*Фол В., Забравената светица, София 1996, 186).*

Consequently the lamb is divided into parts as the right shoulder goes to the one that leads the rite.[377] The first meal is from the intestines – liver, heart, kidneys, and lungs. They are eaten by the people close to the sacred place, i.e. the ones that care for it and the butcher. The remaining meat, if not given away raw, is cut to pieces and boiled in a copper pot. For the ritual meal each family takes a different place, separately from the other families, as the distribution of food is done in a strict hierarchical order according to age. The arrangement of the different families was also done in hierarchy. The families of the ones that care for the sacred area and the one that leads the rite are separated from the other families. As V. Fol writes – *"there is no ritual equality"*.[378]

Description of practice 41 FOR HEALING BY THE SACRED SPRING[379]

Healing rites are performed with the water from the sacred spring, which go in the following order. The requirements for ritual purity, mentioned above, are valid in this case. First one should go to the spring, drop a coin in and place flowers next to it and light some candles. Except for making the sign of the cross when lighting the candles, there is an interesting report that a bow is also made, where both hands touch the ground. The washing is done facing south and in exact order – first the eyes, then the brow, mouth, chest, top of the head and at the end the limbs. The left side is washed first with the right hand and then the right side of the body with the left hand. Finally one should take a sip from the water. After that the offerings are placed – money, flowers and bread.

---

[377] For the meaning of the right shoulder and skin in sacrificial ritual practices we have epigraphic evidences. They appear to be a kind of tax in benefit of the sanctuary or the officiator. In an inscription from Peiraieus connected with the cult of the Thracian Goddess Bendis LSCG 45, 2 -7 (Peiraieus, 4th century BCE) we read the preserved requirement that the one that makes a sacrifice must give to the priestess *"...the skin and the right leg in its entirety"*, see Lupu E., *Sacrifice at the Amphiareion and a Fragmentary Sacred Law from Oropos* // The Journal of the American School of Classical Studies at Athens, Vol. 72, No. 3 (Jul. - Sep., 2003), 321-340.

[378] Fol V., *The Forgotten Saint*, Sofia 1996, 120 (Фол В., *Забравената светица, София 1996, 120*).

[379] The description here is for the sacred spring near the Slivarovo village, Strandzha, see Fol V., *The Forgotten Saint*, Sofia 1996, 184 (Фол В., *Забравената светица, София 1996, 184*).

Description of practice 42 FOR HEALING IN THE SACRED CAVE[380]

The requirements for purity are the same as the ones mentioned above. They go before Sunday, i.e. the evening of Saturday. In front of the cave a candle is lit, which is stuck on a specific place – the so called *odarche*, i.e. seat for rest or on the very rock. The cave is fumigated anticlockwise in a circle. Vessels are placed on the ground so the water dripping from the ceiling of the cave can be gathered. They spend the night in front of the cave and on the next day a candle is lit again and the fumigation is made again in the same way. The gathered water is taken and the ill person takes off their clothes, which are thrown in the gully, and washes their whole body with it. Immediately after that they leave without looking back and fast.

51 - The Cave Of St Marina Near The Slivarovo Village, Strandzha, Personal Archive Of The Author 2011

---

[380] This description is for the ritual actions for healing in the sacred cave near the Slivarovo village, Strandzha, see Fol V., *The Forgotten Saint*, Sofia 1996, 168 (Фол В., *Забравената светица, София 1996, 168*).

52 - Votive Depiction Of A Human Figure, Left As An Offering In The Cave Of St Marina Near The Slivarovo Village, Strandzha – Personal Archive Of The Author 2011[381]

The ritual practice connected with Fiery Marina bears a clearly expressed chthonic nature, because in the first place it is performed during the night, in some places in caves and near rivers. The saint herself is considered as a mistress of snakes, and as sacrifice a number of bloodless offerings are given to her like bread, flowers, coins, but a male lamb is offered too, for which there is a requirement that it must be black. All these records bring the folk image of the saint closer to the honour given in antiquity to the great chthonic Goddesses like the Tauric Virgin, Artemis (in her local hypostases as Phosphoros, Tauropolos or respectively Diana Trivia and others), Hekate, Persephone and Bendis. The Fiery Virgin, who finds her succession in the image of the Christian saint, has preserved her archaic ritual tradition. The mistress of snakes is a well known notion in the Mediterranean, as is attested also in the famous depictions from Crete.[382]

---

[381] The appearance of votives in the cave is very interesting, because according to V. Fol this is an innovation, but in turn shows a return to archaic elements in the ritual practices.

[382] See Caskey L., *A Chryselephantine Statuette of the Cretan Snake Goddess* // American Journal of Archaeology, Vol. 19, No. 3 (Jul. - Sep., 1915), 237-249.

Among the findings in Thrace which are of particular interest are a number of lead snakes from Seuthopolis,[383] which along with other findings give a material expression of the religious notions which the Thracians connected with the snake. If we add the images of snakes on the altar hearths, the connection snake-fire-divinity also becomes clear.

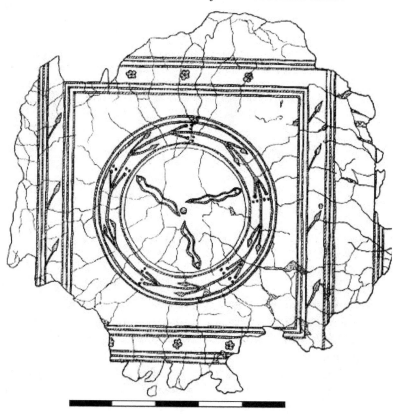

53 - Altar Hearth From Seuthopolis With Three Snakes Emerging From The Centre[384]

According to some researchers of Thracian culture, the snake in the traditional faith is connected with rites and notions which could be attributed to the Thracians.[385] In the

---

[383] See Seuthopolis, *vol. 1*, Sofia 1984, 215 (*Севтополис, Т. 1, София 1984, 215*).

[384] http://1.bp.blogspot.com/_17YFYXayrGs/SQjlaKyORdl/AAAAAAAAAgE/ Kw8QSNIgwaI/s1600-h/Eshar+8.JPG <12.09.2011>.

[385] Ivan Venedikov writes: *"The notions about the snake and the dragon in Bulgaria have a Thracian basis. Almost all the beliefs for the snake are in connection with the old Thracian notions about it – a protector of the home hearth and the cult places, the snake living with the woman and the snake representing a divinity or a mythological creature. A part of the beliefs for the snake, as the ones we just listed, are by the way common for the whole ancient world and the Hellenic and Roman culture have spread them everywhere. However it can be safely said that in the Thracian mythology the*

case of St Marina her relation with snakes from one side and from the other with fire, place her near to the Great Goddess, who is mentioned by the ancient authors as a giver of birth to Zagreus. The chthonic virgin Persephone in a snake form has conceived according to the ancient authors from Zeus, also in the guise of a dragon.[386] On the other hand another great chthonic hypostasis of the Goddess is also, according to me, similar to the folk perception of St Marina. The Goddess Hekate as she is described in the literary fragments is connected with fire and with the snake.

"Like some girding, noetic membrane (s)he divides, the First Fire and the Second Fire, which are eager to mix."[387]

This form of Hekate, also called Artemis by neoplatonists like Proclus, carries one interesting epithet, namely σπειροδρακοντόζωνος *"girt with coils of dragons"*.[388]

St Marina appears as a mistress of the Cosmic fire, and the image of the saint, as it is worshipped by the traditional culture is unifying also for her other manifestations – the darkness of the cave, the connection with water and snakes, protection over youths and children. In this way we see the Christian saint to be perceived by the people as the divinities were perceived in antiquity – as a whole. The parallel with the image of the Goddess Hekate we find also on the basis of another fragment, where the goddess describes her manifestations:

"I come, a virgin of varied forms, wandering through the heavens,
bull-faced, three-headed, ruthless, with golden arrows;
chaste Phoebe bringing light to mortals, Eilethyia;
bearing the three synthemata of a triple nature,
in the aether I appear in fiery forms
and in the aer I sit in a silver chariot;
earth reins in my black brood of puppies."[389]

---

snake had a much greater place, that it has in the Hellenic and that in a great scale the cult of Dionysos, connected with the snake, is typical mostly for the Thracians, where this connection was created and spread with the penetration of the orphic ideas in the whole ancient world." see Venedikov Iv., *The copper threshing-floor of the proto-Bulgarians*, Stara Zagora 1995, 276 (Венедиков Ив., *Медното гумно*, Стара Загора 1995, 276).
[386] Fol A., *The Thracian Dionysos, book 1, Zagreus*, Sofia 1991, 171-174 (Фол А., *Тракийският Дионис, книга 1, Загрей*, София 1991,171-174).
[387] Johnson S., *Hekate Soteira: A Study of Hekate's role in the Chaldean oracles and related literature*. Atlanta 1990, 53.
[388] See Aronen J., *Dragon Cults and νύμφη δράκαινα in IGUR 974* // Zeitschrift für Papyrologie und Epigraphik, Bd. 111 (1996), 128.
[389] Johnson S., *Hekate Soteira: A Study of Hekate's role in the Chaldean oracles and related literature*. Atlanta 1990, 141.

If we use the definition from this ancient fragment, we can say that the saint called Fiery Marina continues in folk belief a worship connected with the Virgin with many faces, who from one side inhabits, guides and appears in and through the fire, and from another fills with her presence the cave depths, too.

This Fiery Virgin is praised in folk songs as a daughter of a very interesting mythological character called Domna queen. In the naming Domna queen, the etymology of which could be derived from the Latin *domina* – 'mistress',[390] we see one of the epithets attributed to the Great Goddesses from antiquity like Demeter,[391] Cybele, Artemis and Hekate[392] - the Latin domina and the Greek δεσποινα.

Domna Queen is depicted in the folk song together with her Son-Sun, referred there with his Christian counterpart – St John:

> *"Oh, Domna, Domna, Domna queen!*
> *Domna queen and swallow!*
> *Before Domna comes pretty Enyo,[393]*
> *after him walks Domna queen,*
> *after him walks, after him flies,*
> *clouds drives white and red."[394]*

---

[390] Here see Venedikov Iv., *The golden pillar of the proto-Bulgarians*, Sofia 1987, 275 (*Венедиков Ив., Златният стожер на прабългарите, София 1987, 275*).

[391] Pausanias, *Description of Greece* 5.15.4:
"Outside the Altis, but on the right of the Leonidaeum, is an altar of Artemis of the Market, and one has also been built for Mistresses, and in my account of Arcadia I will tell you about the goddess they call Mistress."

[392] Aeschylus, fragment 216 (from the sholia of Theocritus, Idyll 2.36): *"Lady (despoina) Hekate, before the portal of the royal halls"*.

[393] Enyo is the folk naming of St John, which is equated with the image of the Son-Sun.

[394] *Collection of Bulgarian Folklore and Folk Studies 28*, 484, Momina tsarkva, Burgas region (*СбНУ 28, 494, Момина църква, област Бургас*). In Bulgarian:
"Ой Домно, Домно, Домно царице!
Домно царице и ластовице!
Пред Домна иде хубави Еньо ,
по него върви Домна царица,
по него върви, по него хвърга,
облаци кера бяли червени."

54 - Depiction On A Vessel From The Thracian Treasure From Rogozen. The Goddess Is On The Right Side And The God On The Left, On Chariots With Winged Horses.[395]

This ritual song is sung on Enyovden (the day of St John – June 24th), i.e. on the Christian celebration which has inherited the worship of the Son-Sun and is connected with the day of the Summer Solstice. The colour code, which is presented in the song – white and red, is another code naming of the Goddess and the God, a colour code which is repeated in other rites and celebrations, for instance in the '*martenitsa*'[396] and others.

According to the folk songs saint Marina is conceived by Domna Queen with the help of the Sun, who gave her a herb for a child. With this story the idea for the self-conceiving of the Great Goddess is represented in code. This belief is significant for the Eastern Mediterranean and is taken in by the Christian religion in the form of the so called virgin birth. In this case it is interesting that Domna queen gives birth to a girl, who is devoted to the sun. According to some songs in her ninth year she is abducted by the sun and in another song she is abducted by the *zmey* (dragon) Perian.[397] Even a replacing of the image of the solar god with that of a dragon can be assumed.[398] According to some scholars this description represents the priestess of the God-Sun,[399] but in my opinion when we talk about the bride of the sun it is

---

[395] Tsatsov P., *Representational problems of Thracian art in early Hellenism* // Archaeology, Sofia 1987, book 4, 21 (Цацов П., *Изобразителни проблеми на тракийското изкуство в ранния елинизъм* // *Археология, София 1987, кн. 4, 21*).

[396] See previous chapter.

[397] I quote the song about the dragon Periyan for a better understanding of the text and for further research (from Fol V., *The Forgotten Saint*, Sofia 1996, 43-44 (Фол В., *Забравената светица, София 1996, 43-44*):

[398] Re. this connection, see Markov V., *Cultural and historical Heritage of the Cult of the Sacred Serpent-Dragon in the Lands of the Thracian Sattri*, Blagoevgrad 2009 (Марков В., *Културно-историческо наследство от култа към сакрализираната змия-змей в земите на тракийските сатри, Благоевград 2009*).

[399] Fol V., *The Forgotten Saint*, Sofia 1996, 42 (Фол В., *Забравената светица, София 1996, 42*).

possible also to suppose a presentation of the Thracian belief of the incest of the Great Goddess with her Son. In this case Domna queen and Marina embody the same image – the Great Goddess, who self-conceives, transforms in her new hypostasis, which she attains by going through a new cycle of nine years, as it is according to the song,[400] and unites with her Son-Sun. The love motifs in these songs are only a part of the love orientation of a number of rites performed during that period. As was mentioned above on the *Goreshtnitsi* (Hot days) the fire of the sedyanki is being lit, as in some places this lighting is done on the day of the Assumption of the Mother of God. Saint Marina is called a saint of the lefteri, i.e. the youths in a premarital age, but she is also the one who watches over their first love thrills and looks after the realisation of social relations. In places an orgiastic ritual practice is known, as the unmarried girls and boys indulge in playful banters in the cave of the saint.[401] This information is interesting, because the unification of the image of the Fiery Virgin, who is honoured in a cave and near water, with a sacrifice of a black lamb and in the same time having an orgiastic element in her ritual practice easily recalls the Thracian goddess with the epiclesis Zerynthia, who some of the ancient authors compare with Hekate, and others with Aphrodite. It is quite possible that this Thracian hypostasis of the Goddess has unified in herself what the Hellenes understood under Hekate – the chthonic and the multifaced nature and under Aphrodite – unifying in love. In this connection the knowing and the depicting of St Marina in the folk cult could in my opinion contribute to the understanding of this hypostasis of the Goddess. We could recall a similar calling of the chthonic virgin mistress of fire and snakes from the ancient magical practices:

---

[400] The song is sung on the Summer Solstice:
From *Collection of Bulgarian Folklore and Folk Studies 28*, 494 (*СбНУ 28, 494*).
[401] See Fol V., *The Forgotten Saint*, Sofia 1996, 92 (*Фол В., Забравената светица, София 1996, 92*).

In Bulgarian:
„Периян Маринки думаше:
- Марино, малка девойко,
мари знаеш ли, повниш ли,
на вашето село Гьоргьово,
какъв панагир ставаше?
- Малка бех, ге го заповних.
Хайде Перияне да подем
панагир да си науче.
 - Ми като конак немаме,
 на конак да кондисаме.
Пък Марина му думаше:
- Сред село конак ще сторим,
сред село на мегданете.
Станали та са тръгнали,
 сред село конак сторили.
Момите хоро сториха,
момите и момчетата.
Кат хи Марина погледна,
че на Периян думаше:
Я дай ми изин, Перияне,
и я на хоро да пода,
хорото да хми оправе.
И кя се фати Марина
между Илия и Петра.
Тие на Марина рекаха:
- Марино, малка девойко,
като те Периян украде,
за любов ли те украде
или те има за хубос,
за хубос да му прилягаш.
 - Той не ме има за любов,
еми ме има за хубос,
госкето да му дочаквам.
Силен се ветер изпена
та дигна бяла Марина
в синьо небо високо
и в доли дълбоки отнесе."

Мари Марино, света Марино!
Домна царица на слънце дума:

In English:
Periyan was saying to Marinka:
- Marina, you little girl,
do you know, do you remember,
in your village Gyorgyovo,
what celebration used to
happen?
- I was little, I didn't remember
it.
Come on, Periyan, let's go
so you could teach me how a
celebration is made.
- Well we don't have a chapel,
in the chapel to have a rest.
And Marina told him:
- In the middle of the village we
will make a chapel,
in the middle of the village, on
the square.
They got up and went,
in the middle of the village a
chapel they made.
The maidens made a line
dance,
the maidens and the lads.
When Marina saw them,
she told Periyan:
- Give me permission Periyan
so I could go to the line dance,
their line dance to put right.
And Marina gripped
between Elijah and Peter.
They told Marina:
- Marina little girl,
when Periyan took you,
did he take you for love
or he has you for beauty,
for beauty to match him.
- He doesn't have me for love,
but he has me for beauty,
his guests to welcome.
Strong wind came out
so it lifted white Marina
in the high blue sky
and took in the deep valleys.

Oh you Marina, saint Marina!
Domna queen speaks to the

- Ой слънце, слънце, ясно
високо!
Като ми грееш ясно високо,
ясно високо, та нашироко,
дали не знаеш биле за рожба,
биле за рожба, за клето сърце?
Ясното слънце тихом говори:
- Зная го, зная, Домно царице,
ала го кажат много далеко,
много далеко и много скъпо:
за торба платно, платно
ленено,
за кило жито, бела пшеница;
овчар го бере, стадо да кърми,
да има стадо ягнета шари,
ягнета шари и пресно млеко.
Домна царица тихом говори:
- Ой слънце, слънце, ясно
високо!
Набери ми го и донеси ми,
та да го варя и да го пия,
дано си стана пълна, непразна.
Ако се добие момиче рожба,
ако е момиче, халал да ти е;
ако е момче, халал да ми е!
Набрало слънце биле за рожба
и го набрало, и го занело,
та го варила Домна царица,
та го варила и го е пила
и е станала пълна, непразна,
и е добила момиче рожба,
момиче рожба, Света Марина.
Гледала го е девет години,
отвънка прага не го е пуснала,
да я не види ясното слънце,
ако ми я види, ке я отнеме.
Щом е сторила девет години,
клепало клепе рано в неделя;
то не било Боже клепало,
нало е била сама змеица,
сама змеица, златокрилица,
та да измами Домна царица.
Измамила е Домна царица,
на църква тръгна, Марини
дума:
- Мари, Марино, хубава керко!
Сичко във къщи да си
почистиш,
отвънка прага да не излизаш,
да не излизаш, сметта да
хвърлиш,
да не излизаш за вода д' идеш,
да не те види ясното слънце;
че ко те види ясното слънце,
ако те види, ке те вземе!
Марининете милните дружки,
те са тръгнали за вода д' идат,

sun:
- Oh sun, sun, clear and high!
As you are shining so high,
clear and high, even wide,
don't you know a herb for child,
a herb for child, for a poor
heart?
The clear sun quietly speaks:
- I know it, I know, Domna
queen,
but they say it is very far,
vary far and very costly:
for a bag of cloth, linen cloth,
for a kilo of wheat, white wheat;
a shepherd picks it, herd to
feed,
so the herd has motley lambs,
motley lambs and milk.
Domna queen quietly speaks:
- Oh sun, sun, clear and high!
Pick it up for me and bring it to
me,
so I could boil it and drink it,
and hopefully become full,
pregnant.
If I have a baby girl,
if it is a girl, it is for you;
if it is a boy, it is for me!
The sun picked the herb for a
child
and it picked it, and it brought
it,
so Domna queen boiled it,
boiled it and drank it
and she became full, pregnant,
and she had a baby girl,
a baby girl, Saint Marina.
She looked after her nine years,
didn't let her outside the
doorstep,
so the clear sun couldn't see
her,
if he sees her, he will take her.
When she became nine years
old,
a semantron beats early on
Sunday;
it wasn't God's semantron,
but it was a dragoness herself,

за вода д' идат, Марина викали:
- Хайде, Марино, за вода д' идем!
Марина забрави майчини думи,
менци е зела, на вода отишла,
вода налела и се върнала.
Ка я виделоясното слънце,
та си посегна от синьото небо,
та си издигна бела Марина,
та я издигна във синьо небо.

a dragoness herself, golden winged,
so she could deceive Domna queen.
She deceived Domna queen,
so she went to church, and spoke to Marina:
- Dear Marina, pretty daughter!
Clean everything in the house,
don't go outside the doorstep,
don't go out, the litter to throw,
don't go out for water,
so the clear sun doesn't see you,
because if the clear sun sees you,
if he sees you, he will take you!
The dear friends of Marina,
they went for water,
for water, they called Marina:
- Come on, Marina, let us go for water!
Marina forgot her mother's words,
she took the cauldrons, for water she went,
water she poured and she came back.
When the clear sun saw her,
he reached out from the blue sky,
he lifted white Marina,
so he lifted her in the blue sky.

Description of practice 43 FOR LOVE PGM XXXVI.187-210[402]

Love spell of attraction: On an unbaked piece of pottery write with a bronze stylus: *"Hekate, you, Hekate, triple-formed, since every seal of every* [love spell of attraction] *has been completed, I adjure you / by the great name of ABLANATHANA and by the power of AGRAMARI because I adjure you, you who possess the fire, ONYR, and those in it, that she, NN, / be set afire, that she come in pursuit of me, NN, because I am holding in my right hand the two serpents and the victory of IAO SABAOTH and the great name BILKATRI MOPHECHE, who brandishes fire, ..., that she love me / completely and be aflame and on fire for me; aye, and tortured too. I am SYNKOUTOUEL."*

[Write] 8 characters like this: *"Grant me, indeed the favour of all, ADONAI.*

In original:[403]

'Αγωγή. εἰς ⟨ὄ⟩cτρακον ὠμὸν χαλκῷ τραφίῳ ‖ ''Εκάτη, c', 'Εκάτη, τρί-μορφοc, πεπληρωμένων | πάντων πάcηc cφραγιcμῶν, ὁρκίζω cε, ‖ τὸν μεγάλον ὄνομα τοῦ 'Αβλαθανα, καὶ | τὴν δύναμιν τοῦ 'Αγραμαρι, ὅτι cε ὁρκίζω, | cε, ⟨ὃc⟩ τὸ πῦρ 'Ονυρ κατέχε[ι]c καὶ τοὺc ἐν αὐτῷ, ⟨τὴν⟩ δεῖνα ‖ πυρωθῆναι, διώκειν πρὸc ἐμὲ τὸν δεῖνα, ὅτι | κατέχω μὲ τὴν δεξιὰν τοὺc δύο δράκωνταc | καὶ τὴν νίκην τοῦ 'Ιαω Cαβαώθ, | καὶ τὸ μεγάλο ὄνομα Βιλκατρι'μοφεχε, | τὸ πῦρ παλλομένη, † cτουτουκατουτου δια|φιλῆ⟨c⟩αί με καιομένην, πυρουμένην πρόc | με, ναί, βαcανιζομένη⟨ν⟩. Cυνκουτουὲλ ἐγώ.' ⟨γράφε⟩ η' χαρι|κτῆραc, οὕτωc· 'δόc γέ

μοι τὴν χάριν πάντων, | 'Αδωναί,

In the described rite the same elements can be seen – fire, snake, inflaming in love. Similar magical ritual practice is preserved also in a folklore environment. The orgiastic finds its magical expression in the very lighting of the festive fires of the *sedyanki*. This act is a collective love magic. In

---

[402] Betz H., *The Greek Magical Papyri in translation, including the Demotical spells*, Chicago/London 1986, 274 and Preisendanz K., Die griechschen Zauberpapyri, II, Leipzig 1931, 169-170.
[403] The text in original is from Preisendanz K., *Die griechschen Zauberpapyri*, II, Leipzig 1931, 169-170.

this connection I'm going to quote one of the ways of performing the rite described in the ethnographic literature.

Description of practice 44 LIGHTING THE *SEDYANKA* FIRE[404]

The lighting of the *sedyanka* fire is done only once each year. It becomes common for the villages (neighbourhoods), whose youths make their sedyanki together. In the first region (the villages around Tryavna, Balkan mountain) the lighting has the following order: some days before the Assumption of the Mother of God (August 28th) every unmarried woman strives to take a stake from the fence and the *pomet*[405] from the oven of the young man's house. A day earlier the unmarried women go around the fields and look for pumpkin stems. In the evening they take all these things and leave them somewhere in the open to *"stay for the night under the stars"*. On the evening of the Assumption of the Mother of God after sunset all the unmarried women gather at the end of the village on a crossroad. They light a fire on the crossroad and arrange in a circle around it. The eldest woman takes the pomet brought by her and makes with it three symbolical moves *'as if she is sweeping'*, and drawls:

> As the oven is swept with the pomet
>
> so the lads should be swept from their houses!
>
> From their houses to be swept,
>
> to come to sedyanka![406]

All the other unmarried women go round the fire three times and jump over it three times. After that the eldest woman throws the pomet in the fire and says:

> As the pomet burns in the fire,
>
> so the lads should burn for the maidens![407]

Again all go round and jump over the fire three times and arrange themselves once more in a circle. Now each woman

---

[404] Goev A., *Lighting the sedyanka fire* // Bulgarian Ethnology, book 1, Sofia 1979, 70-71 (*Гоев А., Заклаждане на седянка* // *Българска етнология кн. 1, София 1979, 70-71*).
[405] *Pomet* is a piece of leather tied to a stick, with which the hearth is cleaned.
[406] In Bulgarian:
Както се измита пещта с помета,
така да се измитат и ергените от къщите!
От къщи да се измитат,
на седянка да дойдат!
[407] In Bulgarian:
Както гори помета в огъня,
така да горят и ергените за момите!

separately makes three independent moves, as if she is sweeping with her pomet and says in her mind with the name of her beloved:

> *As the oven is swept with the pomet,*
>
> *so (the name) should be swept from his house!*
>
> *From his house to be swept – to come to sedyanka!*
>
> *To come to sedyanka – to sit by me!*
>
> *To sit by me – to fall in love with me!*
>
> *To fall in love with me – to take me!*[408]

When she has said that, the woman goes around the fire three times and jumps over it three times. After that she throws the pomet in the fire and says:

> *As the pomet burns in the fire,*
>
> *so (the name) should burn for me!*[409]

And again she makes three rounds and three jumps. When the last woman finishes, all gather round again in a circle. The eldest takes the stake brought by her, throws it in the fire and says:

> *This stake stops the lads.*
>
> *In fire it should burn – hole should open!*
>
> *Hole should open – lads to pass!*
>
> *Lads to pass – to come to sedyanka.*[410]

All the other unmarried women go round the fire three times and jump over it three times at the same time. After that they separately throw their stakes and say in their mind:

> *This stake stops (the name).*
>
> *In a fire it should burn – hole should open!*
>
> *Hole should open (the name) to pass the hole!*
>
> *To pass the hole – to come to sedyanka!*
>
> *To come to sedyanka – to sit by me!*

---

[408] In Bulgarian:
Както се измита пещта с помета,
така да се измита и (т.е. името – бел. моя) от къщи!
От къщи да се измете — на седянка да дойде!
На седянка да дойде -- при мене да седне!
При мене да седне - мене да залюби!
Мене да залюби — мене да вземе!
[409] In Bulgarian:
Както гори помета в огъня,
така да гори и (т.е. името – бел. моя) за мене.
[410] In Bulgarian:
Тоз кол ергените спира.
В огън да изгори - дупка да отвори!
Дупка да отвори - ергени да минат!
Ергени да минат - на седянка да дойдат.

To sit by me – to fall in love with me!

To fall in love with me – to take me![411]

Again the triple rotation and jumping of the fire follows. After that the unmarried women arrange in an open circle. The eldest is in front and the youngest ends it. The last takes the stem and all go round the fire three times, saying in choir:

As the stem drags after us,

so the lads should drag after us![412]

This text is pronounced three times, one time at a round. After the third round the stem is thrown in the fire and all say:

As the stem burns in the fire,

so the lads should burn for the maidens![413]

And again they jump and go round the fire three times.

After finishing the common act an individual dragging is done again by each woman with reference to her beloved, as they do with the pomet and the stake.

In the end all place potatoes[414] in the embers to be baked. Later at an appropriate occasion they give it to their chosen man to eat it. After that they sit by the fire and begin to sing. From this moment on the sedyanki can be made.

In this rite there are a number of ritual elements that are of particular importance, which indicates its archaic ritual origins. The collective magical ritual practice is relatively rare and it is of great importance that in the Bulgarian ethnic territory we find it preserved on such a scale. Its relation to exactly this calendar period suggests that the connection between the celebrations from the end of July to the end of

---

[411] In Bulgarian:

Този кол (т.е. името– бел. моя) спира.

В огън да изгори — дупка да отвори!

Дупка да отвори(т.е. името– бел. моя) дупка да мине!

Дупка да мине - на седянка да дойде!

На седянка да дойде — при мене да седне!

При мене да седне - мене да залюби!

Мене да залюби мене да вземе!

[412] In Bulgarian:

Както се влачи власината след нас,

така да се влачат и ергените след нас!

[413] In Bulgarian:

Както гори власината в огъня,

така да горят и ергените за момите!

[414] The potato as a plant doesn't originate from this latitude so it probably came into use in the practice later, but its symbolism of a root, i.e. to root and the act is a reasonable element. It is possible to suggest that in earlier times another root was used for this final act, probably some sort of turnip or something else.

August have a strong fiery and love focus, as they are believed to be under the protection of the Fiery Virgin – regardless whether she is called Marina or Maria.[415] The aim of the magic rite is to cause love in the unmarried man towards the maidens and it is for this purpose that they are being ritually called, i.e. their feelings, their desire is awaken by means of ritual acts. The inventory used in the rite – pomet from an oven, stake from the fence of his house, stem from a pumpkin, are all connected with liminal places and on the other hand also with love symbolism – to burn, to drag. The place is also not chosen by accident – the crossroad has a sacred symbolism and magical rationalisation from antiquity until today. The ritual ends with the magically charged object being brought into contact with its chosen target – i.e. the men are fed with the potatoes.

The mentioned rites and beliefs in connection with this calendar period and the image of the Fiery Virgin ruling over it give an opportunity for a deeper understanding of the inclusiveness of the ancient Goddess, who the folk belief hides and preserves in a Christian mask and a seemingly Christian hue. Under this new veil are easily seen and expressed the mighty powerful ancient Goddesses, who bear on them the snakes as a decoration, reveal their image in the darkness of the cavern recesses and inflame the skies with fiery tongues.

---

[415] As it was already said in the folk belief the saint herself is called Fiery Marina and Fiery Maria, as the second is connected with the celebration of Mary Magdalene on July 22nd and is called also Maria Oparlia (Maria who singes).

THE SHE-WOLF

With the end of summer and the harvesting of fruits, the year turns to its darker side. With the increasing of the night comes a period during which even in antiquity the Balkan peoples honoured the Goddess in her chthonic hypostasis. The giver of fruits is worshipped also as a receiver of death, as a mistress of the earth's bowels and is called in the rites to give again her all-generating power, which preserves the seed in the darkness of her womb and awakens it again for life when the new agrarian cycle comes. This period could be conventionally related to the months of October, November and December in the contemporary calendar. During antiquity this was the time when the Thesmophoria[416] were held in Ancient Greece, these mysterious rites of the goddess Demeter and her daughter Persephone. In Rome the Good Goddess – Bona Dea was honoured at the beginning of December.[417] The protagonists in these rites were the women, who through sacred deeds and words had to obtain the blessing of the Goddess, who fills the earth's bowels with her presence. The role of the man in these rites is only complementary - he must provide an opportunity for women to honour the Goddess. The blood sacrifice, the chthonic, the mysteriousness and the taboo over the numerous ritual elements assigns these rituals to the mystery acts, which must call the deity. This is a time to meet the tranquillity of

---

[416] Thesmophoria is a festival dedicated to the Goddesses Demeter and Persephone, which was celebrated for three days, resp. 11-13 Pyanepsion (October-November). The ancient authors also accentuate the ancient origin of the festival and claim that it was known to the Pelasgians. It is connected with sowing and its name derives from the Demeter epithet Thesmophoros, i.e. the one, who determined the rules and laws (thesmos), according to which people work hard for their livelihood. The three days are called respectively: the first – Catodos and Anodos, i.e. descent and ascent; the second – Nesteia, i.e. fasting and the third – Kalligeneia, i.e. beautiful birth. Significant for the rite is the sacrifice of a suckling pig in underground abysses and caves called megara, as well as ithyphallic bakery products and mixing the remains of pigs from the previous year with the grains for sowing. In this connection see Harrison J., *Prolegomena to the Study of Greek religion*, Cambridge 1908, 120-131; Burkert W., *Griechische Religion der archaischen und klassischen Zeit*, zweite Auflage, Stuttgart 2011, 364-370; Kotova D., *The Thesmophoria, Women's Festival Complex*, Sofia 1995 (*Котова Д., Тесмофориите. Женски празничен комплекс, София 1995*).

[417] The Good Goddess or Bona Dea is called the Goddess in Rome, who had a nocturnal festival in the beginning of December, which was accessible only for women. The men funded the festival that took place in the home of the senior magistrate and aimed to obtain the blessing of the Goddess over the city and the nation. She is connected even by ancient authors with a number of other great chthonic Goddesses like Hekate, Semele and with regard to the pig that was sacrificed to her also with the goddesses Demeter and Persephone. In connection with the veneration to the Good Goddess see Brouwer H.H.J., *Bona Dea: the sources and a description of the cult*, Leiden 1989.

death occurring in nature, but also a time for rest in human society, which after the harvest of fruits and the sowing of grains, turns its glare to the earth, remembers its ancestors and prepares for the long dark and cold winter nights resounding with the howl of wolves.

In the literature sources there is no evidence whether the Thracians performed similar ritual acts in this period and if such honour to the Goddess was seen, as in Ancient Greece and Rome. But it is possible to suggest that it existed among them too. Similar traces can be sought in the relic ritual practices of the Balkan peoples, which have preserved a memory of those long gone times.

Due to limited space it is impossible to describe in detail the Thesmophoria and the festival of Bona Dea,[418] but as previously mentioned, a significant moment for both of them is the excluding of men from the rite, which is performed only by women. In the ritual acts there is a blood sacrifice and wine drinking, i.e. the women do things that in principle are not allowed to them by social norms.

In both rituals the chthonic is strongly expressed – in the Thesmophoria the going down in underground premises, the so called Megara, and in the rites of Bona Dea the nocturnal celebration.

Examining some of the moments of the autumn-winter ritual calendar of the Bulgarians (and also of other Balkan people) could help in expanding our knowledge of the ancient beliefs connected with this period, because for a great number of them it could be claimed that they are remnants from the pre-Christian age.

---

[418] For comparison of the peculiarities of both festivals see Versnel, Hendrik S., *The Roman Festival for Bona Dea and the Greek Thesmophoria //* Inconsistencies in Greek and Roman Religion. 2. Transition and Reversal in Myth and Ritual, Leiden, 1993, 235–260.

55 - The She-Wolf by Georgi Mishev

56 - The Good Goddess[419]

[419]
http://img0.liveinternet.ru/images/attach/c/0//43/445/43445697_12415
22568_000000.jpg <06.11.2011>.

57 - Saint Petka[420]

According to Bulgarian traditional culture a turning point from which the dark half of the year starts is the celebration of St Petka – October 14th. According to the most widespread beliefs the sowing must have finished by this day.[421] The Christian saint honoured at that time and called Petka (Parascheva of Epivates)[422] bears in her worship a multitude of pre-Christian traits, on which I'm going to focus in detail, because in some of their elements can be seen bright echoes of Paleo-Balkan and Thracian antiquity.

Unlike in the canonical concept, in folk belief the saint bears a number of features that define her as a chthonic

---

[420] http://www.sl-news.sliven.net/index.php?id=53256 <04.11.2011>.
[421] Nokolova V., *Braid in the field*, Sofia 1999, 24-25 (*Николова В., Плитка на нивата, София 1999, 24-25*).
[422] Because of the multiple transfers of the remains of St Petka within the Balkan Peninsula she becomes a common-Balkan saint – Radoslavova D., *The service for reverend Petka in the Bulgarian manuscripts from XVII century* // Christian hagiology and folk beliefs, Sofia 2008, 123 (*Радославова Д., Службата за преподобна Петка в българските ръкописи от XVII век. // Християнска агиология и народни вярвания, София 2008, 123*).

personage.[423] The Christian saint is a successor of a more ancient cult to the female mistress of Friday, which in this case appears also with some other different functions. Unlike in western folklore, where Friday is dedicated to the goddesses of love,[424] in the Bulgarian ritual tradition Friday is connected with a number of prohibitions for performing female activities and is usually connected with fasting.[425] The Christian St Petka, as a personification of the mistress of this day, also adopts a multitude of chthonic features from her ancient predecessor. Unlike the cult of Paraskeva Pyatnitsa among the Eastern Slavs,[426,427] among the

---

[423] In this connection is also one moment of her hagiography and namely the founding of her remains:

Not far from the place where the reverend was buried, a stylite used to dwell. By that time some sailor died. His body was thrown near that place. The stench from the decomposing body was so disgusting, that the stylite was forced to come down from the pillar and beg the nearby residents to bury the body of the unfortunate man.

The devout, but simple people began to dig the grave and found in the earth the body of reverend Petka, which had preserved incorruptible. They got scared. They didn't know what to do. They were ignorant in the spiritual things. In their simplicity they left the incorruptible body in the grave and buried the stinking body in it.

On the next day, one of those devout people, named Georgi, dreamt of a maiden, whole in light, dressed in royal clothes and surrounded by soldiers. One of the soldiers approached Georgi, grabbed his hand and told him:

- Why have you despised the body of reverend Parascheva in such way? Take it out of the stinking grave and lay it in a coffin. The God King wants to glorify her on earth.

Then the divine queen said to the confused Georgi:

- Hurry to take out my remains. I can't stand the stench. My homeland is Epivates, where you live.

In the same night a devout woman, Euphemia, had a similar vision.

On the other day the two appearances were rapidly divulged. The grave was excavated. The incorruptible body was taken out and placed in a reverently solemn manner in the cathedral church "Holy Apostles".

Many healings happened at the holy remains: blind began to see, lame began to walk, those suffering from severe, incurable diseases were healed. (http://www.pravoslavieto.com/life/10.14_sv_Petka_Epivatska_Bulgarska.htm#1 <06.11.2011>).

[424] Among Romans Friday is called the day of Venus - Dies Veneris, in contemporary French is vendredi, and among the Germanic languages the name of the day comes from the goddess of love Freya – in German Freitag, in English Friday.

[425] Vutova V., *The food on Friday – profane and sacred* // The profane and sacred food, Gabrovo 2010, 70-72 (*Вутова В., Храната в петъчния ден – профанна и сакрална* // *Храната сакрална и профанна, Габрово 2010, 70-72*).

[426] See Chicherov V.I., *The Winter Period of the Russian Agricultural Calendar in the XVI to XIX Centuries*, Moscow 1957, 41-43 (*Чичеров В.И., Зимний период русского земледельческого календаря XVI-XIX веков, Москва 1957, 41-43*), as well as Pavlova M., *Wednesday and Friday in connection with the spinning - Ethnogenesis, early history and culture of the Slavs*, Moscow 1985, 66-69 (*Павлова М., Среда и пятница в связи с прядением – Этногенез, ранняя этническая история и культура славян, Москва 1985, 66-69*).

[427] Among the Eastern Slavs the cult of St Petka is connected with that of the Slavic goddess Mokosh. In this relation there St Parascheva-Pyatnitsa is considered as a guardian of springs and wells, she is associated with the

Bulgarians, and also among Romanians, Greeks and Albanians, saint Petka is connected not only with female activities like spinning and weaving, but also with wolves and the snake. In some regions it was believed that her celebration begins the so-called Wolf days, which are dedicated to honouring the wolf and are connected with a number of prohibitions and ritual acts and which will be discussed later in this chapter. In this connection she is believed also to be a mistress of wolves.[428,429] In a number of cases the saint appears as a snake, when a ritual prohibition was violated and she warns or punishes the perpetrator.[430] The saint is believed in the Balkans to be a protectress of spinning and weaving and even in the folk notion she is believed to carry a spindle or a distaff, but once again in a gruesome appearance – dressed in black and with teeth to the knees, awakening the dead and punishing those who don't keep the prohibitions for her day.[431] In some regions in the folk imagination she is even seen with breasts to the knees.[432] Often she is perceived as a part of the three Goddesses of fate and enters into a sacred triad with St Nedelya (St Sunday) and St Mother of God, or with St Nedelya (St Nedelya) and St Sryada (St Wednesday), as according to some ethnographical evidences in some areas the population begins its prayers with addressing St Petka,

---

water element and is honoured with offerings of weaving accessories in sacred wells, see Maksimov S., *Unclean, Unknown and Christian Force*, Saint Petersburg 1903, 516-518 (*Максимов С., Нечистая, неведомая и крестная сила, Санкт Петербург 1903, 516-518*).

[428] Krastanova K., *The Golden loom*, Plovdiv 2007, 96 (*Кръстанова К., Златният стан, Пловдив 2007, 96*)

[429] Popov R., *Saint Menas in the calendar tradition of the Balkan peoples.* // History, 2004, №№ 4-5: 79-88 (*Попов Р., Свети Мина в календарната традиция на балканските народи.* // *История, 2004, №№ 4-5: 79-88*).

[430] In this connection see Krastanova K., *The Golden loom*, Plovdiv 2007, 98 (*Кръстанова К., Златният стан, Пловдив 2007, 98*) and the record which R. Popov gives - Popov R., *Saints and demons on the Balkans*, Plovdiv 2008, 70 (*Попов Р., Светци и демони на балканите, Пловдив 2008, 70*):

Speaks the fierce snake,	Проговори люта змия,
fierce snake, viper:	люта змия, пепелянка:
I am not a fierce snake,	Я не съм си люта змия,
I am Saint Petka,	язе съм си света Петка,
why do you plough on Petkovden (Feast day of saint Petka),	оти ореш на Петковден,
why do you plough to finish your work.	оти ореш да дореш.

Here the saint appears to the perpetrator, who hasn't kept the prohibition for working on her day.

[431] For the above relations and notions see Detelic' M., *St Paraskeve in the Balkan context* – Folklore 121, 2010, 94-105.

[432] Georgieva Iv., *Bulgarian folk mythology*, Sofia 1993, 183 (*Георгиева Ив., Българска народна митология, София 1993, 183*).

St Nedelya and St Mother of God.[433] Along with the chthonic characteristics of the saint she is a healer, especially of ill eyes, infertility and also a guardian of the home altar – the hearth. The calendar period in which the saint is honoured is related with two other personages, namely St Demetrius and the Archangel Michael. Bearing in mind the function of St Demetrius as a horseman and of Archangel Michael as a Soul-reaper,[434] we could presume unification in one sacred period of days honouring the Goddess, the Horseman God and the Guide of souls. In this time span a number of ritual acts are performed, which are related with giving gratitude to the giver of fertility, with ensuring health during winter, with honouring of the ancestors and with sacrifice to the guardian spirit of the home and village. Belonging to this period are also some specific calendar days dedicated to mice (October 27th) and to wolves (different in number, but most often ten days beginning from November 11th), as well as the last day of November, which is dedicated to the bear (November 30th).

To ensure health during the upcoming winter, the Bulgarian people used to perform a number of rites, which are focused on strengthening the personal energy through unification with the divine within the food from the ritual sacrifice shared with it. A significant rite, performed in this period is the so called *Kokosha cherkva* (Hen sacrifice).[435]

Description of practice 45 *KOKOSHA CHERKVA* (HEN SACRIFICE)[436]

This rite is performed entirely by women, and it is not until modern times and only in some regions that men are permitted to it, but only to the ritual meal.

'Hen sacrifice' has a moving date according to the different regions, but it is in the period between the day of St Petka (October 14th) and Archangelovden (from Bulgarian '*day of the Archangels*', the Synaxis of the Archangel Michael

[433] Marinov D., *Living antiquity, book I*, Ruse 1891, 55 (Маринов Д., *Жива старина, кн. I, Русе 1891, 55*).

[434] He is called soul-reaper, because folk belief attributes to him the function of taking out and leading the souls of the dying, which approximates him to Hermes Psychopompos and other deities of death.

[435] Kokosha cherkva is an interesting name, because the very word "*cherkva*" or "*tsarkva*" derives from the Greek kyriakon and means "*God's (place)*", i.e. defines the hen in this case as an offering to the God, i.e. a sacrifice.

[436] The description is made following the article of Popov R., *The rite Kokosha cherkva among the Bulgarians* // Bulgarian Ethnography, book 2, Sofia 1986, 15-22 (Попов Р., *Обичаят "Кокоша черква" у българите* // Българска етнография, кн. 2, София 1986, 15-22).

and the Other Bodiless Powers – November 8th). It is always performed in a detached place – church yard, consecrated ground, under a venerable oak or on a high mound. The ritual protagonists are only women. Every woman brings from her house one black hen, which is the main sacrificial animal for that day. With the hen every woman brings three sourdough breads and wine. Additionally other animals could be sacrificed – ram, lamb, hogget or a barren cow, but they must be black too.

The butchering of the brought black hens is done by the eldest woman among those present. The blood from the butchered hens is gathered and one part from it is buried in the ground, and with another part bread is kneaded, which is consecrated in the church and after that it is distributed among the women who took part in the rite. The heads of the butchered hens are arranged on a stone plate facing east. The birds are boiled together in a cauldron and if there is another sacrificial animal it is boiled separately (in another cauldron). While the sacrificial hens are boiled, the women in festive clothing and with basil bunches play a ritual line dance called 'slyadnoto horo'. This line dance is played as the women align one behind the other, but don't take their hands, and step slowly without music; they go round to the right around the cauldron, where the sacrifice is boiled, and sing the following song:

"*They gathered, they gathered,*
on the high mountain,
eminent celebration to make,
eminent celebration of Kostadin.[437]
They were eating, drinking
and a good word speaking:
-May today doesn't come
Sarandzhe the Wallachian voivode,[438]
our meal to scatter,
our celebration to ruin...
They were still speaking,
and here he is, Sarandzhe is coming,
everyone got up
and greeted him.
One widow's bastard
he didn't get up for Sarandzhe

---

[437] *Kostadin* is the folk name of St Constantine.
[438] *Sarandzhe* is a personal name; Wallachian voivode means a war leader from the north, from Wallachia.

and didn't greet him.
Then Sarandzhe spoke:
- Are you such a hero
or are you so insolent?
- I am not so insolent,
but I am a powerful hero,
come on let's go wrestle!
They wrestled and wrestled
two days and three nights.
Neither the hero defeats,
nor Sarandzhe defeats.
Sarandzhe begged him:
- Loosen up, hero!
Hero doesn't loosen up,
but he hit him in the ground,
so he left him on his place."[439]

After doing this and the line dance is played, the women spread cloths on the ground, used for wrapping the bread, and distribute the sacrifice amongst each other.

---

[439] In Bulgarian:
"Събрали са се, събрали,
на високата планина,
личен панаир да правят,
личен панаир Костадин.
Тъй ми ядяха, пияха
и добра дума думаха:
- Дано му днеска не дойде
Сарандже влашка войвода,
трапезата да ни разпръсне,
панаир да ни раздигне...
Още ми дума думаха,
ей го Сарандже довтаса,
всички му диван станали
и чапраз силям му взели.
Едно вдовиче копелче,
то му диван не стана
и чапраз силям му не взе.
Тогава Сарандже продума:
- Да не си толкоз юначен
или си толкоз ходулче?
– Нито съм толкоз ходулче,
най съм си мощно юначе,
хайде щем да се бориме!
Борили са се, борили,
два дена и три нощи.
Нито юначе надвива,
нита Сарандже надвива.
Сарандже му се молеше:
- Поотпусни се, юначе!
Юначе не се отпуска,
най го в земята удари,
та го на място остави."

In the described rite several elements make an impression, which are also known from the ancient festivals held in this calendar period. Only women participate in it, they make a blood sacrifice, which they taste. The participation of men in the rite is forbidden, and where it is permitted, it is for a little boy who hasn't reached sexual maturity. This doesn't break the ritual prohibition, because that boy is not considered a man, i.e. the prohibition doesn't apply to him. Again we see the inheritance of the sacred areas, often mounds are used for the performing of the ritual. A part of the sacrificial blood is buried and with another part bread is kneaded. This act itself makes a huge impression, because it has no analogue in any other rite, except the tasting of the raw meat in the ritual practices of the nestinari,[440] which in turn is a relic from the Thracian mysteries. Of course in this case we speak of a typological similarity. Placing the heads of the hens on a stone plate facing east associates the practice to the rites connected with the Sun God. His presence in the rite is evidenced also with defining the rite as an *'eminent celebration Kostadin'*, and from the ritual tradition of the nestinari it is known that this Christian saint – St Constantine in the folk notion, continues the belief in the Son of the Great Goddess. Around the vessel with the sacrificial food a ritual dance is played and especially to the right. All these elements find their expression in the lyrics of the song that is sung. In its

---

[440] The *nestinarstvo* is a fiery ritual practice and must not be mistaken with firewalking. This relic from antiquity is preserved in the region of the Strandzha Mountain, in Bulgaria and in Northern Greece. The culmination and most popular moment is the dance on embers by the men and women obsessed by the divine presence, called nestinari. According to their idea, by going in the fire they burn everything unclean and in this way purify the community and assist in its wellbeing and revival. A number of festivals are celebrated in the nestinari ritual tradition, but the most respected is the day of St Constantine and Helen (May 21st/June 3rd), as in this saint couple the nestinari continue the ancient worship of the Great Goddess and her Son Fire/Sun. The nestinari ritual tradition is a complicated complex of beliefs and practices, to which a number of scientific research is dedicated, but I personally would recommend the descriptions of Mihail Arnaudov from 1933 and later, see Arnaudov M., *Essays on Bulgarian folklore*, third facsimile edition, Sofia 1996, 372-531 (Арнаудов М., *Очерци по българския фолклор, трето фототипно издание, София 1996, 372-531*), as well as the most comprehensive survey in my opinion of this problematic area with quoted literature – Fol V., Neykova R., *Fire and music*, Sofia 2000 (Фол В., *Нейкова Р., Огън и музика, София 2000*). Some authors (for instance Xygalatas D., *Ethnography, Historiography, and the Making of History in the Tradition of the Anastenaria*, History and Anthropology 22 (1), 2011, 57–74) don't accept and question the relic nature and ancient origin of the nestinari ritual tradition, but personally I can't agree with them, because they are not familiar with the ethnographic records and the publications on the Bulgarian nestinari, thus they miss a number of significant elements, which are important for the interpretation of the ritual tradition.

contents the main motif is the appearance of the *'Wallachian voivode'*, i.e. a war leader from the north, which according to some scholars is an image of the *hala*,[441] i.e. the destructive force of nature. His opponent is *'widow's bastard' – son of a woman without a man, with unknown father*, who could be interpreted as the residual power of the Son of the Great Goddess – the Sun-God, who defeats the cold coming from the north.

The position of the rite in the period between the day of St Petka and the day of Archangel Michael is also interesting. If in this case St Petka inherits the Goddess of the underworld, Archangel Michael in folk belief is the one who takes the souls and in this connection he is compared with Hermes Psychopompos, but could also be linked with the God of the underworld himself. St Petka and Archangel Michael are mentioned also in a folk song, which has a very clear ancient flavour and which sheds light on the images and their functions according to the people:

Are there thunders, or the earth is shaking,
or the sea fishes are fighting,
or the water is beating the shores?
There are no thunders, nor is the earth shaking,
the sea fishes are not fighting,
nor the water is beating the shores,
but three brothers are dividing a share:
the one is saint Elijah the Thunderer,
the other is the old saint Nicholas,
and the third is saint Rangel.[442]
They divided for three years.
First they gave to saint Elijah,
they gave him the depths of the earth,
they gave him the heights of the sky,
and gave him the fierce thunders.
After him Nicholas took part from the world
and to him they rightfully gave –
they gave him the waters and the fords.
After him give saint Rangel,
they gave him the souls of the people.
The brothers have just separated the world,

---

[441] See Mollov T., *Myth – epos – history. Old-Bulgarian Historical-Apocalyptical Stories* (992-1092-1492), Varna 2002 (*Моллов Т., Мит – епос – история. Старобългарските историко-апокалиптични сказания (992-1092-1492). Варна 2002*). http://liternet.bg/publish/tmollov/mei/5_3.htm <06.11.2011>.
[442] Rangel is a common name for Archangel Michael.

three sisters came flying:

the one is saint Nedelya,[443]

the other is venerable Maria,

and the third is saint Petka.[444]

Spoke venerable Maria:

- Hear me, Thunderer Elijah,

and you, brother Nicholas,

and you, saint Rangel,

the people have forgotten their God:

they don't honour every saint of God,

neither they come to the church for service.

You give me the keys of the padlocks,

so we may lock the earth in the deep,

we may lock the sky in the high,

we may lock the sun in the east,

and we may lock the slush from the sky.

So the sun doesn't shine for three years,

So the rain doesn't fall for three years,

then the people would bow to God,

they would bow, they would pray to God.

And they gave them the keys to the padlocks.

Lock the earth in the depths,

lock the sky in the heights,

they locked the rain in the sky,

they locked the sun in the east.

And for three years the sun didn't shine,

for three years rain didn't fall.

But they didn't obey the God,

they didn't pray to God.

And venerable Maria flied back

and with her came saint Nedelya,

and with her came saint Petka,

and she wanted the keys from the padlocks:

- Oh, give us the keys from the padlocks,

the people don't want to obey God,

---

[443] St Nedelya (Saint Kyriake, from Greek kyriake κυριακη the day of the Lord, i.e. Sunday, in Bulgarian nedelya неделя) is in the folk notion a guardian of the day of Sunday and she often appears only with her sisters saint Sryada (from Bulgarian sryada сряда, i.e. Wednesday) and saint Petka (St Paraskeve from Greek paraskevi παρασκευή literally "Preparation" as the day of preparation for Sabbath, i.e. Friday, in Bulgarian petak петък). In the quoted song in place of St Sryada is St Mother of God, but the identification is not accidental, because in the folk belief the day of Wednesday is dedicated to her.

[444] See previous note.

don't want to pray to God.
Oh, give us the keys from the padlocks,
to unlock black smallpox.
And they gave her the keys from the padlocks,
they released the black smallpox,
released it, brothers, among the people!
Three years the illness beats,
six years the sun didn't shine,
six years the rain didn't fall.
The people got very frightened,
they got frightened, they prayed to God,
they prayed to God, they obeyed God.
And they went to the church, to service: every Friday,
every Sunday and everyone praises every saint of God.
And then venerable Maria flied back,
called the three brothers:
- Give me the keys from the padlock,
to unlock the sun from the east,
to unlock the slush from the sky
and to unlock the earth from the deep.
And they gave her the keys from the padlock,
and she unlocked the sun from the east
and she unlocked the earth from the deep,
and she unlocked the rain from the sky.
Then the sun shined
and the rain began to pour,
and it irrigated this black earth,
and they received plentiful white wheat and this sparkling
wine was born.
With bread the people got fed and sparkling wine they
drank...

In the original Bulgarian: [445]

> *Дали ми гърми, или ми се земля тресе,*
> *или се биу рибе приморкине,*
> *или се биу воде от брегове?*
> *Ни ми гърми, ни се земля тресе,*
> *не ми се биу рибе приморкине,*
> *ни се бие вода от брегове,*
> *но се деле до троица бракя:*
> *едно си е гърмовник свети Илия,*

---

[445] *Collection of Bulgarian Folklore and Folk Studies 10, 24, № 1* (*СбНУ 10, 24,№ 1*).

друго си стари свети Никола,
трекьо е свети Рангел.
Делише се три године дъна.
Най-напред отделите светому Илиу,
отделите му землю у дълбине
и отделите му небо у висине,
и отделите му страшни гърмове.
По нег заделите светоме Николе
и нему право отделите -
отделите му воде и бродове.
По нега заделите светоме Рангели,
отделите му душе от народе.
Тамън му се бракя угодиле,
долетеше до три ми ле сестре:
едно ми е света Неделя,
а другото блажена Мария,
а трекята е света Петка.
Изговори блажена Мария:
- Чуйте мене, гърмовник Илийо,
и ти, брате Николо,
и ти, свети Рангеле,
народ си Бога забравило:
не си служи свак светъц господски,
ни па иду у църкве раване!
Да ми дадете ключи от катанци,
да заключим землю у дълбине,
да заключим небо у висине,
да заключим слънце на изтока
и да заключим киша от небеса.
Да не огрее слънце за три годин,
да не капне киша за три годин,
ега би се народ Богу покорило,
покорило, Богу помолило.
И они вой върлише ключи от катанци.
Заключите землю у дълбине,
заключите небо у висине,
заключише киша от небеса,
заключише слънце на изтока.
И три годин слънце не огрея,
за три годин киша не си паде.
Не стеше се и Богу покоре,
не стеше се ни Богу помоле.
Па долете блажена Мария
и със ню дойде и света Неделя,
и с ню дойде и света Петка,
посакаше па ключи от катанци:
- О, дайте ни ключи от катанци,
народ не сте се Богу покори,
не сте се нити Богу помоли.
О, дайте ни ключи от катанци,
да отключим църну сипаницу.

И дадоше й ключи от катанци,
отпустише църну сипаницу,
отпустише, бракя, у народо!
Та си бие за три годин дъна.
Три годинe сипаница бие,
шест годинe сълнце и не грее,
шест годинe киша и не паде.
Народ се е млогу устрашило,
уплашило, Богу помолило,
помолило, Богу покорило.
И си иде у църкве раване:
сваки петък, свака неделя
и си слави сваки светъц господски.
И долете тъгай блажена Мария,
подвикуе до троица бракя:
- Та дайте ми ключи от катанци,
да отключим сълнце от изтока,
да отключим киша от небеса
и да отключим земле у дълбине.
И дадоше вой ключи от катанци,
па отключи сълнце от изтока
и отключи земле у дълбине,
и отключи кишу от небесе.
Мало си е сълнце огреяло
и мало си е киша увалило,
та запои тия църне земле,
та се роди туя бела ченица
и се роди това руйно вино.
Лебом се е народ заранило
и с руйно винце запоило...

58 - *Depiction Of The Goddess From Babek Village, Southwestern Bulgaria, Which According To Iv. Venedikov[446] Represents The Thracian View Of Persephone[447]*

---

[446] Because the commentary of Iv. Venedikov is relevant to the subject we are viewing, I'm going to quote it in its full: *"She (Persephone) is depicted as a veiled woman between a wheat spike and a vine tendril, stretching her hand over an altar and handing a phiale to the snake-Zeus, which is wriggling over the flame of the altar. The fire itself is depicted as a pine cone."* See Venedikov Iv., *The copper threshing-floor of the proto-Bulgars*, Stara Zagora 1995, 219 (вж. Венедиков Ив., *Медното гумно на прабългарите, II. прераб. изд., Стара Загора 1995, 219*). In this case we have a cross-reference to the link of the Thracian Persephone and the snake-Zeus, which is also a guardian of the home or the so called by the Hellenes Zeus Ktesios ΔΙΟΣ ΚΤΗΣΙΟΥ. For Zeus Ktesios see also Cook A., *Zeus: A study in Ancient religion*. Vol. II, part II, Cambridge 1925, 1059-1065.

[447] Popov D., *The Thracian goddess Bendis*, Sofia 1981, 55 (Попов Д., *Тракийската богиня Бендида, София 1981, 55*).

In this folk song the superficial replacing[448] is very clear. Before us stands a preserved epos, where the naming of the ancient gods are replaced with such of Christian saints, who in their ritual practices have preserved the traits of these divinities and in the rites dedicated to them are worshipped exactly as gods and goddesses, not as mortals (i.e. saints).

Dividing the three worlds between the three divine brothers is known from the ancient mythology and if here the Thunderer is replaced by St Elijah, the master of the seas with St Nicholas, it is Archangel Michael who inherits the rulership of the underworld.[449] The three female saints replace the three Goddesses,[450] who punish the people and then they appear in a single hypostasis and restore the blessing of the divine over the nation. In this case the paredria of the male and female divinities can be seen, who in this connection are defined as brothers and sisters, with no such evidence in the hagiographic literature. Following the ancient belief they appear in couples. Folk belief connects saint Petka with the home and its protection. The inheritance by the Christian saint of the ancient function of the female divinity is clear, because the Goddess is the one who has accepted in her womb the ones before us and through her we give them our honour and pray for their blessing.[451] The breads, prepared for distribution on the commemorations of the deceased, are often called St Petka and St Archangel.[452] Having in mind that Archangel Michael

---

[448]The same practice of replacing of names is done during the period of violent conversion to the religion of Islam among the Bulgarian population during the Ottoman yoke. In the regions with Bulgarian Muslims songs are sung just like in other regions, but the Christian names are replaced with Muslim ones. This has been done so that the performance won't be persecuted by the official authorities. This contemporary example is quite indicative of the existing folk mechanisms for preserving the traditional folklore.

[449]For the dividing of the worlds in the folk belief see also Yankova V., *Between the Spoken and Written Word. The folklore and the folk hagiographies*, V. Tarnovo 2005, 130-177 (Янкова В., *Между устното и писаното слово. Фолклорът и народните жития*, В. Търново 2005, 130-177).

[450]In this case the possibility suggested by some researchers is interesting, that the triple Goddesses are an expression of a strict, chthonic, punishing hypostasis – the Erinyes, the Eumenídes, the triple Hekate, and when they appear in a single form, for instance the single Hekate, they are in their favourable aspect. Of course this thesis needs its proving and reasoning.

[451] Also very interesting is the evidence of a celebration of a local Mother Goddess - μήθηρ θεαν αυτόχτων during October – November in the Thracian area, see Mitrev G., *Religious institutions and communities in the Macedonia province* (148 BC – 284 AC), Sofia 2003, 180 (Митрев Г., *Религиозни институции и общества в провинция Македония (148 г.пр.Хр.-284 г.сл.Хр.)*, София 2003, 180).

[452] For the breads St Petka see Marinov D., *Religious folk customs – selected works in 5 volumes*, v. I, part 2, Sofia 2003, 393-394 (Маринов Д.,

on a great scale inherits the functions and the image of the underworld God, the function of St Petka in this case becomes clear, as well as whose Christian impersonation she is – the Goddess of the underworld.[453] In this sense she appears and protects the home and the relationship with the ancestors. The place where the guardian-spirit is honoured is the hearth. In Bulgarian folk concept the guardian-spirit is a deceased ancestor, who protects the family, the community, the village. It could be a public figure or another prominent person, who becomes a guardian after his death. This folk belief gets the guardian-spirit really near to the ancient concept of the *heroes*.[454] The sacrificial rite, performed in honour of this guardian bears some ritual traits that are identical with the one described above and with the mentioned requirements for the ancient Thesmophoria and rite of the Good Goddess, and that is why it deserves some attention. Its goal, as well as one of its ancient parallels, is to beg for prosperity, which is expressed in the words of the prayer. Only women take part in the rite, again there is a blood sacrifice, ritual breads are kneaded and libations of wine are made in the home altar hearth. The women who take part in the rite must be married; unmarried women are not allowed to participate, which is also a known restriction in the Thesmophoria.

Религиозни народни обичаи – избрани произведения в 5 тома, том I, част 2, София 2003, 393-394).

[453] In this sense the possible connection on a linguistic level is quite interesting, between the naming Persephone, respectively Proserpina (with their local variations Περσεφονη, Περσεφασσα, Φερσεφασσα, Φερρεφαττα, Πηριφονα, Περεφονεια and the Etruscan Phersipnei) and St. Parascheva (Παρασκευη) on the basis of the beginning p-r-s, see Toporov V., *On the paleo-Balkan connections in the field of language and mythology* // Balkan linguistic collection, Moscow 1977, 52 (*Топоров В., К древнебалканским связям в области языка и мифологии // Балканский лингвистический сборник, Москва 1977, 52).*

[454] In his research of the hero cults in antiquity Farnell (see Farnell L., *Greek hero cults and ideas of immortality*, Oxford 1921, 3) shares his opinion that while among the Hellenes there is a lack of evidence for honouring the heroes in the prehistoric age, i.e. around 11th century BCE, among their neighbours the Thracians and the Phrygians this veneration could be traced with certainty to the second millennium BCE.

Description of practice 46 SACRIFICIAL RITE FOR THE GUARDIAN SPIRIT OF THE HOUSE (*STOPANOVA GOZBA*)[455]

The youngest woman in the house brings in undrunk and unspoken water in white cauldrons. This water is used for preparing the meals and for kneading dough for breads, *banitsa*[456] and *pogacha*.[457] The wheat, from which the flour is prepared, must be washed in the river three times and the flour must be sieved through three sieves. Three women, who are no longer of childbearing age, are called from three houses. When these three women come, they must stand next to the hearth, where a dent is made, i.e. like a pit, and over it a black hen, prepared by the household, is butchered. After the hen is butchered they try to ensure that all the blood runs into the dent dug in the hearth. After that it is buried and slurred over with mud. The hen is plucked. The plumage is preserved and is used for healing purposes and the intestines are buried in the garden. The meat is cooked or baked whole, i.e. it is not torn into pieces.

From the prepared dough one piece is separated for making banitsa and from the rest a pogacha is made. The top of the pogacha is decorated using a fork and is baked very carefully so it doesn't burn.

When the banitsa, the pogacha and the hen are ready, the youngest <u>married</u> woman in the house puts the table next to the hearth and on it she places the hen, the banitsa, the pogacha and a vessel with wine. The eldest woman fumigates everything placed on the table with frankincense and after that she puts in an empty plate for the divine householder.

First of all she takes the vessel with wine, pours some in the fire and says:

"Be happy divine householder, be merry house!"[458]

After that she takes the pogacha, places it on her head and breaks it into two parts, she then breaks these two parts

---

[455] The description is made following Marinov D., *Religious folk customs – selected works in 5 volumes*, v. I, part 2, Sofia 2003, 454-457 (Маринов Д., *Религиозни народни обичаи – избрани произведения в 5 тома, том I, част 2, София 2003, 454-457*), and the same rite is described also by Mihail Arnaudov with some differences, see Arnaudov M., *Essays on Bulgarian folklore*, Sofia 1996, 532-536 (Арнаудов М., *Очерци по българския фолклор, София 1996, 532-536*).
[456] A traditional food prepared by layering a mixture of whisked eggs and pieces of cheese between filo pastry and then baking it in an oven.
[457] A type of round puff pastry.
[458] In Bulgarian: *"Радувай се, стопане, весели се къщо!"*

into another two to make a total of four pieces. One quarter is separated for the divine householder and the others are for the meal. The quarter for him is spread with butter and honey and is placed separately on a plate. A piece from the banitsa is also put aside on the plate of the divine householder. The hen is torn and a leg from it is separated for the divine householder and placed on his plate. After that three small cups are filled with wine and they are also placed on the divine householder's plate.

The eldest woman, who has fumigated the table, takes the plate with the things for the divine householder and with the other two women goes to the attic and places them in the four corners: in the first corner the pogacha and one cup of wine, in the second the banitsa piece and a cup of wine, in the third corner – the thigh from the hen, and in the fourth corner the third cup of wine. After she does that and before coming down from the attic, she bows and says:

"Be happy divine householder, be merry house!"[459]

The other two women do the same. After that they come down from the attic and sit on the table.

Before they start to eat, the eldest woman takes a cup of wine and pours half of it in the fire and the other half she splatters on the fireplace of the hearth and says:

"Bloom house, be merry divine householder!

Where you go, go, but here you should come back to bring dew.

If you come from a field, here you should come back – to bring wheat;

if you come from a vineyard, here you should come back – to bring grapes!"[460]

After that they sit to eat. When they feed, if someone wants to drink wine, instead of saying cheers they should pour some in the hearth and say:

"Bloom house, be merry householder!"[461]

Finally when they are about to clear the table and drink the last cup of wine, the housewife pours half of it in the fire and says:

---

[459] In Bulgarian: *"Радувай се, стопане, весели се къщо!"*
[460] In Bulgarian:
"Цъфти къщо, весели се, стопане!
Къде ходиш, да ходиш, тук да се връщаш, роса да доводиш.
От поле ако идеш, тука да се връщаш – жито да донасяш;
от лозе ако идеш, тука да се връщаш – грозде да доносиш!"
[461] In Bulgarian: *"Цъфти, къщо, весели се, стопане!"*

"Bloom house, be merry divine householder,

Where you go, go,

but here you should come back and bring in the house:

to the brood health and long life,

help the brides to give birth easily;

protect and guard the sheep, the cattle, the horses, the bees

and other livestock;

protect the fields, the vineyards, the sesame, the cotton, the tobacco, the corn

and all that yields in the field!"[462]

The other women stay and keep silent while the housewife says that, and then they - say:

"Bloom house, be merry divine householder!"[463]

With this the rite is considered finished and the table is cleaned and the guests leave.

The fact that the officiating is done by the women deserves our attention. It is obligatory that they are only married women, i.e. bonded with the home hearth and in this sense having the ritual right to venerate it and call its guardian. The connection of the woman with the home is a notion which has formed in antiquity[464] and is preserved even today. Ritual tradition and the ritual acts described above are expressions of the sustainability of these beliefs.

---

[462] In Bulgarian:
"Цъфти, къщо, весели се, стопане!
Къде ходиш, да ходиш,
тука да се връщаш и да донасяш в къщата:
на челядта здраве и дълъг живот,
на булките да помагаш леко да раждат;
да пазиш и закриляш овците, говедата, конете, пчелите
и друга стока живина;
да пазиш нивите, лозята, сусамите, памуците, тютюните, царевиците
и всичко, що се ражда в полето!"
[463] In Bulgarian: *"Цъфти, къщо, весели се, стопане!"*
[464] See Naumov G., *The vessel, the oven and the house in a symbolic relation with the womb and the woman (Neolithic examples and ethnographic implications)* // Studia mythologica slavica 9, Ljubljana 2006, 59-95 (Наумов Г., *"Садот, печката и куката во симболичка релација со матката и жената (неолитски предлошки и етнографски импликации)"* // Studia mythologica slavica 9, Ljubljana 2006, 59-95).

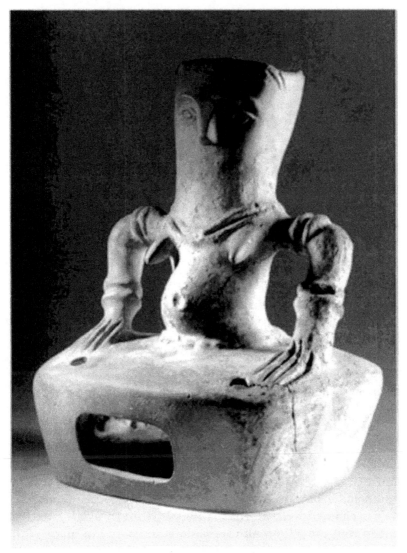

59 - Pregnant Goddess, Depicted As A Personification Of The Home[465]

The blood sacrifice, the ritual bread and the libation of wine in the home hearth are elements which clearly prove the rite as pre-Christian. In this case the home is the temple, the home hearth is the altar and the women are the priestesses who perform the sacred act and honour the ancestors. The guardian-spirit is considered as completely real and that is why after a week people check to see if the food and wine for him were tasted.

---

[465] Chausidis N., *The woman as a personification of the living space* // Macedonian theatre: Balkan context, Skopje 2007, 66 (Чаусидис Н., *Жената како персонификација на просторот за живеење* // *Македонскиот театар: балкански контекст, Скопје 2007, 66*).

The family guardian is called in other cases, too. According to folk belief he could also grant health and that is why, when there is a serious illness, another rite is performed, which aims to beg for the health of the ill person. In this case a man and a woman participate in the ritual act, which in a way distinguishes it from the female only practices described above. The essence of the rite as a chthonic sacrifice likens it to those actions that aim to beg a blessing from the ancestors. The rite is called namestnik and it is possible that the etymology *'na myastoto na'* (from the Bulgarian, meaning *'on the place of somebody'*), i.e. to replace them, is connected with the idea of a sacrifice that represents a substitute for the ill person.

Description of practice 47 NAMESTNIK[466]

Namestnik is the name of the sacrifice made for the health of an ill person. This action is always done on Saturday. The purpose is to beg the divine householder (the mythical ancestor and guardian) of the home for health for the ill. For this rite a man and a woman are specially chosen. They shouldn't be spouses. After this rite the man becomes a sworn brother of the ill person, and the woman – a sworn sister.

First the man will choose a completely black ram from the sheep of the person, for whom the namestnik is being made, and then he will take it to the house of that person and will dig a pit on the right side of the hearth; then he'll butcher the ram and let the blood pour in the pit. When the ram is cleaned well, all that is usually thrown away must be put in that pit. When all this is done, crosses are made with the blood in the opposite corners of the hearth, i.e. on the left side. After that the person washes and the meat and intestines of the ram are also washed and given to the women to cook them.

While the man makes the sacrifice women prepare bread, ten to fifteen breads are made as a whole, i.e. a whole oven. The breads are made of sourdough. Additionally other meals are made too: meat with cabbage, potatoes, rice, grits and other.

---

[466] The description is made following *Collection of Bulgarian Folklore and Folk Studies* – v. 2, 275 (СбНУ - т. 2, 275) and Marinov D., *Religious folk customs – selected works in 5 volumes*, v. I, part 2, Sofia 2003, 457-459 (*Маринов Д., Религиозни народни обичаи – избрани произведения в 5 тома, том I, част 2, София 2003, 457-459*).

All this is prepared for dinner and not for lunch, because the rite itself is done in the evening.

When lunchtime passes, they fill a wooden wine vessel with wine and send a girl around the village, and she goes from house to house and calls the villagers with the words:

"Plenty of health for you, come tonight on a namestnik!"[467]

The girl hands the wine vessel to the invited person, who drinks and gives it back. After dark all the invited villagers begin to arrive. When all of them are in the house, they start with the following: two candles are lit, one on the north side of the room (midnight) and one on the south (midday) and the meal is served, the meat with the bread. When all the food is prepared a bowl with wine is taken and is covered on top with a small bread, so the bowl can't be seen, and they grab it from below using some wool or wool cloth, so the hand won't touch the bowl. When everything is prepared and everyone gathered, the eldest from the invited takes the bowl and spins it three times, so some wine spills from it on the table. The same thing is repeated by the rest of the people – guests and household, until all take a turn. After that they place the bowl with the wine and the wool on a shelf where it stays until the next week.

Then they take a plate with kolivo[468] – boiled wheat, and put a loaf of bread on top of it. On another plate they place meat and liver, and they distribute them from person to person until there is none. The bread and the kolivo are given away by the housewife and the meat by a man. Then they start to eat and drink and all sit at the table, because until now there was a requirement for all to stand. When everyone finishes eating they go home.

On the next Saturday the same people gather again. Now they take the bowl with wine from the last Saturday and cover it with new bread. They twist it again each one three times, just like the previous Saturday. After that they eat the two breads and with this the rite is over.

In spite of its distinction from the circle of rites to which only women are permitted, this ritual act deserves some attention because it has also preserved material in its archaic appearance. An absence of any Christianisation element can be noticed in the whole description. The rite is related to Saturday, because according to folk belief this day

---

[467] In Bulgarian: *"Много Ви здраве, да дойдете довечера на наместник!"*
[468] From the Greek κόλλυβα, meaning ritual food made mainly from wheat, sugar and walnuts and used for commemorations of the deceased.

is considered as dedicated to the deceased.[469] Additionally the ritual meal is done in the evening, which one again gives a hint of the connection with the night and the afterlife. The man and the woman, who make the ritual preparations, assume a completely sacred function, which is additionally emphasised from the belief that subsequently they turn into a sworn brother and sister of the ill person. The ritual commitment is preserved as a sacred fact also in the social context. For the chthonic role of the black ram in the sacrificial rites and for the calling of the ancestors' souls we have to recall the famous moment with Odysseus in the underworld, who following the advice of Circe calls the souls of the dead with the same sacrifice and has to promise to Teiresias the finest black ram (Hom. Od. XI). This rite is preserved in later times in the magical papyri in a similar way:

Description of practice 48 FOR CALLING THE SOULS OF THE DEAD PGM XXIII.1-70[470]

"[But' when with vows] and prayers [I had appealed]
[To them], the tribes of dead, I took [the] sheep
And slit their throats [beside the trough, and down]
The dark blood [flowed. From out of Ere]bos
5   Came gathering [the spirits] of the dead: /
(5) [New brides, unmarried youths,] toil-worn old men,
[And] tender [maidens] with fresh-mourning hearts,
[And many] pierced by bronze-tipped spears, [men] slain
In battle, still in armour stained with gore.
10 [These many] thronged from ev'ry side around
(10) The trough I with [awful] cry. Pale fear seized me.
[But] having drawn the sharp sword at my thigh,
[I sat,] allowing not the flitting heads
Of the dead to draw nearer to [the blood],
15 And I in conversation spoke with them.
(He has said what must be done:) I
(15)"O rivers, earth, and you below, punish
Men done with life, whoe'er has falsely sworn;
Be witnesses, fulfill for us this charm.

---

[469] Even in antiquity Saturday was dedicated to Saturn - dies Saturni, and subsequently in the Eastern Orthodoxy is considered as the day on which Jesus was dead in his grave (between the crucifixion on Friday and the resurrection on Sunday).

[470] Betz H., *The Greek Magical Papyri in translation, including the Demotical spells*, Chicago/London 1986, 262-263.

20 I've come to ask how I may reach the land
Of that Telemachus, my own son whom I
(20) I left still in a nurse's arms." For in
This fashion went the charm most excellent.
(He tells what charms must be sung:)
25 "[Hear] me, gracious and guardian, well-born
[An]ubis; [hear, sly] one, O secret mate,
Osiris' saviour; come, Hermes, come, robber,
(25) Well-trussed, infernal Zeus; / Grant [my desire],
Fulfill this charm. [Come hither, Hades,] Earth,
30 Unfailing Fire, O Titan Helios;
[Come,] Iaweh, Phthas, Phre, guardian of laws,
[And Neph]tho, much revered; Ablanatho,
In blessings rich, with [fiery] serpents girded,
(30) Earth-ploughing, goddess with head high, [Abrax]as,
35 A daimon famous by your cosmic name,
Who rule earth's [axis], starry dance, the Bears'
Cold light. [And come] to me, surpassing all
In self-control, O Phren. I'm calling [you],
O B[r]i[ar]eus and Ph[r]asios and you,
40 O Ixion and Birth and youth's decline,
(35)Fair-burning Fire, I [and may you come,] Infernal
And Heav'nly One, and [you who govern] dreams,
And Sirius, who..."
Standing beside the trough, I cried [these words],
45 [For well] did I remember Circe's counsels,
[Who] knew [all] poisons which the broad earth grows./
(40)   [Then came] a lofty wave of Acheron
Which fights with lions, [Cocytus] and Lethe
And mighty Polyphlegethon. A host
50 [Of dead] stood round the trough, [and first] there came
The spirit of Elpenor, my comrade.
(And so on.)

The place where the animal is sacrificed is the hearth, because it is believed to be a dwelling of the guardian-spirit – he lives underneath it. This belief as well as the mythological explanation most probably also keeps the memory of the times when burials took place in the homes and in a number of cases exactly under the home hearth, which according to some scholars is identified also with the womb of the

Goddess and is analogical with the burial pit.[471] In the womb of the Goddess the light is being born – the celestial, as well as the earthly, so that is why the hearth belongs to the same semantic plan and turns to be a proper place for officiation connected with the ancestors. The pit, where the blood is left to pour is dug on the right side of the hearth and additionally on the left side of the same hearth marks are made with that blood, particularly crosses, i.e. solar signs. In this way both hemispheres are included – over and under the earth. In this case it is clearly defined that the right is underground (hypo-chthonic) and the left is celestial (uranic). The sacredness of the left among the Thracians has been observed in scientific literature,[472] and in this case in ritual context manifests the same meaning of the actions. The movement is done from right to left, i.e. expected sequence for a blood chthonic sacrificial ritual practice, which is concentrated around the earthly hypostasis of the light – the fire. It is unlikely that the crosses in this case have any connection with the Christian symbolism, but rather have preserved their ancient symbolism, and depict and introduce solarity in the rite. The order of the actions – first burying and libating in the pit, and after that marking in height with a solar symbol, is an expression of a prayer through actions so in the same way the ill person should stand up and be filled with power. The rite is performed in the evening, i.e. it is a nocturnal rite and is a joint meal of mortal people and the divine guardian. Lighting the candles in the north and south end of the room could be viewed as inherited, because in Thracian antiquity these two directions are evidenced to be really sacred. Interesting in this case is the specification of the recorder of the rite that not using east and west is strange, which would be explicable in one Christian context.[473] Bearing in mind the belief of the

---

[471] See Bachvarov K., *Neolithic mortuary practices*, Sofia 2003, 143-144 (*Бъчваров К., Неолитни погребални обреди, София 2003, 143-144*), as well as in relation to the burials performed in the homes during the Mycenaean Age see Cook A., *Zeus: A study in Ancient religion*. Vol. II, part II, Cambridge 1925, 1059-1065.

[472] For the meaning of the left direction, as an invisible motion of the sun see Teodorov E., *Ancient Thracian heritage in Bulgarian folklore*, Sofia 1999, 15 (*Теодоров Е., Древнотракийско наследство в българския фолклор, София 1999, 15*); for the directions in the nestinari ritual tradition see Fol V., Neykova R., *Fire and music*, Sofia 2000, 82 (*Фол В., Нейкова Р.,. Огън и музика, София 2000, 82*); for the Thracian tribe skaioi *"left"* and the left greaves in Thrace see Marazov Iv., *Thracian mythology*, Sofia 1994, 39-40 (*Маразов Ив., Митология на траките, София 1994, 39-40*).

[473] Noted by Dimitar Marinov, who writes: *"Remarkable here is the rare phenomenon that the candles are stuck from North and South, while usually they are stuck from East and West."* Marinov D., *Religious folk customs – selected works in 5 volumes*, v. I, part 2, Sofia 2003, 459 (*Маринов Д.,*

ancients that the south is the place where the souls of the blessed dwell,[474] its presence in the rite becomes absolutely understandable. These two world directions are marked in order to show the way both to gods and mortals.[475] Because earlier we paid attention to the meaning of the ritual breads, I won't stop on them now. An interesting element in this case is the way of making the wine libation. The bowl is placed on wool and in such a way that it won't be touched with the hand, i.e. it must stay sacred and untouched. Wool was forbidden in antiquity for Egyptian priests, the Orphics and the Pythagoreans.[476] In my view its use in this case is because of another reason and namely because it is an important ritual element as a cult object in a number of ritual acts dedicated to the subterranean deities. Except for the prohibition quoted by Herodotus there are records of its role in the Orphic ritual tradition. There it is one of the cult objects of Dionysos, the so-called toys, which the Titans gave to the God according to the information given by Clement of Alexandria:

"The mysteries of Dionysos are wholly inhuman; for while still a child, and the Curetes danced around [his cradle] clashing their weapons, and the Titans having come upon them by stealth, and having beguiled him with childish toys, these very Titans tore him limb from limb when but a child, as the bard of this mystery, the Thracian Orpheus, says:

Религиозни народни обичаи – избрани произведения в 5 тома, том I, част 2, София 2003, 459).

[474] One fragment from Homer is popular, that has been discussed by Porphyry in his work *"The Cave of the Nymphs"*, where it is described that in this cave the North is dedicated to the mortals and the sacred South is dedicated to the immortals – see Porphyry, *On the cave of the Nymphs, Selected works of Porphyry* transl. by Thomas Taylor, London 1823, 171. In his work Porphyry himself asks a question to the reader – *"...and why the poet did not rather make use of the west and the east for this purpose, since nearly all temples have their statues and entrances turned towards the east;"* (Porphyry, *On the cave of the Nymphs, Selected works of Porphyry* transl. by Thomas Taylor, London 1823, 173). In this connection we learn that even in Hellenic antiquity such signification of South and North would have been surprising, but in a Thracian context this is completely grounded, having in mind the numerous archeological findings, which prove it – in built temples, as well as on rock sanctuaries and cave-wombs, see Fol V., *Rock topoi of faith in Southeastern Europe and Asia Minor during Antiquity.* Studia Thracica 10, Sofia 2007, 185-186 (*Фол В., Скални топоси на вярата в Югоизточна Европа и в Мала Азия през древността. Studia Thracica 10. София 2007, 185-186*).

[475] See previous note.

[476] Herodotus, *Histories*, book 2, 81: *"But woollen fabrics are not taken into shrines, or buried with them, for it is not considered holy. They agree in this with the observances which are called Orphic and Bacchic, but are in fact Egyptian and Pythagorean; for neither is it considered holy for a participant in these rites to be buried in woollen garments, and there is a sacred story told on the subject."*

"Cone, and spinning-top, and limb-moving rattles,

And fair golden apples from the clear-toned Hesperides."

And the useless symbols of this mystic rite it will not be useless to exhibit for condemnation. These are dice, ball, hoop, apples, top, one looking-glass, tuft of wool."[477]

Along with that record, which is quite late and bent through the Christian view of the author seeking 'exposure', there are also records from earlier ages from the region of the Eastern Mediterranean, which confirm the connection of wool with the divinities of the underworld and fit in the same semantic circle as the rite quoted above. In the Hittite ritual texts the usage of wool is evidenced repeatedly, but most often it is connected with the female deity, the underworld and the idea of fertility and prosperity. In these rites the wool is used in a number of cases to draw the deities near, i.e. it ensures the thread of transition. In some Hittite rituals, during the calling of the Goddesses of destiny, the priest symbolically draws ways on which they must come back and bring prosperity again. Drawing near and calling the Goddesses he does with a wool thread, wool cloth, another thread and an eagle feather.[478] The important role of the wool we find in the ritual of Kamrusepa, where three types of wool are used in a rite for healing an ill person.[479] As a whole in the Hittite ritual texts the usage of wool is evidenced with a different symbolism according to its colour. The purpose of mentioning this was to note that even in early antiquity the usage of wool in cult ritual practices is widespread and it has been preserved in the relic ritual tradition until today, as in a number of cases its ritual function is to accomplish a possibility for transition and symbolic calling of the deities. These examples from the Hittite texts make it very possible to suggest that among stockbreeding people like the Thracians such examples have also existed and it is likely that the described rite is one such example.

The rest of the sacrificial rite shows the belief that the divine powers, including the ancestors, appear to be commensals. Repeating the rite on the next Saturday is interesting, because there is no triple recurrence, which is typical for healing practices. The double performance of the rite marks the dual orientation, which was mentioned even

---

[477] Clement, *Protreptikos* 2.17.2-18.2, *The writings of Clement of Alexandria*, transl. Wilson W., London 1867, 29-30.
[478] See Haas V., *Die hethitische Literatur: Texte, Stilistik, Motive*, Berlin 2006, 110
[479] Ibid. 241

in the initial ritual actions – marking the two corners of the hearth – right and left, marking the two directions – north and south. It could be suggested as a rite which includes both spheres of the Cosmos – the space over and under the earth and aims for their unification with a certain idea, which in this case is the healing.

The image of the Goddess is not named directly in these two rites, but she is present through the ritual actions and objects, as well as through the hearth, which appears as her depiction. The hearth, the oven as a place where the fire is born, i.e. the earthly manifestation of the God-Sun is an aniconic image of the Divine Genetrix. Following the ancient tradition to honour the hearth as a place of divine presence, the new Christian religion also accredits the protecting functions over it to its saints. The winter festival of St Petka as well as being related with honouring the feminine principle, which gives fertility, is also connected with reverence for the ancestors. This reverence, although it might be expressed in other circumstances, in some regions is attached to the calendar date November 14th.[480] Folk culture and spirituality have preserved the connection between the end of autumn, the gathering of fruits, the beginning of winter and the time for giving reverence to the mythical ancestors and guardians. It is not by chance that this is exactly the time of the biggest feast for the dead – the one on the day of Archangel Michael (November 8th).[481]

---

[480] Marinov D., *Religious folk customs – selected works in 5 volumes*, v. I, part 2, Sofia 2003, 459 (*Маринов Д., Религиозни народни обичаи – избрани произведения в 5 тома, том I, част 2, София 2003, 459*).
[481] Which in turn is also absolutely grounded bearing in mind that Archangel Michael inherits the role of god of the underworld, just as this is expressed in the folk song and was discussed earlier in this chapter.

*60 - The Great Goddess, Depicted On A Vessel
From The Rogozen[482] Ritual Set*

*61 - Winged Mother Of God Painted By Bulgarian Iconographers From
Samokov, Located In The Sukovo Monastery
"Dormition Of The Theotokos"
Near Dimitrovgrad, Republic Of Serbia,
Photograph – I. Mishkova 2011*

The connection of St Petka with the prohibition for spinning on Friday, with her transformation into a snake, with her protection of home and healing, and at the same time with her protection over wolves, depicts one concept for divinities related with the underworld. In Balkan ritual practice and faith the divine spinner is often connected with the wolf and death. The spindle and its connection with death can be seen among the Romanians, where for protection against vampirism of the deceased a spindle is stuck in three places of the grave – by the head, in the middle and in the feet. For the relation of the spindle and the female image of death some texts give evidence:

"Bark around me the dogs bark,

like they're hearing a mad wolf,

but it is not a mad wolf,

it is a samodiva with a cudgel,

and with a distaff in her belt, with a wool sliver"[483]

The wolf as a chthonic character and guide of souls is also known in the folklore texts of the Balkan peoples. In Romanian texts it is said to the soul of the deceased:

"And in front of you a wolf will appear, it will scare you.

Don't be scared, become his brother, because the wolf knows all forests and paths.

He will guide you to a big road, towards the king's son,

he will guide you to heaven, there you will live."[484]

This concept of the wolf and the underworld is preserved until today although in one faded appearance, as in some moments the ritual actions are isolated and are performed only with a protective function. Nevertheless the rites preserve the basic, because the ancient gods could rightfully be called divinities of the rite. In it the connection is realised and the notion of the divine is formed.

---

[483] The translation in English is made by Ekaterina Ilieva using the Bulgarian translation of G. Mishev from the Russian edition of Sveshnikova T., *The wolf in the context of the Romanian burial rite. Research on the Balto-Slavic spiritual culture.* // Burial rite, 1990, 131 (Свешникова Т., *Волк в контексте румынского погребального обряда* в Исследования балто-славянской духовной культуры // Погребальный обряд, Москва 1990, 131).

[484] The translation in English is made by Ekaterina Ilieva using the Bulgarian translation of G. Mishev from the Russian edition of Sveshnikova T., *The wolf in the context of the Romanian burial rite. Research on the Balto-Slavic spiritual culture.* // Burial rite, 1990, 130 (Свешникова Т., *Волк в контексте румынского погребального обряда* в Исследования балто-славянской духовной культуры // Погребальный обряд, Москва 1990, 130).

With the celebration of St Petka begins a calendar period in which the so-called Wolf days appear. In a number of regions in Bulgaria the continuation and the dates of this period vary, as in some of them its initial date is the celebration of St Petka and in others it is November 11th.[485] Its continuation could be also different – three, seven, nine, ten or twelve days. In spite of the different records regarding the continuation of the celebration, the most complete description which could be accepted is given by D. Marinov, respectively from November 11th to 21st,[486] as this period is divided in parts. Along with the fact that this time period was called Wolf days, it also carries the naming Mrata nights. Folk belief accredits to those days dangerous characteristics and that is why a great part of the performed rites have a protective function.

Mrata nights or Wolf days begin with a blood sacrifice of a black rooster, which is considered as dedicated to the spirit Mrata, which the people imagine as a huge black bird (hen) with big eyes and wings. The rite is again performed by women; they butcher the sacrifice on the doorstep – the main liminal point in the house. The blood sacrifice in this case aims to protect, but also to sanctify the doorstep, i.e. so it could become inaccessible for invasion by evil influences and powers. Along with that parts of the sacrifice are used for healing during the year, and the woman performing the rite uses it to beg for an increase of her healing powers.

---

[485] Additionally there are such days dedicated to the wolf also in February – February 1st to 3rd, for which the same ritual prohibitions are valid, but they are going to be examined further in connection with the celebrations of Dionysos, because they coincide with the cutting of the vine. For this days see Marinov D., *Religious folk customs – selected works in 5 volumes*, v. I, part 2, Sofia 2003, 150-152 (Маринов Д., *Религиозни народни обичаи – избрани произведения в 5 тома, том I, част 2, София 2003, 150-152*).

[486] Marinov D., *Religious folk customs – selected works in 5 volumes*, v. I, part 2, Sofia 2003, 397-402 (Маринов Д., *Религиозни народни обичаи – избрани произведения в 5 тома, том I, част 2, София 2003, 397-402*).

Description of practice 49 SACRIFICE TO MRATA[487]

The hostess in the community chooses the best, the biggest and most fed among all the chickens; the chicken must be black as a raven and furthermore a rooster, i.e. male. If it happens that there is no black rooster, it could be another colour.

The evening of November 11th, before St Menas,[488] they take that chicken and butcher it in this way: one grabs the chicken's legs, and another grabs its head; the one that holds the head will stand inside the house and he holds the knife to butcher it, and the other, who holds the chicken's legs will stay in front of the doorstep, outside the house. When the knife is raised to perform the butchery, the person, standing outside asks: *"What do you butcher?"* *"We butcher mrata"*,[489] answers the one standing inside and in the same time cuts the head of the chicken, while saying: *"We are not butchering you, but mrata butchers you"*[490] and holds tight the beak of the chicken, so it is not open.

---

[487] The description is made following Marinov D., *Living antiquity, book 1*, Ruse 1891, 62-63 (*Маринов Д., Жива старина, кн. 1, Русе 1891, 62- 63*), but there are some differences with the description given in Marinov D., *Religious folk customs – selected works in 5 volumes*, v. I, part 2, Sofia 2003, 396-397 (*Маринов Д., Религиозни народни обичаи – избрани произведения в 5 тома, том I, част 2, София 2003, 396-397*), where the rite is performed during the day: *"Very early in the morning the housewife gets up and her first job is to go in the coop and to catch the rooster, she has chosen. When she catches it, she will go back in her house and will tie its legs so it doesn't run. After that she makes a fire and prepares the knife for butchering the sacrifice."* In this case I have quoted the description the way it is given in the older source and the way it is quoted from other researchers, for instance see Plotnikova A., *Ethnolinguistic geography of the South Slavs*, Moscow 2004, 76 (*Плотникова А., Этнолингвистическая география Южной Славии, Москва 2004, 76*). Additionally the same tradition of butchering a black chicken on the doorstep is described also for the region of Eastern Serbia; as the butchering is done again in the dark, before sunrise on the day of St Menas, i.e. before dawn on November 11th, see Popov R., *Saint Menas in the calendar tradition of the Balkan peoples. – History*, 2004, №№ 4-5: 79-88 (*Попов Р., Свети Мина в календарната традиция на балканските народи. –История, 2004, №№ 4-5: 79-88*). This is confirmed also by the research of Serbian scholars, who clearly situate the sacrifice in the dark part of the day – the evening after dusk on November 10th or the morning before dawn on November 11th: *"In the morning before the sun every house on saint Mrata (i.e. St Martin) or in the eve of the celebration, after sunset, butchers either a black chicken "mratinche", or "black" hen, rooster, most often without any sign."* – Petrovich S., *Serbian mythology. System of the Serbian mythology, I book*, first edition, Nish 1999, 62 (*Петровић С., Српска митологија систем српске митологије, I књига Прво издање, Ниш 1999, 62).*

[488] This is probably an inaccuracy, which the describer D. Marinov makes, because the eve of the celebration of St Menas is on November 10th before 11th and not on November 11th itself.

[489] In Bulgarian: *"Какво колиш?" "Колим мратиняк"*

[490] In Bulgarian: *"Не колим те ние, ами те коли мратиняк"*

When the chicken is butchered it is given to the women, who pluck it. The plumage is stored and is used as a remedy: women who have recently given birth and children are fumigated with it, when they have fever. The head, the legs and the gizzard (the stomach) are threaded on a red thread and are hung behind the door to protect from evil. In some villages (those in the mountains) an ember and feathers are placed in the beak of the chicken and along with the gizzard and the legs it is hung on the beam, on which the cooking pot is hung on the hearth, so no evil can enter the house. The meat is cooked and eaten.

The rite is also described in another variation.

Description of practice 50 SACRIFICE TO MRATA - VARIATION[491]

The mrata rooster is butchered in the house, behind the door, where the person sits who has entered the house first on the day of Ignazhden.[493] The mrata (the rooster) is butchered with the scissors that are used for cutting cloth. The housewife, who butchers it, after cutting its head says:

"Whatever I touch, it should become healing!"[494]

After cutting the head, she ties the scissors and they stay tied until November 21st, i.e. until the last Mrata night.

Sacrificing a chicken is commented by most researchers as a redemptive sacrifice[495] and in this case it is possible to suppose a similar connotation of the rite. Tracing the ritual actions makes other features become visible, which lend the rite another different rationalisation. First of all the parts of the sacrifice are preserved and are used for healing through the year, i.e. they possess cathartic (purifying) properties. The sacrifice is eaten, i.e. there is a ritual meal, which makes it differ from a number of purification rites in antiquity, where the redemptive sacrifices were burnt or buried, but were not shared between those who performed it. In the Hellenic notion the two types of sacrificial rites are divided

---

[491] Marinov D., *Religious folk customs – selected works in 5 volumes*, v. I, part 2, Sofia 2003, 396 (Маринов Д., *Религиозни народни обичаи – избрани произведения в 5 тома, том I, част 2, София 2003, 396*).

[493] Ignazhden is the day of St Ignatius of Antioch, which is celebrated on December 20th.

[494] In Bulgarian: *"Що пофана, да е лековито!"*

[495] Scheftelowitz, I., *Das stellvertretende Huhnopfer, mit besonderer Berücksichtigung des jüdischen Volksglaubens*, Giessen 1914; Henninger J., *"Über Huhnopfer und Verwandtes in Arabien und seinen Randgebieten, "* Anthropos, 41-44/1946-1949.

into θεραπεία – serving and ἀποτροπή – rites for protection.[496] In the protective rites the sacrifice is not shared between those who perform it, because its aim is to unify them with the divinities for whom it is made. In this sense the difference, which we find in this case and in the ones described above, becomes clear. Regardless of the protective nature of the sacrifice, the connection and unification with the divinity are sought again. A possible reason for the absence of such differentiation could be the difference between the Hellenic and Thracian divine concept. Among the Thracians the divinities have two sides and are perceived as dual, but are not dualistic, i.e. there is no division of the image. This blood sacrifice, as well as the one described in *Kokosha cherkva* (Hen sacrifice), aims through the blood as a carrier of life to strengthen the sustainability of the liminal point of the home (the doorstep),[497] and also of the vital powers of the participants in the rite – from one side through sharing the sacrifice on the ritual meal (see the rite *Kokosha cherkva*) and from the other through the verbal formula: *"Whatever I touch, it should become healing!"*

As was mentioned above, with this rite begins the so-called Wolf days.[498] Among the Balkan peoples this period is saturated with numerous magical actions[499,500] aiming to

---

[496] See Harrison J., *Prolegomena to the Study of Greek Religion*, Cambridge 1908, 10-12.

[497] See Yerkes R., *Sacrifice in Greek and Roman religions and early Judaism*, New York 1959, 2.

[498] For this calendar period see Mencej M., *Wolf holidays among Southern Slavs in the Balkans* // Acta Ethnographica Hungarica, 2009 54 (2), 337–358 and among the Romanians see Sveshnikova T., *Under the sign of the wolf. Features of the Balkan-Romance culture.* // Time in the space of the Balkans. Evidences of the language, Moscow 1994, 64-74 (Свешникова Т., Под знаком волка. Черты балканороманской народной культуры // Время в пространстве Балкан. Свидетельства языка, Москва 1994, 64-74).

[499] See Popov R., *St Menas in the calendar tradition of the Balkan peoples.* // History, 2004, №№ 4-5: 79-88 (Попов Р., *Свети Мина в календарната традиция на балканските народи.* // История, 2004, №№ 4-5: 79-88) according to Kitevski M., *Summer rites from Deburtsa (Ohrid region).* // Macedonian folklore, № 19-20, 1979, 56 (Китевски М., *Летни обичаји от Дебърца (Охридско).* // Македонски фолклор, № 19-20, 1979, 56): "The shepherds from the region of Ohrid perform a special magical ritual: On the eve of the celebration they pick a briar stick and cut it in two parts. The one they hide under the doorstep together with a hemp comb and the other they place above the door with another comb. After that they let the sheep one by one through the scrapers and cut from each some fleece. From the wool they make a thread, which they tie on both briar sticks saying: "I shall tie the eyes and the mouth of the wild one (the wolf), so it doesn't see the sheep!" The briar sticks are put in the sheep pen and are kept until the next year. Other times, when the shepherds are gathering the sheep in the sheep pen, they put under the doorstep and above the door two open hemp or wool combs. After they gather the animals, they close the mouth of the combs and leave them like that until the end of the "wolf days"."

assure the protection of the people and livestock from this much feared predator. Along with this completely everyday life moment, in the beliefs and rituals we find also a lot more of an ancient mythological layer. The connection wolf-underworld-ancestors[501] is known throughout Eurasia. In the region of the Eastern Mediterranean the wolf is a cult animal from antiquity.[502] The thesis, that among Thracians the wolf is connected with the winter sun[503] - *"chthonic fiery image of Apollo"*,[504,505] has been amplified in scientific circles. Along with that in antiquity the wolf is related also to the image of the Goddess. In the guise of a she-wolf the Goddess Leto goes from the lands of the Hyperboreans to Lykia, which until then has another name, and because wolves greet her there she renames the land Lykia (Antonius Liberalis, *Metamorphoses* 35). Porphyry writes that in the language of the mysteries Artemis is called she-wolf λύκαινα.[506] The name of one Thracian heroine Harpalyke (Ἁρπαλύκη) is derived etymologically with the meaning *"predatory she-wolf"*.[507] It is not uncommon for the Goddess to take the guise of a she-wolf or to have wolf traits – ankle of a wolf or an image of a dog (which appears as its substitute).[508] The

---

[500] See Popov R., *St Menas in the calendar tradition of the Balkan peoples.* – History, 2004, №№ 4-5: 79-88 (*Попов Р., Свети Мина в календарната традиция на балканските народи // История, 2004, №№ 4-5: 79-88*) according to Ghinoiu, I. Op. cit., 321-325; Pamfile, T. *Sârbătorile la români.* Studii etnografic. Bucuresti, 1997, 211-213: *"On the last day of the cycle the women gloze again the hearth, the floor and the doors while saying: "As I am glozing the mouth of the oven, so I gloze the eyes of the enemies!" In Bukovina they rub with garlic the door frames and the sashes to prevent themselves from illnesses and magic."*

[501] In this line of thought we find a lot of widely known concepts of the she-wolf that has nurtured Romulus and Remus in the Roman mythology; among the Turkic peoples, too see Ilimbetova A., *The cult of the wolf among the Bashkirs (Илимбетова А., Культ волка у башкир)*, http://turkportal.ru/culturearticles/6-kult-volka-bashkir.html <10.12.2011>.

[502] See Kagarov Evg., *The cult of fetishes, plants and animals in ancient Greece*, Saint Petersburg *1913, 218-226 (Кагаров Евг., Культ фетишей, растений и животных в древней Греции, Санкт Петербург 1913, 218-226)*.

[503] Fol V., *The wolf/the dog and the North as the direction of wisdom.* // Studia archeologiae et historiae antiquae. Doctissimo viro Scientiarum Archeologiae et Historiae Ion Nikuliță, anno septuagesimo aetatis suae, dedicator. Chișinău 2009, 149-158.

[504] Fol A., *Orphica magica*, Sofia 2004, 140 (*Фол А., Orphica magica, София 2004, 140*).

[505] For the connection between Apollo and the wolf see also in Graf Fr., *Apollo*, London/New York 2008, 97.

[506] *Porphyrius de Abstin.* IV. 16, 155: *Selected works of Porphyry*, transl. Thomas Taylor, London 1823.

[507] See Ivanov V., *Dionysos and Pre-Dionysianism*, Saint Petersburg 1994, 97 (*Иванов В., Дионис и прадионисийство, Санкт Петербург 1994, 97*).

[508] In this connection see West D., *Some cults of Greek goddesses and female daemons of oriental origin: especially in relation to the mythology of*

Trojan queen Hecuba turns into a bitch[509] attendant of the *"ruling over the Strymon kingdom Zerynthian goddess"*,[510] and her tomb is called *"the sign of the dog"* (κυνος σημα). The role of the wolf, respectively the dog, as a mediator of the Goddess and her image, is reflected also in the legend of the saving of Byzantium (which is an old Thracian settlement)[511] because of the barking of dogs,[512] and therefore the worship of the Goddess there as torchbearer (Λαμπαδηφόρος). In ancient magic the Goddess is called as wolf taming[513] - δαμνο[514] λύκαινα.[515]

*62 - Archaic Ionic Seal With Theriomorphic
Depiction Of The Goddess As A She-Wolf[516]*

---

goddesses and demons in the Semitic world. PhD thesis, University of Glasgow 1990, 278-281, 326, 329, 331, 336, 351, 354, 363, 377, 383, 385, 402, 404, 405, 429,430. online: http://theses.gla.ac.uk/1263/ <10.12.2011>.

[509] See Schlesier R., *Die Bakchen des Hades. Dionysische Aspekte von Euripides Hekabe – Metis. Antropologie des mondes grecs anciens Vol. 3*, n 1-2, 1988, 111-135 and also Reitler R., *A Theriomorphic Representation of Hekate-Artemis* - American Journal of Archaeology, Vol. 53, No. 1 (Jan. - Mar., 1949), 29-31.

[510] *Lykophron*, Alexandra 1178-1179 - Holzinger C., Leipzig 1895, 149-151.

[511] For its founder is considered Byzas, who is called 'Byzas , the Thracian king' (Βύζας ὁ Θράκης βασιλεύς), see Tomaschek W., *Die alten Thraker. Eine ethnologische Untersuchung*, Neudruck der Ausgaben von 1893 und 189, Osnabrück 1975, II, 16.

[512] Limberis V., *Divine Heiress. The Virgin Mary and the creation of Christian Constantinople*, London/New York 1994, 127.

[513] See Gager J., *Curse Tablets and Binding Spells from the Ancient World*, New York/Oxford 1992, 267.

[514] Δαμνο is derived as etymology from δαμάω, δάμνημι, which means *'tame'*, in German *zähmen*, see Hofmann J., *Etymologisches Wörterbuch des Griechischen*, München 1950, 58-59.

[515] PGM III 434-435 - Preisendanz K,. *Die griechischen Zauberpapyri*, Leipzig 1928, 50.

[516] Reitler R., *A Theriomorphic Representation of Hekate-Artemis* // American Journal of Archaeology, Vol. 53, No. 1 (Jan. - Mar., 1949), 29-31.

A similar function in Bulgarian traditional faith is the so-called Wolf Mother of God. According to the folklore data three 'Mothers of God' are worshipped – the Little, the Middle and the Big.[517] The Middle is honoured on November 21st and is considered to be a mistress of wolves – "*This Mother of God gives orders to the wolves.*"[518] According to the folk belief these three '*Mothers of God*' are *sisters.*[519] The Triple Faced Mother of God provokes interest, because it is absolutely unacceptable from the perspective of the Christian canon, but obviously in the folk notion there is no obstacle for her existence,[520] because the cultural memory preserves the idea of the image of the triple-faced Goddess. The very Wolf days in most of the regions are considered to end on November 21st, which is celebrated in honour of the Limping wolf and bread spread with honey is given away.

The Wolf celebrations are connected with the mating season of wolves. In this regard in traditional Bulgarian culture the belief exists that the she-wolf could become pregnant only if she has tasted the meat of a dog or a person wearing clothing sewed during this period.[521] According to variations of this belief the requirement is that the she-wolf tastes a coal from the hearth and that is why a prohibition exists for throwing the ash outside the house.[522] These beliefs show the association of the she-wolf's fertility with the sacrifice of a dog or a person, as well as with the fertile power of the home hearth fire. Of great interest are some magic rites, which represent in unity the she-wolf and the hearth and in this connection I think it is necessary that they are examined in a more detailed way.

---

[517] The Wolf Mother of God is considered to be the middle one, because the other two celebrations dedicated to Mother of God are respectively Little Mother of God on September 8th, i.e. the birth of St Mother of God and Big Mother of God on August 15th, i.e. her Assumption. Thus the Wolf Mother of God is the middle one, because she is situated between the other two, i.e. between her birth and her death.

[518] For the continuity of this calendar cycle and the information about the Wolf Mother of God see Marinov D., *Religious folk customs – selected works in 5 volumes*, v. I, part 2, Sofia 2003, 397-402 (*Маринов Д., Религиозни народни обичаи – избрани произведения в 5 тома, том I, част 2, София 2003, 397-402*).

[519] Ibid 398.

[520] The double and triple images of saints are an interesting phenomenon in the folk beliefs and usually it is due to strong pre-Christian groundings of the worship, in this connection see Popov R., *Twin Saints in the Bulgarian Folk Calendar*, Sofia 1991 (*Попов Р., Светци близнаци в българския народен календар, София 1991*).

[521] Georgieva Iv., *Bulgarian folk mythology*, Sofia 1993, 55-57 (*Георгиева Ив., Българска народна митология, София 1993, 55-57*).

[522] Ibid. 96-97.

Description of practice 51 HEALING A CHILD FROM EVIL FORCES (EVIL EYE, MAGIC)[523]

The child is healed in front of the hearth, where its face is washed and the water is splashed into the fire. When the 'ograma[524] is tough, the following should be said:

> *"Sits a she-wolf on a chimney,*
>
> *on a chimney in front of the fire,*
>
> *around her are the wolf cubs*
>
> *to protect this child*
>
> *from children's mischief,*
>
> *from evening fears.*
>
> *If they have come in the evening,*
>
> *in the evening they should leave,*
>
> *if they have come in the morning,*
>
> *in the morning they should leave!*
>
> *Because our child has thorny character,*
>
> *that's why you go in the forest,*
>
> *there are food and drinks,*
>
> *there are pipes and drums,*
>
> *there is a big line dance,*
>
> *there you go, eat and drink,*
>
> *there you play and rejoice!*
>
> *Are you're from eyes, are you from words,*

---

[523] Koshov S., *Spells from Razlog region* // Bulgarian folklore, Sofia 1980, № 4, 104 (Кошов С., Магии от Разложко // *Български фолклор, София 1980, № 4, 104*).
In Bulgarian:
"Седи въчица на кумине,
на кумине пред огъине,
около неа са въчетата
да си чуваа детето
от подетини лошави,
от вечерни стреищници.
Ако са вечер дошли,
вечер да си бегаа,
ако са сутрин дошли,
сутрин да си бегаа!
Куд детето ни е зглаве трънливо,
затава връвете в гората,
там има ядене и пиене,
там има свирьки и тапане,
там има оро големо,
там идете, та яште и пийте,
там играите и се веселете!
От очи ле сте, от думи ле сте,
от фърлено в дворо ле сте
от настапищина ле сте?
От щеето и да сте,
от детето ни се уведете,
в честа гора се вденете!"
[524] *Ograma* is the name for this kind of sickness.

are you from thrown in the yard,
are you from stepped over?
From whatever you are,
go away from our child,
in a dense forest you go!"

In the presented rite some moments are of particular interest. The purification is performed at the hearth, which as a sacred centre of the house is an expected element. Fire and water are used in the rite, which is also absolutely reasonable bearing in mind their strong purifying rationalisation in ritual practice. In this case what is untypical is the unification in an interesting way of the fire and the water. The child is being washed and the water is splashed into the fire. This practice is known also in the nestinar ritual tradition and bearing in mind the strong archaic layer in it, the same could be assumed in this case too.[525] Of particular interest is the ritual formula in which the she-wolf is called as a protector of the child. It is recognised as one of her cubs and that is why she must be its protectress. This technique is known in the initiatory ritual traditions, where the newly initiated is recognised as an offspring of the divinity and is placed under its protection. Surely this deep connection has been forgotten with time, but it has remained preserved in the magical ritual practices, because it operates with another way of thinking, namely the mythological, where the ritual act is not always rationalised because this is not a requirement for its realisation.

Similar to the described above is the following practice.

---

[525] For the description of the washing of the hands over the fire of the boys who carry the nestinari icons see Arnaudov M., *Essays on Bulgarian folklore*, Sofia 1996, 463 (Арнаудов М., *Очерци по българския фолклор*, София 1996, 463).

Description of practice 52 HEALING OF NIGHT FEAR[526]

"An incantation is made over the child. The woman that makes the incantation is called baiachka. The incantation is repeated three times. A pinch of ash is taken from nine places to be mixed with water and has to be drunk before dawn. As the incantations are made, so the ash is drunk. The piece spends the night on the circle, so it could be seen from what the fear has come.

"They found her, cursed things stroke her down,

so they broke her waist, her brain, her joints,

her veins, her abdomen, her intestines, her head, her leg

from where learned the bitch born on Saturday

with nine puppies born on Saturday

and rushes through fire and through blaze

so she chases the curses and havocs of (the name),

she chases to chase them away,

so they go in desolated forests,

where no dog barks,

where a woman doesn't twist a crutch for yarn,

where no rooster sings".[527]

(The ritual actions in this case are not described clearly enough, but during my fieldwork in the village of Starosel in the years 2009/2010, I came across a healer, whose grandmother was familiar with that incantation and in this connection I attach her description of the actions, which are done for the incantation.)

Ash is taken from the hearth and is sieved. A plank and the chain from the hearth are also used. When beginning the incantation a pile of ash is made and the plank is placed

---

[526] *Archive of the Ethnographic Institute and Museum*, inv. № 880 II, Ethnographic materials from the village of Starosel, gathered by Zhivka Stamenova, Tatyana Koleva, 1974 (*АЕИМ инв. № 880 II, Етнографски материали от с. Старосел, събрани от Живка Стаменова, Татяна Колева, 1974*).

[527] In Bulgarian:

"Намерили я, поразили я проклетии,

та я трошили в снагъ, в мозък, в стави,

в жили, в курем, в чирвъ, в главъ, в крак

де съ научила кучка съботница

с девет кучета съботничета

и припка през огън и през пожар

та гони на (името) поразии и проклетии,

гони да ги изгони,

да идат в пусти гори

дето куче не лай,

дето жена мотовилка не мотай,

дето петел не пее."

over, the healer takes the chain from the hearth in her right hand and holding it over the plank covering the ash pronounces the ritual formula. After the incantation is repeated three times, the plank is lifted up and the healer looks at the figures in the ash and identifies from them the cause of the fear. After that nine pinches are taken from the ash using the thumb and the forefinger, so that as the pinches are made an 'I' shape is formed.

The pinches are made in the following order:

I 6	I 1	I 8
I 4	I 2	I 5
I 7	I 3	I 9

The ash is put into a spoon with some water and this is given to the ill person to drink, as he or she is standing at the door, but outside the doorstep, with the healer inside and she says:

"Fear outside, heart on its place!"[528]

And she throws the spoon over the person's left shoulder, behind his or her back and watches; if the spoon is upside down there is fear, and if it has fallen with the hollow up that means that the fear has been healed. This procedure is repeated three times, as the incantations are made on Wednesday, Friday and Sunday.

In relation to the incantation above, which is against night fear, the piece is left to spend the night over the ash and during the night to leave a sign for the reason.)

The hearth, substituted with the ash, is also an element in this rite. In the incantation, assistance is called from a bitch born on Saturday with nine puppies born on Saturday. According to the traditional belief a dog, which is born on Saturday possesses the power to see and chase away evil forces. Saturday, as a day of the dead, lends the ones born on it the ability to see the dead, because they are closer to them. The protective force is called in the guise of a bitch to chase away the evil from the ill person.

---

[528] In Bulgarian: *"Страх навън, сърце на място!"*

The commonality between the two rites presented is that the female image of the wolf and dog is sought as a protector, and through it purification is called. In this connection the bitch and the she-wolf are a substitute for a mythological parent (represented with wolf cubs or with puppies), who protects the ill person and accepts him or her as one of her offspring. Binding the image of the mother-wolf or bitch and the idea of purification and healing in combination with the fire (as an earthly projection of the celestial luminary the Sun), reflects an old mythological notion, which most probably belongs to the archaic layer of folk culture. The mother and the woman recently given birth are compared with the she-wolf herself for which the following rite gives evidence, where the she-wolf integrates the four cosmic elements in order to reinstate the order:

Description of practice 53 FOR HEALING A YOUNG MOTHER[529]

If the young mother suffers from an evil spirit and becomes ill, her eyes become blue like gaunt and she has screaming in her ears, then they carry her over a fire and say:

"A she-wolf passed through fire,
wolf cub carries in the mouth,
neither the she-wolf got burned,
nor drops the wolf cub.
A she-wolf passed through water,
wolf cub carries in the mouth,
neither the she-wolf got drowned,
nor drops the wolf cub.
A she-wolf passed through forest,
wolf cub carries in the mouth,
neither the she-wolf got lost,
nor drops the wolf cub."[530]

---

[529] *Collection of Bulgarian Folklore and Folk Studies book 21*, Sofia 1905, 54 (*СбНУ кн. 21, София 1905, 54*).
[530] In Bulgarian:
"Вълк мина през огън,
вълче носи в уста,
ни се вълк изгори
ни вълче изпуща.
Вълк мина през вода,
вълче носи в уста,
ни се вълк удави,
ни вълче изпуска.
Вълк мина през гора,
вълче носи в уста,

Along with the purification rites, which contain the mythical notion of the she-wolf protectress and helper, of particular interest is one practice connected with the sacrifice of puppies for ensuring the safe birth of a baby and protection over the pregnant woman. This rite is extremely interesting, because we have evidence for the sacrifices of dogs among the Thracians, but even further for a sacrifice of dogs in the cult of the Goddess of women in labour for ensuring a safe birth.[531] The role of the dog in rites of passage is very important and is attested also through archaeological data in the Thracian's lands, even if in this case it is more commonly detected in funeral ritual practices.[532]

Description of practice 54 TO PREVENT MISCARRIAGE[533]

Immediately after she finds out that she is pregnant the woman girdles herself with a thread. This thread is taken from the shedding of a loom of a girl that is going to weave for the first time. The thread is girdled next to the skin and is not removed until the end of the pregnancy. About three months after the beginning of the pregnancy a second procedure is performed. This happens with the help of an elderly woman, who has passed the menopause. She finds three or at least one recently born puppies. At dawn she takes the pregnant woman by the river and both turn to face east. The elderly woman takes one of the puppies and drops it under the chemise of the pregnant woman. It falls between her body and the chemise into the river, which carries it away. While dropping it the elderly woman says and the pregnant woman repeats after her:

"I will drown it! I gave to you – now you give to me!"[534]

After that the women separate. If there were three puppies the elderly woman leaves the remaining two

---

ни се вълк изгуби,
ни вълче изпуска."

[531] In this connection see De Grossi Mazzorin J., Minniti C., *Dog Sacrifice in the Ancient World: A Ritual Passage?*, // L.M. Snyder & E.A. Moore (eds.), *Dogs and People in Social, Working, Economic or Symbolic Interaction*, 9th ICAZ Conference, Durham 2002, 62-64.

[532] Georgieva R., *Opfergabe von Tieren im thrakischen Bestattungsbrauchtum* (Ende des II - I Jahrtausend v.Chr.). // Prähistorische Zeitschrift, Bd. 70, Heft 1. Berlin, 1995, 115-135.

[533] *Sofia region. Ethnographic and linguistic researches.*, Sofia 1993, 198 (Софийски край. Етнографски и езикови проучвания., София 1993, 198).

[534] In Bulgarian:
"Оно негу био да удава! Я тебе даде – на си ти мене!"

somewhere in the bushes, far from the road. Neither the pregnant woman nor the elderly woman go straight back into their homes. First of all each one of them goes to visit the home of some elderly people who no longer have the ability to have children.

The quoted ritual practice has no other known parallels in the Bulgarian lands and its conservation until such a late period makes it an exceptional example of the sustainability of ritual actions. It is hard to suppose another origin for this operation except an echo from antiquity, because there we find very close parallels. The role of the sacrifice of a dog, and even further of a little puppy, is to ensure the rite of passage which the pregnant woman is entering. In essence this rite is sacrificial, as the words in the ritual formula show – *"I gave to you, now you give to me!"* The addressee of this formula is not named, but is easy to guess why, because with time and under the influence of official religious ideas, this type of rite enters the sphere of the hidden and is performed secretly. The sacrifice is made by a river, which is a known liminal location connected with the feminine.

The image of the wolf is saturated with a lot of mythological rationalisation and in this connection parts of its body are believed to be carriers of magical power.[535] In the traditions of the Balkan peoples ritual procession of the villages with the body of a killed wolf are known, which is greeted with gifts and the very rite has apotropaic rationalisation to protect the village from a wolf attack. In Balkan ritual practice a lot of the wolf's body parts are used for healing. Widely known is the use of *'wolf's mouth'* – a thin strip of leather cut from the snout of the wolf, around the mouth. This practice is known to all the southern Slavs and most probably belongs to the relics of the ancient traditions of Balkan folklore. Because there are numerous known publications on this subject,[536] I'm not going to discuss it in

---

[535] Of course these beliefs are widespread and can be seen also among other peoples, and not only those of the Balkans; for the role of the parts of the wolf's body as apotropaic see Black W., *Folk-medicine: chapter of the History of Culture*, London 1883, 153-154; също вж. Seligmann S., *Der böse Blick und Verwandtes*, Berlin 1910, I, 121, 175, 211.

[536] See Plas P., *The songs of the Vučari: Relations between text and ritual-mythological context.* // Slavica Gandensia 26, Gent 1999, 85-116; Plas P., *Falling Sickness, Descending Wolf: Some Notes on Popular Etymology, Symptomatology, and 'Predicate Synonymy' in Western Balkan Slavic Folk Tradition.* // Zeitschrift für Slawistik 49.3, Potsdam 2004, 253-72; Plas P., *Wolf texts' in Western Balkan Slavic folk tradition: outlines of an ethnolinguistic/ethnopoetic inquiry* // Slavica Gandensia 30, Gent 2006, 77-88; Mencej M., *Funkcija gospodarja volkov v povedkah, zagovorih, verovanjih in šegah* // Etnolog številka 10, Ljubljana 2000, 163-178; Nenov N., *Valchari. Healing with wolf's mouth.* // Etar. Ethnological researches IV,

detail and I'm going to only quote some of the known ritual practices from the Bulgarian ethnic territory, that most probably have their parallels among other Balkan peoples.

Description of practice 55 HEALING OF FEAR WITH WATER POURED THROUGH A WOLF'S MOUTH[537]

"Pour water through a wolf's mouth and give this water to the ill person to drink. (The wolf's mouth is considered among people to be healing, that is why after killing a wolf they twist the mouth in the shape of a circle and use it for healing different illnesses). If it is possible the wolf should be killed on a Saturday before sunrise. In cases when wolf cubs are found in the woods on a different day, for instance Wednesday or Thursday, people take them into their homes and feed them until Saturday, and on Saturday morning before sunrise they butcher it and take its mouth."

Description of practice 56 HEALING OF A CHILD EPILEPSY WITH WOLF'S MOUTH[538]

"Flowers brought on Easter to the church are taken, along with valerian (*Valeriana officinalis*) and German Iris (*Iris germanica*) and they are all placed outside in a cauldron, *'under the stars'*. On the next day the naked child has that water poured over it, then it is dressed and passed through a wolf's mouth, *'mouth of a killed wolf'*. This is made *'facing the sun, before noon, while the day is going forward'*. The little children are passed through seven times and the big ones nine. After that, the ill child steps on a clean cloth and the healer sprinkles it with millet as she is going around its face and puts some millet in its bosom, and the child sleeps with the millet, without taking off its clothes. The millet that has fallen down on the cloth during the sprinkling is shaken out on a rose (*Rosa multiflora*) in the garden." During the whole time the healer speaks the same words as for the evil eye (Hlebarovo region).

The presented ritual practices show the role of the wolf and its connection with maternal care in a very interesting way. The chthonic nature of the wild beast is related in a

---

Gabrovo 2002, 69-78 (Ненов Н., *Вълчарите. Лекуване с вълча паст //* *Етър. Етноложки изследвания IV*, Габрово 2002, 69-78).

[537] Marinova G., *An old healing book from Asenovgrad //* Etar. Ethnological researches IV, Gabrovo 2002, 176 (Маринова Г., *Един стар лекарственик* *от Асеновград //* *Етър. Етноложки изследвания IV*, Габрово 2002, 176).

[538] Kapantsi. *Lifestyle and culture of the Bulgarian population in Northeastern Bulgaria*. Sofia, 1985, 306 (*Капанци. Бит и култура на старото* *българско население в Североизточна България. София, 1985, 306*).

number of rites with the protection given from the feminine principle, which is represented in part by the killed wolf. In this way, the healing of the small child is bound through the delivery from a she-wolf. Although according to most researchers of the rite it is more like a warrior initiation, I personally do not agree with that, because in the warrior rites as a whole there is rarely a woman-healer or priestess, and in this case of the healing with wolf's mouth women are also admitted. One part of the valchari[539] are men, but for the passing through a wolf's mouth there is no requirement for the sex of the ill person, i.e. it could be also a girl, which makes it impossible to see this as a case of male ritual war initiation. Of course this couldn't be completely rejected, because including women in this case could be a consequence of a late profanity of the rite, such as is seen in some other traditional rites.

The dark side of the year and the apparent death in nature are unsurprisingly reflected in traditional ritual practices. From ancient times humans, who worship the Goddess as a Genetrix, aim to live and organise their society in tune with her cycles. In the region of the Eastern Mediterranean the late autumn and the beginning of winter have been from antiquity that calendar period when the human community, just like nature, turned its stare down to the bowels of the earth and inward to itself. During that time mortals gave their honour to the Goddess, who fills the black soil with her power, who manifests in the lurking fertility of the sleeping seed. Women, as carriers of fertility in society and as keepers of the home hearth, were the main officiators in the calling of the Goddess. Just like the wolf – the zoomorphic representation of the Winter sun, spills the blood of the deer - the representation of the God of the summer, the ancient priestesses spilled the blood of the sacrificial animals and moistened the earth with it.

The end of the single life had to ensure the non-mortality and revival of the whole life, to move again the fertile power of the earth, but also to connect the mortals with the immortals, the living with the dead and what has been created to continue its cycle. The Divine Spinner weaves the ties horizontally in society and vertically in the three worlds. Accompanied by the beast of prey – the wolf, which is also her offspring and which she tames with her presence, she organizes order again in the home and in the Cosmos, i.e. in herself.

---

[539] Healers who use wolf's mouths in their practice.

63 - Statue Of A Wolf, 1st-3rd Century CE[540]

---

[540] *"Vassil Bozhkov" Collection, inv. № 297.*

Even with the passing of linear time, with the change in the composition of the nationalities and organisation of the communities which have inhabited and still inhabit the lands of the ancient Thracians, the essence of the rites from antiquity performed in this calendar period is transferred in our time, even if they are externally modified. Traditional societies, such as the Balkan ones including Bulgarian, retained the connection of the ritual with the natural cycle despite the official religious doctrine (Christianity or Islam) until the middle of the past century. Keeping this connection and performing the rites that have marked the sowing of crops, the increasing of night, the time when the howling of wolves can be heard, has enabled the preservation of strongly archaic ritual practices. They call the mythical concept of a force, which appears as a spinner, as a healer, punishing in the guise of a snake, receiver of souls and womb of fire, dangerous and predaceous, spilling blood, but also called as a zealous mother-guardian in the image of a She-wolf.

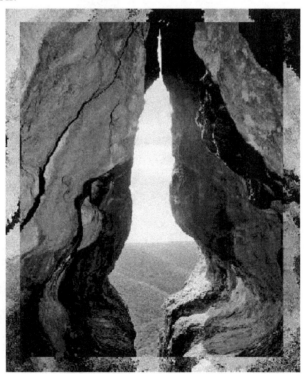

64 - View From The Inside Of The Womb-Cave – Sanctuary Of The Great Goddess, Tangardak Kaya, Kardzhali Region[541]

---

[541] http://lions-kardzhali.org/lions/kardzhali/ <20.08.2011>.

The concept of the divine expressed in a female form is attested in the Eastern Mediterranean from antiquity (sixth millennium BCE). Throughout its genesis, the Thracian ethnicity continues this ancient veneration and subsequently passes it to the newly arrived other ethnicities like Slavs, proto-Bulgarians etc., who for their part additionally enrich it with beliefs and rituals of their own. The overlay of ideas and practices does not prevent the survival of the native ones; in some cases turns out to be a favourable ground for the endurance of many highly archaic rituals and beliefs which have typological parallels in the corresponding geographical region.

The natural features and the outside world as visible manifestation of the deities continue even today to shape the beliefs of the Thracian land's inhabitant in similar ways. Arriving and departing religious structures give a different outer appearance. Ever since ancient times, the primordial, all-embracing Great Goddess has been named in various ways and called in different ritual manifestations. These names and images altered according to time and its trends. The Thracian epithets of the Goddess during the Hellenistic and the Roman age are 'translated' with their pantheon conformities. The ancient authors translate the Thracian ideas according to their own, therefore, they are calling the Thracian Great Goddess with divine names, familiar for them – Hera (Polyaen. 7, 22), Queen Artemis (Hdt. 4, 33), Athena (Athen. 12, 531e-532a), Hestia (Diod. 1, 94, 2). On the monuments from this age she is known as – Artemis, Diana, Cybele, Hekate, Aphrodite, Demeter and others.[542] In later times, for the Slavs, she is named Mokosh, Lada and others. For the Slavs and their pantheon, we possess only scarce information, which is primarily from the written tradition, but there are not enough material finds. From the literary sources we understand that the ancient authors also identified the Goddesses worshiped by the Slavs with their ancient parallels. An example for this is the finding of a relation between the Slavic Goddess Mokosh and the Goddess Hekate.[543] Most likely, the proto-Bulgarians also brought with themselves their concept, which was connected with the image of the Great Goddess they found in the Thracian lands, but this assumption is also lacking evidence.

---

[542] Fol V., Popov D., *The Deities of the Thracians*, Sofia 2010, 66-68.
[543] See *Sermon of St Gregory the Theologian* (893 y.): "*Goddess Ekatia (Hekate) for virgin they proclaim her and Mokosh they venerate....*"online: http://liternet.bg/publish/akaloianov/slovo.htm <20.10.2011>.

With the adoption of Christianity, the ancient images and concepts of the Goddess assumed new names. The folk kept their far-off beliefs and rites, but transformed them once again in order to preserve them. It is unlikely that this process was conducted deliberately and on purpose. More likely, the natural admiration and the necessity of unity with nature were the reasons for seeking ways of preserving the rituals and beliefs which provided the possibility to interact with it. There are preserved evidences for the performing of pre-Christian rituals after the adoption of Christianity. Of particular interest is some information from the hagiography of St George the Hagiorite (Tenth-Eleventh century CE) concerning a village in the Rhodope Mountains where at that time[544] a marble Goddess statue[545] was worshipped by the local population and the saint broke it down to pieces in order to enforce Christianity. This evidence confirms once more the stability of folk's inner necessity for their Goddess. The marble image might be broken down to pieces, but the sacred springs, the sacred caves, the sacred home hearths, remain and continue to be the places, where to the present day, the proximity of this power, which the ancient sometimes just called the Great Goddess, keeps on being sought and experienced. In ancient times she was called Bendis, Hekate, Zerynthia, Cotyto and in numerous other ways, now she is called Maria, Marina, Helen or in a different way. But the Goddess today continues to be sought and venerated in ritual.

For the ancient Thracians the vertical model of the world is of three parts, therefore, the trinity is a common method as a formation of the sacred area. This is the place where the seekers have the chance to send their spiritual power in katabasis (going down, i.e. into the underworld) and anabasis (going up), in order to search for knowledge and union with the deities. The horizontal model of the world is sustained by the tetrad which most easily gets its explanation in the cardinal directions. The representation of the Goddess' image in four chapters is conditional. Undoubtedly she could be seen and believed as an infinite

---

[544] This happens about two centuries after the adoption of Christianity in the First Bulgarian State in 864.
[545] T. Gerasimov, *Information about a marble idol among the Bulgarian Slavs in the Thessaloniki region* // Linguistic-ethnographic research in memoriam Acad. St. Romanski, Sofia, 1960, 557-561 (*Т. Герасимов, Сведение за един мраморен идол у българските славяни в Солунско* // *Езиковедско-етнографски изследвания в памет на акад. Ст. Романски, София, 1960, 557—561*).

multitude and all-containing Monad. Pythagoras[546] defines four manifestations of the feminine:

- the woman who had not known a man – Kore (a virgin);
- the woman ready to become married – Nymph (a bride);
- the woman who gave birth to children – Mater (a mother);
- the woman who has passed the menopause and moved on in old age - Maia (an elderly woman).

In this case, I chose the method with the four faces of the feminine principle, in order to present the veneration to the Goddess that is professed in the horizontal model of the world and in the annual circle. These images are constantly connected and interweaving. The Christian female saint remains a Goddess in the ritual. This Goddess preserves her trans-functionality. The fertility of plants, animals and humans depends on her. She gives health to the body and soul to those who pray to her. She is also a fearsome dispensator of illnesses and death, who holds the keys of the All. And through the whole path of the year - from the new birth of the sun, during its radiance above and the revival of earth's power, when the mountains are filling with the lively sounds of spring, during the scorching heat of the summer and grain entering the soil with the setting of autumn and the memory of death - the Great Goddess is called for her divine appearance even to the present day.

---

[546] Iamblichus, *Life of Pythagoras*, transl. Thomas Taylor, London 1818, 27.

CONCLUSION

The present book does not claim to be exhaustive on the relics of ancient magical ritual practices in Bulgarian traditional culture. The richness of archaic practices and beliefs is a very important moment in the examination of Balkan traditional culture as a whole. Therefore it is my desire to introduce the contemporary reader to authentic representations of the magical ritual practices, which have preserved a multitude of archaic elements. Following the perpetuity of cyclical time, venerated in the calendar circle of the year, this book mainly examines the traces of honour to the Great Goddess, which are preserved in the traditional culture of the Balkans and particularly in the Bulgarian ethnic territory.

Basic moments in the beliefs and rituals are described in very short form, which call the image of the Goddess. For the ancient Thracians the primordial is exactly she, who is the Genetrix of the Sun, the Mountain Mother of mortals and immortals, the Virgin, the She-Wolf and she was believed in and venerated in many other images and namings. That is why the first book dedicated to Thracian magic in the past and the present mainly discusses the image of the Goddess, as she is perceived even today in folklore culture. Although today she is officially degraded to the status of a saint (i.e. of a mortal), in the rite, in the ritual words, in the belief of the ritual persons she continues to reveal herself as a deity, who controls all the elements and has power over them. This same Goddess is not accidentally called by the ancients the *'Almighty'*.

The present book does not claim to be exhaustive on the matter, because this would be practically impossible, but I hope that it is an incentive and useful source for research to follow.

INDEX OF HERBS

Herb 1 Black poplar
Populus nigra

Herb 2 'Borisii' (Avens)
Geum coccineum

Herb 3 Burning-bush
Dictamnus albus

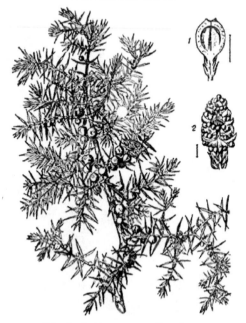

Herb 4 Common Juniper
Juniperus communis

Herb 5 Common Primrose
Primula veris

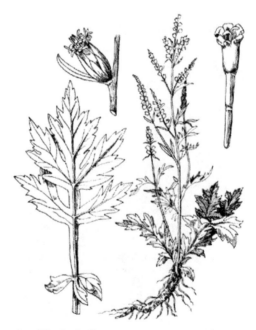

Herb 6 Common wormwood
Artemisia vulgaris

Herb 7 Cretan dittany
Origanum dictamnus

Herb 8 Cross gentian
Gentiana cruciata

Herb 9 Dog rose
Rosa canina

Herb 10 Dog's tooth violet
Erythronium dens-cans

Herb 11 False helleborine
Veratrum lobelianum

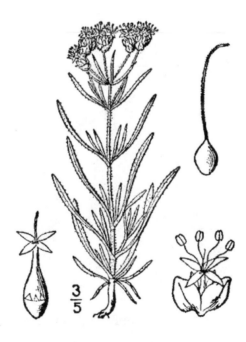

Herb 12 Fleawort
Plantago psyllium

Herb 13 German Iris
Iris germanica

Herb 14 Hart's-tongue Fern (Bronze-plant)
Phyllitis scolopend

Herb 15 Herb Paris
Paris quadrifolia

Herb 16 Horse Tongue Lily
Ruscus hypoglossum

Herb 17 Ivy
Hedera helix

Herb 18 Lesser honeywort
Cerinthe minor

Herb 19 Maidenhair spleenwort
Asplenium trichomanes

Herb 20 Purging Buckthorn
Rhamnus catharticus

Herb 21 Red alkanet
Anchusa officinalis

Herb 22 Safflower
Carthamus tinctorius

Herb 23 Small meadow rue
Thalictrum minus

Herb 24 Soapwort
Saponaria officinalis

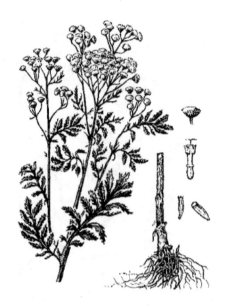

Herb 25 Tansy
Tanacetum vulgare

Herb 26 Valerian
Valeriana officinalis

Herb 27 Yellow melilot
Melilotus officinalis

HERB IMAGE CREDITS:

Herb 1
http://luirig.altervista.org/naturaitaliana/viewpics2.php?rcn=43180
Herb 2
http://www.pflanzen-shop.ch/geum-coccineum-cooky-nelkenwurz-.html
Herb 3
http://caliban.mpiz-koeln.mpg.de/oltmanns02/tafeln/Tafel_112.html
Herb 4 http://en.wikisource.org/wiki/File:Britannica_1911_Juniper_-_J._communis.jpg
Herb 5 http://upload.wikimedia.org/wikipedia/commons/f/fb/Nsr-slika-384.png
Herb 6 http://alamut.info/Lexikon/Pflanzen/Artemisia%20vulgaris.htm
Herb 7 http://www.desert-tropicals.com/Plants/Lamiaceae/Origanum_dictamnus2.jpg
Herb 8 http://www.redbubble.com/people/kirke/works/247482-cross-gentian-gentiana-cruciata
Herb 9 http://alamut.info/Lexikon/Pflanzen/Rosa%20canina.htm
Herb 10 http://etc.usf.edu/clipart/81900/81967/81967_erythronium_lg.gif
Herb 11
http://plant.geoman.ru/books/item/f00/s00/z0000004/pic/000149.gif
Herb 12 http://luirig.altervista.org/photos-search/index.php?title=Plantago+psyllium
Herb 14 http://hardyfernlibrary.com/ferns/tind/asplenium%20sco.jpg
Herb 15
http://www.visualphotos.com/image/1x6044824/herb_paris_plant_paris_quadrifolia_1857_artwork
Herb 16 http://chestofbooks.com/gardening-horticulture/Commercial-Gardening-1/images/Plants-with-Leaf-like-Branches.jpg
Herb 17 http://www.anbg.gov.au/poison-plants/600_wide/Hedera_helix.jpg
Herb 18
http://species.wikimedia.org/wiki/File:Cerinthe_minor_Sturm11.jpg
Herb 19 http://hardyfernlibrary.com/ferns/tind/asplenium%20tr.jpg
Herb 20 http://luirig.altervista.org/pics/display.php?pos=44445
Herb 21 http://luirig.altervista.org/naturaitaliana/viewpics2.php?rcn=4297
Herb 22 http://pulib.if.ua/part/10573
Herb 23
http://lh5.ggpht.com/_vULWN1oSjXw/SWhPLFZsnuI/AAAAAAAAYQg/7cfZCtKMwGk/s800/wal-hoo00003.jpg
Herb 24 http://bilki.bg/index.php?m=1&ws_m=2088
Herb 25
http://plant.geoman.ru/books/item/f00/s00/z0000004/pic/000107.gif
Herb 26 http://www.swsbm.com/Illustrations/Valeriana_officinalis-2.gif
Herb 27 http://alamut.info/Lexikon/Pflanzen/Melilotus%20officinalis.htm

INDEX OF IMAGES

BIBLIOGRAPHY

IN LATIN SCRIPT:

Abbot G., *Macedonian Folklore*, Cambridge 1903

Abel E., *Orphica*, Leipzig 1885

Abt A., *Die Apologie Des Apuleius Von Madaura Und Die Antike Zauberei*, Gießen 1908

Angeletti L., Agrimi A., French D , Curia C., Mariani-Costantini R., *Healing Rituals And Sacred Serpents* // The Lancet Volume 340, Issue 8813, 1992

Aristophanes. *Wealth. The Complete Greek Drama*, Vol. 2. Eugene O'Neill Jr., New York 1938

Aronen J., *Dragon Cults And Νύμφη Δράκαινα In Igur 974* // Zeitschrift Für Papyrologie Und Epigraphik, Bd. 111, 1996

Bawanypeck D., (Ed.), Hethiter.Net/: *Cth 393* (Trde 2008-10-30) // Http://Www.Hethport.Uni-Wuerzburg.De/Txhet_Besrit/Translatio.Php?Xst=Cth 393&Expl=&Lg=De&Ed= <29.12.2011>

Benko St., *The Virgin Goddess: Studies In The Pagan And Christian Roots Of Mariology*, Leiden 1993

Betegh G., *The Derveni Papyrus: Cosmology, Theology, And Interpretation*, New York 2004

Betz H., *Fragments From A Catabasis Ritual In A Greek Magical Papyrus* // History Of Religions, Vol. 19, No. 4, Chicago 1980

Betz H., *The Greek Magical Papyri In Translation, Including The Demotic Spells*, Chicago/London 1986

Black W., *Folk-Medicine: Chapter Of The History Of Culture*, London 1883

Bloch R., *Orpheus Als Lehrer Des Musaios, Moses Als Lehrer Des Orpheus* // Antike Mysterien. Medien, Transformation Und Kunst, Dill U., Walde Chr., Berlin/New York, 2009

Bocev Vl., *Kurban Among The Macedonians* // Kurban In The Balkans, Belgrade 2007

Bossert H., *Die Schicksalsgöttinnen Der Hethiter* // Die Welt Des Orients, Bd. 2, H. 4, 1957

Brouwer H., *Bona Dea: The Sources And A Description Of The Cult*, Leiden 1989

Burkert W., *Griechische Religion Der Archaischen Und Klassischen Zeit*, Zweite Auflage, Stuttgart 2011

Burkert W., *Weisheit Und Wissenschaft: Studien Zu Pythagoras, Philolaos Und Platon*, Nürnberg 1962

Caskey L., *A Chryselephantine Statuette Of The Cretan Snake Goddess* // American Journal Of Archaeology, Vol. 19, No. 3, 1915

Clement, Protreptikos 2.17.2-18.2, *The Writings Of Clement Of Alexandria*, Transl. Wilson W., London 1867

Clinton K., *The Sacred Officials Of The Eleusinian Mysteries* // Transactions Of The American Philosophical Society, Vol. 64, 1974

Collins. B., *The Puppy In Hittite Ritual* // Journal Of Cuneiform Studies, Vol. 42, No. 2, 1990

Cook A., *Zeus: A Study In Ancient Religion*. Vol. Ii, Part Ii, Cambridge 1925

Dalipaj G., *Kurban And Its Celebration In The Shapti Region* // Kurban In The Balkans, Belgrade 2007

De Grossi Mazzorin J., Minniti C., *Dog Sacrifice In The Ancient World: A Ritual Passage?* // L.M. Snyder & E.A. Moore (Eds.), Dogs And People In Social, Working, Economic Or Symbolic Interaction, 9th Icaz Conference, Durham 2002

Detelic' M., *St Paraskeve In The Balkan Context* // Folklore 121, 2010

Diels H., *Die Fragmente Der Vorsokratiker*, Berlin 1903

Dimitrova N., *Theoroi And Initiates In Samothrace: The Epigraphical Evidence*, Princeton 2008

Dukova U., *Die Bezeichnung Der Dämonen Im Bulgarischen*, München 1997

Eitrem S., *Opferritus Und Voropfer Der Griechen Und Römer*, Kristiania 1915

Eliade M., *Images And Symbols: Studies In Religious Symbolism*, Princeton 1999

Farkas A. *Style And Subject Matter In Native Thracian Art* // Metropolitan Museum Journal, Vol. 16, 1981

Farnell L., *Cults Of The Greek States*, Vol. V, Oxford 1909

Farnell L., *Greek Hero Cults And Ideas Of Immortality*, Oxford 1921

Fol Al., Jordanov K., Porozhanov K., Fol V., *Ancient Thrace*, Sofia 2000

Fol V. *The Wolf/The Dog And The North As The Direction Of Wisdom* // Studia Archeologiae Et Historiae Antiquae. Doctissimo Viro Scientiarum Archeologiae Et Historiae Ion Nikuliţă, Anno Septuagesimo Aetatis Suae, Dedicator, Chişinău 2009

Fol V., Popov D., *The Deities Of The Thracians*, Sofia 2010

Fol V., *The Rock Antiquity Of Eleusis* // Von Domica Bis Drama. Gedenkschrift Für Jan Lichardus, Sofia 2004

Foley F., *Word – Power, Performance And Tradition* // The Journal Of American Folklore, Vol. 105, No 417

Gager J., *Curse Tablets And Binding Spells From The Ancient World*, New York/ Oxford 1992

Gamkrelidze T., Ivanov V., *Indo-European And The Indoeuropeans*, Berlin/New York 1995

Georgieva R., *Opfergabe Von Tieren Im Thrakischen Bestattungsbrauchtum (Ende Des II - I Jahrtausend V.Chr.).* // Prähistorische Zeitschrift, Bd. 70, Heft 1. Berlin, 1995

Graf F., *Derveni And Ritual* // Proceedings Of The Derveni Papyrus Conference 2008, Online: Http://Chs.Harvard.Edu/Wb/1/Wo/6wszedsoifka6abqoyud cg/0.1 <10.01.2012>

Graf F., *Magic In The Ancient World*, Cambridge/ Massachusetts/London 1997

Graf Fr., *Apollo*, London/New York 2008

Grattius, Transl. J. W. Duff And A. M. Duff, *Minor Latin Poets*, Loeb Classical Library, Cambridge 1934

Haas V., *Die Hethitische Literatur: Texte, Stilistik, Motive*, Berlin 2006

Halpern B., Foley J., *The Power Of The Word: Healing Charms As An Oral Genre* // The Journal Of American Folklore, Vol. 91, No 362

Hamilton M., *Incubation Or The Cure Of Disease In Pagan Temples And Christian Churches*, London 1906

Harrison E., *Eumolpos Arrives In Eleusis* // Hesperia: The Journal Of The American School Of Classical Studies At Athens, Vol. 69, No. 3, 2000

Harrison J., *Prolegomena To The Study Of Greek Religion*, Cambridge 1908

Henninger J., *Über Huhnopfer Und Verwandtes In Arabien Und Seinen Randgebieten* // Anthropos, 1946-1949

Henrichs A., *Zur Genealogie Des Musaios* // Zeitschrift Für Papyrologie Und Epigraphik, Bd. 58, 1985

Hofmann J., *Etymologisches Wörterbuch Des Griechischen*, München 1950

Hopfner Th., *Griechisch-Ägyptischer Offenbarungszauber*, Bd. II, Amsterdam 1983

Hordern J., *Notes On The Orphic Papyrus From Gurôb (P. Gurôb 1; Pack² 2464)* // Zeitschrift Für Papyrologie Und Epigraphik, Bd. 129, 2000

Hristova P., *How To Call Down The Moon Or Cultural Continuity In South-eastern Europe* // Orpheus. Journal Of Indo-European And Thracian Studies, Vol. 7, Sofia 1999

Iamblichus, *Life Of Pythagoras*, Transl. Thomas Taylor, London 1818

Isaac B., *The Greek Settlements In Thrace Until The Macedonian Conquest*, Leiden 1986

Jacoby F., *Die Fragmente Der Griechischen Historiker 4*, Leiden/Boston/Köln 1999

Jauregui M., *Orphism And Christianity In Late Antiquity*, Berlin/New York 2007

Johnson S., *Hekate Soteira: A Study Of Hekate's Role In The Chaldean Oracles And Related Literature*, Atlanta 1990

Kaindl R., *Die Wetterzauberei Bei Den Rutenen Und Huzulen*, Mittheilungen Der Kaiserlich-Königlichen Geographischen Gesellschaft In Wien, Xxxvii, Wien 1894

Kerenyi K., *Eleusis. Archetypal Image Of Mother And Daughter*, Princeton 1991

Kern O., *Das Prooimion Des Orphischen Hymnenbuches* // Hermes, 75 Bd., H. 1, 1940

Koiva M., *The Transmission Of Knowledge Among Estonian Witch Doctors* // Folklore: Electronic Journal Of Folklore, No 2 /1996

Köppen P., Die *Dreigestaltete Hekate Und Ihre Rolle In Den Mysterien*, Wien 1823

Kowalzig B., *Singing For The Gods*, New York 2007

Kraemer R., *Women´s Religions In The Greco-Roman World*, New York / Oxford 2004

Krauss F., *Südslawische Hexensagen* // Mitteilungen Der Antropologischen Gesellschaft In Wien, Band Xiv, Wien 1884

Lalonde G., *Pagan Cult To Christian Ritual: The Case Of Agia Marina Theseiou* // Greek, Roman, And Byzantine Studies 45, 2005

Lawson J., *Modern Greek Folklore And Ancient Greek Religion*, Cambridge 1910

Lazaridis D., *Amphipolis*, Archaeological Receipts Fund, Athens 1997

Limberis V., *Divine Heiress. The Virgin Mary And The Creation Of Christian Constantinople*, London/New York 1994

List E., *Is Frau Holda The Virgin Mary?* // The German Quarterly, Vol. 29, No. 2, 1956

Luppe W., *[Σεληνογενησ]* // Zeitschrift Für Papyrologie Und Epigraphik, Bd. 55, 1984

Lupu E., *Sacrifice At The Amphiareion And A Fragmentary Sacred Law From Oropos* // The Journal Of The American School Of Classical Studies At Athens, Vol. 72, No. 3,,2003

Lykophron, *Alexandra* - Holzinger C., Leipzig 1895

Marinus Of Samaria, *The Life Of Proclus Or Concerning Happiness,* 28, Online: Http://Www.Tertullian.Org/Fathers/Marinus_01_Life_Of_Proclus.Htm <10.02.2012>

Mccown C., *The Ephesia Grammata In Popular Belief* // Transactions And Proceedings Of The American Philological Association 54, 1923, 128-31

Mcpherran M., *Socrates And Zalmoxis On Drugs, Charms, And Purification* // Apeiron: A Journal For Ancient Philosophy And Science, Vol. 37, 1, 2004

Mencej M., *Funkcija Gospodarja Volkov V Povedkah, Zagovorih, Verovanjih In Šegah* // Etnolog Številka 10, Ljubljana 2000

Mencej M., *Wolf Holidays Among Southern Slavs In The Balkans* // Acta Ethnographica Hungarica 54 (2), 2009

Moore C., *On The Origin Of The Taurobolium* // Harvard Studies In Classical Philology, Vol. 17, 1906

Mouton A., *Hittite Witchcraft* // A. Süel (Ed.), Acts Of The Viith International Congress Of Hittitology, Ankara 2010

Nieto F., *Visogothic Charm From Asturias And The Classic Tradition Of Phylacteries Against Hail* // Magical Practice In The Latin West, Leiden-Boston 2010

Nilson M., *Greek Mysteries In The Confession Of St. Cyprian* // The Harvard Theological Review, Vol. 40, No 3, 1947

Oliver J., *On The Exegetes And The Mantic Or Manic Chresmologians* // The American Journal Of Philology, Vol. 73, No. 4, 1952

Passalis H., *Secrecy And Ritual Restrictions On Verbal Charms Transmission In Greek Traditional Culture* // Incantatio, Tartu 2011

Persson A., *Der Ursprung Der Eleusinischen Mysterien* // Archiv Für Religionswissenschaft Bd. 21, Leipzig/Berlin 1922

Petreska V., *The Secret Knowledge Of Folk Healers In Macedonian Traditional Culture* // Folklorica. Journal Of The Slavic And East European Folklore Association, Vol. Xiii 2008

Plas P., *Falling Sickness, Descending Wolf: Some Notes On Popular Etymology, Symptomatology, And 'Predicate Synonymy' In Western Balkan Slavic Folk Tradition.* // Zeitschrift Für Slawistik 49.3, Potsdam 2004

Plas P., *The Songs Of The Vučari: Relations Between Text And Ritual-Mythological Context.* // Slavica Gandensia 26, Gent 1999

Plas P., *Wolf Texts' In Western Balkan Slavic Folk Tradition: Outlines Of An Ethnolinguistic/Ethnopoetic Inquiry* // Slavica Gandensia 30, Gent 2006

Poper J., *Towards A Poetics, Rhetorics And Proxemis Of Verbal Charms* // Folklore: Electronic Journal Of Folklore, No 24, 2003

Popov R., *Kurban Sacrificial Offerings On The Feastdays Of The Summertime Saints In The Calendar Tradition Of The Bulgarians* // Kurban In The Balkans, Belgrade 2007

Porphyrius *De Abstin.* Iv. 16, 155: *Selected Works Of Porphyry*, Transl. Thomas Taylor, London 1823

Porphyry, *On The Cave Of The Nymphs, Selected Works Of Porphyry*, Transl. By Thomas Taylor, London 1823

Preisendanz K., *Die Griechschen Zauberpapyri*, I, Leipzig 1928

Preisendanz K., *Die Griechschen Zauberpapyri*, II, Leipzig 1931

Proclus, *In Tim.*, Iii Ed. E Diehl, Vol 2, Bt, 1904

Reitler R., *A Theriomorphic Representation Of Hekate-Artemis* // American Journal Of Archaeology, Vol. 53, No. 1, 1949

Risteski L., *The Orgiastic Elements In The Rituals Connected With The Cult Of The Moon Among The Balkan Slavs* // Studia Mythologica Slavica 5, Ljubljana 2002

Robertson N., *Hittite Ritual At Sardis* // Classical Antiquity, Vol. 1, No. 1, 1982

Rusten J., *Unlocking The Orphic Doors: Interpretation Of Poetry In The Derveni Papyrus Between Pre-Socratics And Alexandrians* // Proceedings Of The Derveni Papyrus Conference 2008, Online: Http://Chs.Harvard.Edu/Wb/1/Wo/4zfcx3intvrs5mdk0bpnim/0.1 10.01.2012>

Scheftelowitz, I., *Das Stellvertretende Huhnopfer, Mit Besonderer Berücksichtigung Des Jüdischen Volksglaubens*, Giessen 1914

Schlesier R., *Die Bakchen Des Hades. Dionysische Aspekte Von Euripides Hekabe* // Metis. Antropologie Des Mondes Grecs Anciens Vol. 3, N 1-2, 1988

Schmidt B., *Das Volksleben Der Neugriechen Und Das Hellenische Alterthum*, Leipzig 1871

Schütz O., *Zwei Orphische Liturgien* // Rheinisches Museum Für Philologie 87, Frankfurt Am Main 1938

Selare R., *A Collection Of Saliva Superstitions* // Folklore, Vol. 50, No. 4, 1939

Seligmann S., *Der Böse Blick Und Verwandtes*, Berlin 1910

Smalwood T., *The Transmission Of Charms In English, Medieval And Modern* // Charms And Charming In Europe, New York 2004

Sobolev A., *On Balkan Names For The Sacrificial Animal On St George's Day* // Kurban In The Balkans, Belgrade 2007

Sturtevant E., *A Hittite Text On The Duties Of Priests And Temple Servants* // Journal Of The American Oriental Society, Vol. 54, No. 4, 1934

Theodossiev N. *"Κοτεογς Ηλιου And Κοτεογς Μητροс Ορεας"* // Hermes, Vol. 129, No. 2, 2001

Tomaschek W., *Die Alten Thraker. Eine Ethnologische Untersuchung*, Neudruck Der Ausgaben Von 1893 Und 189, Osnabrück 1975

Toohey P., *Epic Lessons: An Introduction To Ancient Didactic Poetry*, London/New York 1996

Trepanier S., *Empedocles: An Interpretation*, New York 2004

Ustinova Y., *"Either A Daimon, Or A Hero, Or Perhaps A God:" Mythical Residents Of Subterranean Chambers* // Kernos 15, 2002

Ustinova Y., *Caves And The Ancient Greek Mind*, Oxford/New York 2009

Ustinova Y., *Greek Knowledge Of The Thracian And Scythian Healing Practices And Ideas Of Afterlife And Immortality* // Ephemeris Napocensis, Xiv-Xv, Bucarest 2004-2005

Ustinova Y., *Truth Lies At The Bottom Of A Cave: Apollo Pholeuterios, The Pholarchs Of The Eleats, And Subterranean Oracles* // La Parola Del Passato 59, Naples 2004

Versnel H., *The Roman Festival For Bona Dea And The Greek Thesmophoria* // Inconsistencies In Greek And Roman Religion. 2. Transition And Reversal In Myth And Ritual, Leiden 1993

Watkins C., *How To Kill A Dragon: Aspects Of Indo-European Poetics*, New York 1995

Wessely K., *Ephesia Grammata Aus Papyrusrollen*, Inschriften, Gemmen Etc., Wien 1886

West D., *Some Cults Of Greek Goddesses And Female Daemons Of Oriental Origin: Especially In Relation To The Mythology Of Goddesses And Demons In The Semitic World*. Phd Thesis, University Of Glasgow 1990, Online: Http://Theses.Gla.Ac.Uk/1263/ <10.12.2011>

Wünsch R., *Antikes Zaubergerät Aus Pergamon*, Berlin 1909

Yerkes R., *Sacrifice In Greek And Roman Religions And Early Judaism*, New York 1959

In Cyrillic script:

First the name of the author and the title of the book are given in English translation, and in brackets and italic is the name of the author and the original title in Cyrillic.

Aleksieva M., *Hellenic orphic sources*, Sofia 2004 (Алексиева М., Елински орфически свидетелства, София 2004)

Arnaudov M., *Essays on Bulgarian folklore*, third facsimile edition, Sofia 1996 (Арнаудов М., Очерци по българския фолклор, трето фототипно издание, София 1996)

Bachvarov K., *Neolithic mortuary practices*, Sofia 2003 (Бъчваров К., Неолитни погребални обреди, София 2003)

Baeva V., *Holy Zona: a specific local cult in the region of Melnik*// Ideas and terrenes in ethnology, folkloristics and anthropology 2010 (Баева В., Света Зона: един специфичен местен култ от Мелнишко // Идеи и терени: етнология, фолклористика, антропология 2010)

Batakliev G., *Orpheus. Hymns. Argonautica*, Plovdiv 1989 (Батаклиев Г., Орфей. Химни. Аргонавтика, Пловдив 1989)

Bozhinova V., *South-western university "Neofit Rilski" - Report on subject: St Mother of God – golden apple*, Blagoevgrad 2009, online: http://satrae.swu.bg/media/5366/st.%20virgin.pdf <29.12.2011> (Божинова В., Югозападен университет „Неофит Рилски" – Доклад на тема: Света Богородица-златна ябълка, Благоевград 2009)

Bulgarian etymological dictionary, Sofia 1971 (Български етимологичен речник, Издателство на БАН, София 1971)

Chausidis N., *The woman as a personification of the living space* // Macedonian theatre: Balkan context, Skopje 2007 (Чаусидис Н., Жената како персонификација на просторот за живеење // Македонскиот театар: балкански контекст, Скопје 2007)

Chaykanovich V., *The magic and religion*, Belgrade 1985 (Чајкановић В., О магији и религији, Београд 1985)

Chicherov V., *The Winter Period of the Russian Agricultural Calendar in the XVI to XIX Centuries*, Moscow 1957 (Чичеров В.И., Зимний период русского земледельческого календаря XVI-XIX веков, Москва 1957)

Chichikova M., *New discovered epigraphic evidence for the cult of Phosphoros in northeast Thrace* // Terra Antiqua Balcanica IV, Sofia 1990 (Чичикова М., Новооткрит епиграфски паметник за култа на Фосфорос в Североизточна Тракия – TAB,4, София 1990)

Chohadzhiev A., *Weights and/or Spools: Distribution and interpretation of the Neolithic "cocoon-like loom-weights".* // Prehistoric Thrace, Sofia/Stara Zagora, 2004 (Чохаджиев А., Макари и/или тежести: разпространение и интерпретация на неолитните "пашкуловидни тежести за стан". // Праисторическа Тракия, София/Стара Загора 2004)

Fol A., *The Hymns of Orpheus*, Sofia 1995 (Фол Ал., Химните на Орфей, София 1995)

Fol A., *The Thracian Dionysos. Book one: Zagreus*, Sofia 1991 (Фол Ал., Тракийският Дионис. Книга първа. Загрей, София 1991).

Fol A., *The Thracian Dionysos. Book three: Naming and faith*, Sofia 2002 (Фол А., Тракийският Дионис. Книга трета: Назоваване и вяра, София 2002)

Fol A., *The Thracian Orphism*, Sofia 1986 (Фол Ал., Тракийският орфизъм, София 1986)

Fol Al., Fol V., *The Thracians*, Sofia 2005 (Фол Ал., Фол В., Траките, София 2005)

Fol Al., *History of the Bulgarian lands in Antiquity*, Sofia 2008 (Фол Ал., История на българските земи в древността, София 2008)

Fol Al., *Orphica magica*, Sofia 2004 (Фол Ал., Orphica magica, София 2004)

Fol V., *Cultural and historical heritage of ancient Thrace* // Preservation of the cultural and historical heritage in Republic of Bulgaria, Sofia 2010 (Фол В., Културно-историческо наследство на Древна Тракия // Защита на културно-историчекото наследство в Република България, София 2010)

Georgi Mishev

Fol V., *Megalithic and Rock-cut Monuments in Ancient Thrace*, Sofia 2000, 138 (Фол В., Мегалитни и скално-изсечени паметници в Древна Тракия, София 2000, 138)

Fol V., Neykova R., *Fire and music*, Sofia 2000 (Фол В., Нейкова Р., Огън и музика, София 2000)

Fol V., *Orpheus the Thracian*, Sofia 2008 (Фол В., Орфей тракиецът, София 2008)

Fol V., *Rock topoi of faith in South-eastern Europe and Asia Minor during the Antiquity*. Studia Thracia 10, Sofia 2007 (Фол В., Скални топоси на вяра в Югоизточна Европа и Мала Азия през древността, София 2007)

Fol V., *The Forgotten Saint*, Sofia 1996 (Фол В., Забравената светица, София 1996)

Fol V., *The worship of St Marina in Strandzha* // Myth-Art-Folklore, 1, Sofia 1985, 128-130 (Фол В., Почитането на св. Марина в Странджа.// Мит-изкуство-фолклор, 1, София 1985, 128—130)

Georgieva Iv., *An ancient cult in the Rhodopes, Strandzha and Nestos* // Rhodopes collection, vol. 3, Sofia 1972, 159-174 (Георгиева Ив., Един старинен култ в Родопите, Странджа и Места // Родопски сб., Т. 3. София 1972, 159-174)

Georgieva Iv., *Bulgarian folk mythology*, Sofia 1981 (Георгиева Ив., Българска народна митология, София 1981)

Georgieva Iv., *The bread of the Bulgarians: bread without sourdough, bread with sourdough.* // Bulgarian ethnology issue 3, 1993, 15-23 (Георгиева, Ив. Хлябът на българина: хляб без квас, хляб с квас. // Българска етнология № 3, 1993, 15-23)

Gerasimov T., *Information about a marble idol among the Bulgarian Slavs in the Thessaloniki region* // Linguistic-ethnographic research in memoriam Acad. St. Romanski, Sofia, 1960, 557-561 (Герасимов Т., Сведение за един мраморен идол у българските славяни в Солунско // Езиковедско-етнографски изследвания в памет на акад. Ст. Романски, София, 1960, 557—561)

Gerov N., *Dictionary of the Bulgarian language*, Sofia 1977 (Геров Н., Речник на българския език, София 1977)

Goev A., *Lighting the sedyanka fire* // Bulgarian Ethnology, book 1, Sofia 1979, 70-71 (Гоев А., Заклаждане на седянка // Българска етнология кн. 1, София 1979, 70-71)

316

Goev A., *Ritual healing through incantation in the Bulgarian folk medicine* // Ethnographic problems of the folk culture, vol. 1, Sofia 1989, 130 (Гоев А., Обредното лечение чрез баене в българската народна медицина // Етнографски проблеми на народната култура, т. 1, София 1989, 130)

Gorov G., *Strandzha folklore*, Sofia 1983 (Горов Г., Странджански фолклор, София 1983)

Gyuzelev V, *Knyaz Boris the First. Bulgaria during the second half of IX c.*, Sofia 1969 (Гюзелев В., Княз Борис Първи. България през втората половина на IX в., София 1969)

History of Bulgaria, v.1, Primitive communal and Slave system. Thracians, Sofia 1979 (История на България, т.1, Първообщинен и робовладелски строй. Траки, София 1979)

Hristov Iv., *Temple of the Immortals*, Sofia 2010 (Христов Ив., Храмът на безсмъртните, София 2010)

Ilimbetova A., *The cult of the wolf among the Bashkirs* (Илимбетова А., Култ волка у башкир) online: http://turkportal.ru/culturearticles/6-kult-volka-bashkir.html <10.12.2011>

Ivanov V., *Dionysos and Pre-Dionysianism*, Saint Petersburg 1994 (Иванов В., Дионис и прадионисийство, Санкт Петербург 1994)

Kabakova G., *Structure and geography of the legends for Baba Dokia* // Balkans in the Mediterranean context, Moscow 1986, 146 (Кабакова Г., Структура и география легенды о Бабе Докии // Балканы в контексте Средиземноморья, Москва 1986, 146)

Kagarov Evg., *The cult of fetishes, plants and animals in ancient Greece*, Saint Petersburg 1913 (Кагаров Евг., Культ фетишей, растений и животных в древней Греции, Санкт Петербург 1913)

Kapantsi. *Lifestyle and culture of the Bulgarian population in North-eastern Bulgaria*. Sofia, 1985 (Капанци. Бит и култура на старото българско население в Североизточна България. София, 1985)

Kasabova-Dincheva A., *Magic – social necessity* // Ethnographic problems of the folk culture 5, Sofia 1998 (Касабова-Динчева А., Магията – социална необходимост // Етнографски проблеми на народната култура 5, София 1998)

Kazasova R., *Secret incantations and divinations*, Gabrovo 2003 (Казасова Р., Тайни баилки и гадания, Габрово 2003)

Kitevski M., *Summer rites from Deburtsa (Ohrid region). //* Macedonian folklore, № 19-20, 1979, 56 (Китевски М., Летни обичаји от Дебърца (Охридско).// Македонски фолклор, № 19-20, 1979, 56)

Konova L., *Magic and funeral rites. Clay cult objects from the necropolis of Apollonia Pontica //* Heros Hephaistos. Studia in Honorem Liubae Ognenova-Marinova, Veliko Turnovo 2005, 148-164 (Конова Л., Магия и погребален обред. Глинени култови фигурки от некропола на Аполония Понтика // HEROS HEPHAISTOS. Studia in Honorem Liubae Ognenova-Marinova, Велико Търново 2005, 148-164).

Koshov S., *Spells from Razlog region //* Bulgarian folklore, Sofia 1980, № 4, 105-106 (Кошов С., Магии от Разложко // Български фолклор, София 1980, № 4, 105-106)

Kotova D., *The Thesmophoria, Women's Festival Complex*, Sofia 1995 (Котова Д., Тесмофориите. Женски празничен комплекс, София 1995)

Krastanova K., *The Golden loom*, Plovdiv 2007 (Кръстанова К., Златният стан, Пловдив 2007)

Lebedev A., *Fragments of ancient Greek philosophers, part I*, Moscow 1989 (Лебедев А., Фрагменты ранних греческих философов, часть I, Москва 1989)

Lyubenov P., *Baba Ega: Collection of different beliefs, folk healings, spells, incantations and customs from the region of Kyustendil*, Tarnovo 1887 (Любенов П., Баба Ега. Сборник от различни вярвания, народни лекувания, магии, баяния и обичаи от Кюстендилско, Търново 1887)

Maksimov S., *Unclean, Unknown and Christian Forces*, Saint Petersburg 1903 (Максимов С., Нечистая, неведомая и крестная сила, Санкт Петербург 1903)

Marazov Iv., *Thracian mythology*, Sofia 1994 (Маразов Ив., Митология на траките, София 1994)

Marinov D., *Living antiquity, book I*, Ruse 1891 (Маринов Д.,. Жива старина, кн. I, Русе 1891)

Marinov D., *Religious folk customs – selected works in 5 volumes*, vol. I, part 1, Sofia 2003 (Маринов Д., Религиозни народни обичаи – избрани произведения в 5 тома, том I, част 1, София 2003)

Marinov D., *Religious folk customs – selected works in 5 volumes*, vol. I, part 2, Sofia 2003 (Маринов Д., Религиозни народни обичаи – избрани произведения в 5 тома, том I, част 1, София 2003)

Marinova G., *An old healing book from Asenovgrad //* Etar. Ethnological research IV, Gabrovo 2002, 176 (Маринова Г., Един стар лекарственик от Асеновград // Етър. Етноложки изследвания IV, Габрово 2002, 176)

Markov Gr., *Folk spells from Godech region as a means for psychotherapy //* Bulgarian ethnology 56, Sofia 1992, 102 (Марков Гр., Народни баяния от Годечко като средство за психотерапия // Българска етнология 56, София 1992, 102)

Markov V., *Cultural and historical Heritage of the Cult of the Sacred Serpent-Dragon in the Lands of the Thracian Satri*, Blagoevgrad 2009 (Марков В., Културно-историческо наследство от култа към сакрализираната змия-змей в земите на тракийските сатри, Благоевград 2009).

Markov V., *Cultural heritage and succession. Heritage from the ancient pagan holy places in Bulgarian folk culture*, Blagoevgrad 2007 (Марков В., Културно наследство и приемственост. Наследство от древноезическите свети места в българската народна култура, Благоевград 2007)

Maykov L., *Great Russian spells*, Saint Petersburg, 1994 (Майков Л., Великорусские заклинания, Санкт Петербург, 1994)

Meszaros D., *The monuments of ancient Chuvash religion*, Cheboksary 2000 (Месарош Д., Памятники старой чувашской веры, Чебоксары 2000)

Mihaylov N., *The witch as an archetypical character //* Balkan readings 2, Symposium on the structure of the text, Moscow 1992, 50-52 (Михайлов Н., Ведьма как архетипический персонаж // Балканские чтения 2. Симпозиум по структуре текста, Москва 1992, 50-52),

Mihaylova G., *Are the masked ones masked*, Sofia 2002 (Михайлова Г., Маскирани ли са маскираните, София 2002)

Mikov L., *First of March rituality*, Sofia 1985 (Миков Л., Първомартенска обредност, София 1985)

Miltenova A., Toncheva I., Barlieva Sl., The *speech of Thomas the Apostle for exaltation of the Holy Panagia: textological observations – Marina Yordanova in Pyati dostoit. Collection in memory of Stefan Kozhuharov.* Sofia 2003 (Милтенова А., Тончева И., Бърлиева Сл., Словото на апостол Тома за въздвижение на Светата Панагия: текстологически наблюдения - Марина Йорданова в Пяти достоитъ. Сборник в памет на Стефан Кожухаров, София 2003)

Minkov Tsv., *I am loved by a zmey, mother. Mythical folk songs*, Sofia 1956 (Минков Цв., Мене ме, мамо, змей люби. Митически народни песни, София 1956

Mishev G., *Cultural memory in the region of Thracian cult centre Starosel* // The Bulletin of the National Museum of Bulgarian History, XXII, Veliko Tarnovo 2010 (Мишев Г., Културна памет в района на тракийски култов център Старосел // Известия на националния исторически музей, XXII, Велико Търново 2010)

Mitrev G., *Religious institutions and communities in the Macedonia province (148 BC – 284 AC)*, Sofia 2003 (Митрев Г., Религиозни институции и общества в провинция Македония (148 г.пр.Хр.-284 г.сл.Хр.), София 2003)

Mladenova Ya., *Images of Hekate in our lands*, Archaeology magazine 1961, book 3 (Младенова Я., Паметници на Хеката от нашите земи, сп. Археология 1961, кн. 3)

Mochulskiy V., *Sermons and teachings against the pagan beliefs and rites. On the traditional history of the Bulgarians*, Odessa 1903 (Мочульский В., Слова и поучения, направленные против языческих верований и обрядов. К бытовой истории болгар, Одесса 1903)

Mollov T., *Bulgarian Christmas blessings*, Varna 2005-2009, online: http://liternet.bg/folklor/sbornici/blagoslovii/nova_kamena.htm <29.12.2011> (Моллов Т., Български коледни благословии, Варна 2005-2009, online: http://liternet.bg/folklor/sbornici/blagoslovii/nova_kamena.htm <29.12.2011>)

Mollov T., *Bulgarian folklore motifs. Vol. I. Ritual songs*, Varna 2006-2010, online: http://liternet.bg/folklor/motivi/maika_diri_sina_si/vabel_3.htm <29.12.2011> (Моллов Т., Български фолклорни мотиви. Т. I. Обредни песни, Варна 2006-2010, online: http://liternet.bg/folklor/sbornici/blagoslovii/nova_kamena.htm <29.12.2011>)

Mollov T., *Myth – epos – history. Old-Bulgarian Historical-Apocalyptical Stories (992-1092-1492)*, Varna 2002 (Моллов Т., Мит - епос –история. Старобългарските историко-апокалиптични сказания (992-1092-1492), Варна 2002).

http://liternet.bg/publish/tmollov/mei/5_3.htm
<06.11.2011>

Nachov D., *Vili and samovili.* / Chitalishte, 1871, №7, 310 (Начов Д., Вили и самовили. / Читалище, 1871, №7, 310)

Naumov G., *The vessel, the oven and the house in a symbolic relation with the womb and the woman (Neolithic examples and ethnographic implications)* // Studia mythologica slavica 9, Ljubljana 2006, 59-95 (Наумов Г., "Садот, печката и куќата во симболичка релација со матката и жената (неолитски предлошки и етнографски импликации)" // Studia mythologica slavica 9, Ljubljana 2006, 59-95)

Nenov N., *Valchari. Healing with wolf's mouth.* // Etar. Ethnological research IV, Gabrovo 2002, 69-78 (Ненов Н., Вълчарите. Лекуване с вълча паст // Етър. Етноложки изследвания IV, Габрово 2002, 69-78).

Nesheva V., *Melnik – the town build by god*, Sofia 2008 (Нешева В., Мелник – богозиданият град, София 2008)

Neykova R., *Shamans – Did They Exist in the Balkans?*, Sofia 2006 (Нейкова Р., Имало ли е шамани на Балканите?, София 2006)

Nikolova M., *Pagan and Christian motifs in the Christmas song about the birth of the "Young God"* // Crypto-Christianity and religious syncretism on the Balkans, Sofia 2002, 69-76 (Николова М., Езически и християнски мотиви в коледните песни за раждането на "Млада Бога" // Криптохристиянство и религиозен синкретизъм на Балканите, София 2002, 69-76)

Nikolova V., *Braid in the field*, Sofia 1999 (Николова В., Плитка на нивата, София 1999)

Ovcharov D., *For the essence of the pagan cult centre Madara* // Madara. Excavations and research. Book 3, Shumen 1992, 99-108 (Овчаров Д., За същността на езическия култов център Мадара. // Мадара. Разкопки и проучвания. Кн. 3, Шумен 1992, 99-108)

Pankova Y., *Terminology and ritual functions of bread in South-Slavic folk rites* // Symbolic language of traditional culture. Balkan studies II, 1993 (Панкова Ю., Терминология и ритуальные функции хлеба в южнославянских родинных обрядах // Символический язык традиционной культуры. Балканские чтения II, 1993)

Pavlova M., *Wednesday and Friday in connection with the spinning - Ethnogenesis, early history and culture of the*

Slavs, Moscow 1985 (Павлова М., Среда и пятница в связи с прядением // Этногенез, ранняя этническая история и культура славян, Москва 1985)

Petrova M., *On the cult and hagiographic tradition of St Marina* // Christian hagiology and folk beliefs, Sofia 2008 (Петрова М., За култа и агиографската традиция на св Марина // Християнска агиология и народни вярвания, София 2008)

Petrovich S., *Serbian mythology. System of the Serbian mythology*, I book, first edition, Nish 1999 (Петровић С., Српска митологија систем српске митологије, I књига Прво издање, Ниш 1999)

Plotnikova A., *Christmas symbols in the terminology of ritual bread among Serbians* // Symbolical language of traditional culture. Balkan studies II, Moscow 1993 (Плотникова А., Рождественская символика в терминологии обрядового хлеба у сербов // Символический язык традиционной культуры. Балканские чтения II, Москва 1993)

Plotnikova A., *Ethnolinguistic geography of the South Slavs*, Moscow 2004 (Плотникова А., Этнолингвистическая география Южной Славии, Москва 2004)

Plotnikova A., *Ethnolinguistic geography of the Balkan* // Blood sacrifice. Transformation of one ritual, Belgrade 2008 (Плотникова А., Етнолингвистичка географија Балкана // Крвна жртва. Трансформације једног ритуала, Београд 2008)

Popov D., *The Thracian goddess Bendis*, Sofia 1981 (Попов Д., Тракийската богиня Бендида, София 1981)

Popov D., *Zalmoxis. Religion and society of the Thracians*, Sofia 1989 (Попов Д., Залмоксис. Религия и общество на траките, София 1989)

Popov R., *Calendar folk celebrations and customs from the region of Troyan* // Cultural-historical heritage of the region of Troyan, Sofia 1991, 77-78 (Попов Р., Народни календарни празници и обичаи в троянския Край // Културно-историческото наследство на Троянския край, София 1991, 77-78)

Popov R., *Saint Menas in the calendar tradition of the Balkan peoples* // History 2004, 4-5 (Попов Р., Свети Мина в календарната традиция на балканските народи.//История 2004, №№ 4-5)

Popov R., *Saints and demons on the Balkans*, Plovdiv 2008 (Попов Р., Светци и демони на балканите, Пловдив 2008)

Popov R., *The rite Kokosha cherkva among the Bulgarians* // Bulgarian Ethnography, book 2, Sofia 1986, 15-22 (Попов Р., Обичаят "Кокоша черква" у българите // Българска етнография, кн. 2, София 1986, 15-22)

Popov R., *Twin Saints in the Bulgarian Folk Calendar*, Sofia 1991 (Попов Р., Светци близнаци в българския народен календар, София 1991)

Radenkovic L., *Folk spells and incantations*, Nis-Pristina-Kragujevats, 1982 (Раденковић. Љ., Народне басме и бајања. Ниш-Приштина-Крагујевац, 1982)

Radoslavova D., *The service for reverend Petka in the Bulgarian manuscripts from XVII century* // Christian hagiology and folk beliefs, Sofia 2008 (Радославова Д., Службата за преподобна Петка в българските ръкописи от XVII век. // Християнска агиология и народни вярвания, София 2008)

Seuthopolis, *Vol. 1*, Sofia, 1984 (Севтополис. т. 1. София, 1984)

Sofia region. *Ethnographic and linguistic research.*, Sofia 1993 (Софийски край. Етнографски и езикови проучвания., София 1993)

Stareva L., *Bulgarian spells and divination methods*, Sofia 2007 (Старева Л., Български магии и гадания. София 2007)

Strandzha. *Material and spiritual culture.*, Sofia 1996 (Странджа. Материална и духовна култура., София 1996)

Sveshnikova T., *The wolf in the context of the Romanian burial rite. Research on the Balto-Slavic spiritual culture* // Burial rite, 1990 (Свешникова Т., Волк в контексте румынского погребального обряда в Исследования балто-славянской духовной культуры // Погребальный обряд, Москва 1990)

Sveshnikova T., *Under the sign of the wolf. Features of the Balkan-Romance culture.* // Time in the space of the Balkans. Evidences of the language, Moscow 1994 (Свешникова Т., Под знаком волка. Черты балканороманской народной культуры // Время в пространстве Балкан. Свидетельства языка, Москва 1994)

Taho-Godi A., *Antique hymns*, Moscow 1988 (Тахо-Годи А., Античные гимны, Москва 1988)

Teodorov E., *Ancient Thracian heritage in Bulgarian folklore*, Sofia 1999 (Теодоров Е., Древнотракийско наследство в българския фолклор, София 1999)

The Rhodopes. Traditional Folk Spiritual and Socio-Normative Culture, Sofia 1994 (Родопи. Традиционна народна духовна и социалнонормативна култура, София 1994)

Todorova-Pirgova Iv., *Traditional healing rituals and magical practices*, Sofia 2003 (Тодорова-Пиргова Ив., Баяния и магии, София 2003)

Tolstoy N., *Balkan-Slavic badnik in a Slav perspective* // Balkans in the context of the Mediterranean, Moscow 1986 (Толстой Н., Балкано-славянския бадняк в общеславянской перспективе // Балканы в контексте Средиземноморья, Москва 1986)

Tolstye N.I. and S.M., *Protection from hail in Dragacheve and other Serbian regions* // Slavic and Balkan folklore, Moscow 1981 (Толстые Н.И. и С.М., Защита от града в Драгачеве и других сербских зонах // Славянский и балканский фольклор, Москва 1981)

Toporkova A., *Russian erotic folklore. Songs. Rituals and ritual folklore. Folk theatre. Spells. Riddles.* Chastushki, Moscow 1995 (Топоркова А., Русский эротический фольклор. Песни. Обряды и обрядовый фольклор. Народный театр. Заговоры. Загадки. Частушки. Составление и научное редактирование, Москва 1995)

Toporov V., *On the paleo-Balkan connections in the field of language and mythology* // Balkan linguistic collection, Moscow 1977 (Топоров В., К древнебалканским связям в области языка и мифологии // Балканский лингвистический сборник, Москва 1977)

Tsatsov P., *Representational problems of the Thracian art in the early Hellenism* // Archaeology, Sofia 1987, book 4 (Цацов П., Изобразителни проблеми на тракийското изкуство в ранния елинизъм // Археология, София 1987, кн. 4)

Vakarelski Hr., *Bulgarian burial customs*, Sofia 2008 (Вакарелски Хр., Български погребални обичаи, София 2008)

Venedikov Iv., *The copper threshing-floor of the proto-Bulgarians*, Stara Zagora 1995 (Венедиков Ив., Медното гумно, Стара Загора 1995)

Venedikov Iv., *The golden pillar of the proto-Bulgarians*, Sofia 1987 (Венедиков Ив., Златният стожер на прабългарите, София 1987)

Vetuhov A., *Charms, spells, amulets*, Warsaw 1907 (Ветухов А. Заговоры, заклинания, обереги, Варшава 1907)

Vlahov K., *Thraco-Slavic parallels*, Sofia 1969 (Влахов К., Трако-славянски успоредици, София 1969)

Vutova V., *The food on Friday – profane and sacred* // The profane and sacred food, Gabrovo 2010 (Вутова В., Храната в петъчния ден – профанна и сакрална // Храната сакрална и профанна, Габрово 2010)

Yanakieva S., *Thracian hydronymy*, Sofia 2009 (Янакиева С., Тракийска хидронимия, София 2009)

Yaneva St., *Varieties of Bulgarian Ritual Bread*, Sofia 1989 (Янева Ст., Български обредни хлябове, София 1989)

Yankova V., *Between the Spoken and Written Word. The folklore and the folk hagiographies*, V. Tarnovo 2005 (Янкова В., Между устното и писаното слово. Фолклорът и народните жития, В. Търново 20057)

Yordanova-Aleksieva M., *Hellenic Orphic evidences*, Sofia 2004, 179 (Йорданова-Алексиева М., Елински орфически свидетелства, София 2004, 179)

Zabyilin M., *Russian people: their customs, rituals, legends, superstitions and poetics. In four books*, Moscow 1880 (Забылин М. Русский народ: Его обычаи, обряды, предания, суеверия и поэзия. В четырех частях, Москва 1880)

INDEX

N

O

P

R

Threskeia- Θρησκεια

65 - The Symbol of Threskeia

Threskeia is an informal group of people, who share common beliefs, practices of divine worship and ideas related to Thracian culture.

To find out more about this organisation please e-mail: dadaleme@abv.bg

If you enjoyed this book, you may also enjoy some of the other titles published by Avalonia.

A Collection of Magical Secrets by David Rankine (editor)

Artemis: Virgin Goddess of the Sun & Moon by Sorita d'Este

Defences Against the Witches' Craft by John Canard

From a Drop of Water (anthology, various contributors) edited by Kim Huggens

Heka: Egyptian Magic by David Rankine

Hekate Her Sacred Fires (anthology) edited by Sorita d'Este

Hekate Liminal Rites (history) by Sorita d'Este & David Rankine

Odin's Gateways by Katie Gerrard

The Priory of Sion by Jean-luc Chaumeil

Seidr: The Gate is Open by Katie Gerrard

Stellar Magic by Payam Nabarz

The Book of Gold by David Rankine (editor) & Paul Harry Barron (translator)

The Cosmic Shekinah by Sorita d'Este & David Rankine

The Gods of the Vikings by Marion Pearce

The Grimoire of Arthur Gauntlet by David Rankine (editor)

The Guises of the Morrigan by David Rankine & Sorita d'Este

The Isles of the Many Gods by David Rankine & Sorita d'Este

The Temple of Hekate by Tara Sanchez

Thoth: The Ancient Egyptian God of Wisdom by Lesley Jackson

Visions of the Cailleach by Sorita d'Este & David Rankine

Vs. (anthology, various contributors) edited by Kim Huggens

Wicca Magickal Beginnings by Sorita d'Este & David Rankine

These and many other titles are available from our website, **www.avaloniabooks.co.uk** and all good metaphysical bookshops.

CPSIA information can be obtained
at www.ICGtesting.com
Printed in the USA
FSHW021333150621
82329FS